Wineries of the
Eastern States

The Gazebo at Pellegrini Vineyards, Cutchogue, Long Island.

WINERIES
OF THE
EASTERN STATES

Marguerite Thomas

Berkshire House Publishers
Lee, Massachusetts

On the cover: Photographs by Marguerite Thomas:
Front Cover: *Vineyard at Chamard, Clinton, Connecticut.*
Back Cover: *The White Inn, Fredonia, New York; Native American Grapes; Larry McCullough, winemaker, in the cellar at Chamard.*

Frontispiece: *The gazebo at Pellegrini Vineyards, Cutchoque, Long Island,* photograph by Suzi Forbes Chase.

Wineries of the Eastern States
Copyright © 1996 by Berkshire House Publishers
Cover and interior photographs © 1996 by Marguerite Thomas and other credited sources
All wine labels courtesy of the wineries and vineyards

Library of Congress Cataloging-in-Publication Data
Thomas, Marguerite, 1939-
      Wineries of the eastern states / Marguerite Thomas
         p.   cm. — (The great destinations series, ISSN 1056-7968)
      Includes bibliographical references and index.
      ISBN 0-936399-77-5
          1. Wine and wine making—East (U.S.). I. Title. II. Series
    TP557.T474 1996
    641.2′2′0974—dc20   95-47950
                                              CIP

ISBN: 0-936399-77-5
ISSN: 1056-7968 (series)

Editor: Suzi Forbes Chase. Managing Editor: Philip Rich. Original design for Great Destinations™ series: Janice Lindstrom. Cover design: Jane McWhorter. Maps by Ron Toelke.

Berkshire House books are available at substantial discounts for bulk purchases by corporations and other organizations for promotions and premiums. Special personalized editions can also be produced in large quantities. For more information, contact:

Berkshire House Publishers
480 Pleasant St., Suite 5; Lee, Massachusetts 01238
800-321-8526

Manufactured in the United States of America

10 9 8 7 6 5 4 3 2

GREAT DESTINATIONS™ Series

The Berkshire Book: A Complete Guide
The Santa Fe & Taos Book: A Complete Guide
The Napa & Sonoma Book: A Complete Guide
The Chesapeake Bay Book: A Complete Guide
The Coast of Maine Book: A Complete Guide
The Aspen Book: A Complete Guide
The Charleston, Savannah & Coastal Islands Book:
   A Complete Guide
The Gulf Coast of Florida Book: A Complete Guide
The Central Coast of California Book : A Complete Guide
The Newport & Narragansett Bay Book: A Complete Guide
The Hamptons Book: A Complete Guide
Wineries of the Eastern States

The Great Destinations™ series features regions in the United States rich in natural beauty and culture. Each Great Destinations™ guidebook reviews an extensive selection of lodgings, restaurants, cultural events, historic sites, shops, and recreational opportunities, and outlines the region's natural and social history. Written by resident authors, the guides are a resource for visitor and resident alike. All books contain maps, photographs, directions to and around the region, lists of helpful phone numbers and addresses, and indexes.

To the memory of my late husband,

Frank S. Jewett,

who made everything possible.

Contents

INTRODUCTION
HISTORY, GRAPES, AND MARKETING
1
History 1
From Vineyard to Table 3

PART ONE
THE BENCHLANDS
7
Southeastern New England 10
Long Island 18
Eastern New Jersey and Coastal Virginia 34
Lake Erie Region 44

PART TWO
ATLANTIC UPLANDS
63
Northern New Jersey and the Delaware River Region 66
Southern Pennsylvania and Maryland 80
Northern and Central Virginia 96
Western Connecticut 115
The Hudson River Valley 120
The Finger Lakes 134

PART THREE
THE MOUNTAINS
171
The Virginia Highlands 174
Central Pennsylvania 187

Acknowledgments

With deepest thanks to the many people who encouraged, advised, and shared their knowledge and time with me. First, to the vintners whose expertise and enthusiasms for this project helped to steer me in the right directions. To Marsha Palanci, Lila Gault, Lynn O'Hare Berkson, and the many others who guided and inspired me with their common sense and creative ideas. To my family, friends, and colleagues who helped me taste and evaluate the wines. And special thanks to Jean Rousseau, publisher of Berkshire House, for his concepts for the book; to Suzi Forbes Chase for her patient editing; and to Philip Rich who, in addition to his editorial skills, is blessed with unfailing diligence, resourcefulness, and good humor.

Preface

Why did it take almost 350 years for the eastern United States to develop a competitive wine industry? It certainly wasn't because there was little interest, for we've been striving for viticultural success from the very beginning.

When Peter Stuyvesant was governor of New Netherland more than three centuries ago, he planted grapes on Manhattan Island in an attempt to develop a wine industry. In 1662, Lord Baltimore called his land grant in Maryland "The Vineyard" and, in his enthusiasm for wine, planted his own 300-acre plot of vines. Connecticut's official seal depicts three grapevines bearing fruit, a symbol of that state's early viticultural aspirations. George Washington grew grapes at Mount Vernon, but it was Thomas Jefferson who proved to be the most zealous early proponent. He yearned to see serious wine produced in America. "It is desirable that it should be made here, and we have every soil, aspect, and climate of the best wine countries," he wrote. For thirty years Jefferson tried unsuccessfully to grow European grapes at Monticello.

What went wrong? Until recently, wine produced in the eastern United States failed to attract the praise West Coast wines have garnered for decades. It's not just that California is better at promoting its product. The reason eastern wineries failed to receive unconditional thumbs up from critics and consumers is, to put it bluntly, because their wine simply wasn't as good. To be sure, a few isolated examples of superior wine were made in the East, but on the whole, wines from East Coast states had not, until now, exhibited the dry character and clean, fruity flavors that consumers want today. The reasons are fascinating and complex.

I have been as prejudiced against East Coast wines as anyone. Because I spent my childhood in France and much of my adult life in California's wine country, I may even have been more biased than others. When I first moved to New York, and then to Connecticut, I *wanted* to like New England wines — after all, the notion of drinking wine from one's own locale was a tradition I believed in. In addition, I strongly believe in supporting local grape farmers, partly because wineries help to keep agricultural land from being overrun by housing developments and shopping malls, and also because I believe it's important for children to witness the practice of local farming. Furthermore, I think children should be part of an environment where sensible wine consumption keeps family and friends gathered around the dinner table fostering relaxed and extended conversation.

Nevertheless, after a few attempts to find an eastern wine I liked, I gave up and went back to the California and European wines I love. Despite a couple of Long Island vintages which, I admit, showed promise, I thought the odds were against the East Coast ever developing into a region of world-class wine-making.

And then, several years ago, a funny thing happened. Through a mutual friend, my husband and I were introduced to Susan and Earl Samson, who own Sakonnet Vineyards in Rhode Island. We hit it off, and so, when Susan and Earl invited us to spend the weekend at their home in Little Compton, my only concern was that I wouldn't be able to come up with anything nice to say about their wine.

Sitting in the Samson's cozy kitchen, I swirled my first glass of Sakonnet Chardonnay nervously. I took a sniff, thankful that at least the wine smelled pretty good. With the first sip, I was amazed. I sipped again. Why, this stuff tasted just like *real* wine! By the end of the weekend, I knew something interesting was going on in winemaking, at least in Rhode Island.

After more research, I called several of the editors at the wine magazines I write for and told them I wanted to write about New England wines. Since then, I have written several articles about wines from the eastern states, and I have been a judge in national competitions where East Coast wineries have beaten out competitors from the West Coast. Although only a small percentage of the wine made in the East can be considered premium, the picture has changed so rapidly over the past few years that instead of counting the number of premium eastern wineries on the fingers of one hand, there are enough now to actually fill a book. Furthermore, these should continue to improve as the vines become more mature, the winemakers more knowledgeable, and the public more discerning.

While most of the wine in the East is still made from the hardy native American grape varieties (serious wine drinkers consider these to be inferior), the number of winemakers who are using the best European grapes and French-American hybrids is increasing. Furthermore, although most eastern wine is still white, winemakers have begun to experiment with such grapes as Cabernet Franc, Cabernet Sauvignon, Merlot, Pinot Noir, and other red wine grapes favored by sophisticated wine drinkers.

California, with its temperate climate and hospitable environment, has been turning out rivers of premium wine for several decades, while the rest of the country — where temperatures regularly range from root-splitting sub-zero to wilting stretches of high humidity in the upper nineties — lagged behind. Now, thanks to a host of factors coming together at the same time: technological advances, agricultural improvements, and more progressive winery licensing regulations, we are at the dawn of a new era in American winemaking, particularly in the eastern states.

It is an exciting time for writers such as myself, who specialize in wine. It is also an exciting time for winemakers, who suddenly have a whole new universe of possibilities open to them. Above all, it is an exciting time for consumers, who love good wine and who love the excitement of discovering new wineries and new varieties of wine.

For those of us who love to travel, the birth of scores of new wineries gives us new reasons to visit the American countryside. The eastern segment of the country, where the concentration of wineries is greater than anywhere except California, is a particularly rewarding travel destination. The vines seem to grow best in places where the landscape is spectacular. From the comely beauty of New York's Finger Lakes, to the maritime attraction of New England's coast, to the lush and fertile plateau of the Shenandoah Valley, there's dramatic scenery to explore. A sojourn in the eastern wine regions is also an opportunity to become reacquainted with the history of the birth of our country.

In addition, as wine is meant to accompany food, visits to the wine country should also include samplings of the best regional foods. As the public's palate has become more refined, gastronomic entrepreneurs and small-scale farmers, like the wine producers, are responding by growing, producing, and preparing more sophisticated ingredients and dishes.

The unpredictable climate and weather, and the variety of plant pests and diseases, will always make winemaking in the eastern states a challenge. It is now undeniable, however, that the supreme effort will pay off for both the winemaker and the consumer, especially in the best viticultural regions. With a greater number of wineries producing better and better wines, today's wine enthusiast can visit more cellars and sample the product in more tasting rooms than ever before. In fact, as most wineries in the East are small, producing anywhere from several hundred to a few thousand cases a year, the only way most of us will ever have a chance to taste some wines is by visiting the wineries themselves. If we come home with an extra case of wine in the trunk, it will be a vacation to remember every time we pour a glass for ourselves and our friends.

Happy travels, and *Santé*!

THE WAY THIS BOOK WORKS

THE WINE REGIONS

When we contemplate travel in this country, we tend to think in terms of various states. But where wine is concerned, this doesn't make much sense, particularly in the East where state lines have not been drawn according to the climactic and geologic criteria that influence grape production. Wine from the Connecticut coast, for example, has more in common with Long Island wine than with anything made in the far western section of Connecticut, where the climate is not moderated by the Atlantic. Grapes grown in the fertile farmland of eastern Pennsylvania will taste more like those in neighboring New Jersey than like anything from the rugged northeastern part of the state. Think of the differences between Sonoma and Santa Barbara, or Burgundy and Bordeaux to understand how important the image, as well as the different flavors, of separate wine regions can be. And so, the

problem remains as to how to delineate the eastern region into separate viticultural areas.

One useful method of defining eastern wine regions is based on the ideas of
Eric Miller, winemaker-owner of Chaddsford Winery in southeastern
Pennsylvania. Under Miller's system, the East is divided into three distinct
geologic regions: the Benchlands, the Atlantic Uplands, and the Mountains.
Each of these regions has its own characteristic climate and soil type. In each,
vines perform in a relatively similar fashion and the wines reflect the individ-
uality of the land.

I have organized this book around these three separate divisions, which
have been further broken up into smaller sub-sections based on American
Viticultural Appellations (AVA's). Like the *appéllations contrôlées* that desig-
nate and control France's geographically based names, the labels on wines
from official AVA's specify quality according to geographical regions, such as:
Napa Valley, southeastern New England, Hudson River.

THE WINE AND WINERIES

The intent of this book is to identify the best wine made from grapes in the
eastern states rather than to provide a definitive guide to every single winery in the East. A few of the places that are included produce wine that is as
good as any in the world. Others make wine that may not win first place in
wine tasting contests, but is still a pleasant enough beverage to accompany
meals. Those wineries that make mediocre wine, bad wine, or wine that would
appeal to a limited audience, have not been included. Similarly, I have not
included wineries that concentrate more on tour attendance than on making
wine.

In addition, although I have included some wineries that produce wine
made from fruit in addition to grape wine, places that make *only* fruit wine
have not been included. Similarly wineries whose entire production consists
of wine made from the native American labrusca and rotundifolia grapes have
not been included. While these were the only wines that could be produced in
the East until about a hundred years ago — and many people certainly continue to enjoy these wines — most contemporary wine drinkers do not find the
flavor of wines made from Concord or Catawba grapes appealing.

A few wineries make all of their wine from grapes or grape juice that has
been purchased from other viticultural regions such as California or Michigan.
These have not been included either. There is nothing wrong with this — in
fact, many wineries use grapes or juice from somewhere else (usually as a
blender) for *some* of their wines. But an important goal of this book is to capture the spirit of winemaking — from the grapes in the vineyard through the
final nectar created in the winery.

One of the characteristics of wine that attracts discerning consumers is the
element the French call *"terroir"* — the individual characteristics imparted to
wine by specific types of climate, soil, and other geologic factors. For example,

the crisp, mineral-scented wines from the cool Burgundy region of Chablis are typically very different from the richer, flowery white wines from the Côte de Nuits section of Burgundy, although they are made from the same Chardonnay grape. A robust, intensely colored Cabernet from Long Island is unlike the light, delicate Cabernet produced in the Finger Lakes. Some of these differences are a result of the deliberate stylistic imprint of individual wine-makers, but much of the character of wine is a consequence of the locale where the vines grow.

In the eastern United States, as in much of Europe, *terroir* is more important than in California, where variations in climate are less pronounced. Here, individual micro-climates have a profound effect on the grapes, which means that wine made from fruit grown in a specific region is more apt to possess a personality of *place*. The reflection of locale in wine contributes some of the subtle charm and mystery, as well as the individual character that we look for in the best wines. And so, the wineries included in this book grow at least a portion of their grapes on their own property or purchase them from vineyards in the same viticultural region.

Although most of the wine was sampled by various tasting panels whose judgment I took into account, when all else is said and done, the final decision about which wineries to include were based entirely on my own subjective reactions. If I liked the wine, if I thought it would in some way enhance one's dining experience, and if I believed that a majority of wine drinkers would also have a favorable impression of it, that winery was included in this book. In all cases, I have given my own brief subjective description of the wines and the wineries.

THE FOOD, LODGING, AND PLACES OF INTEREST

Wine regions tend to attract good restaurants. Among these eateries there is often at least one in the community with top-notch food and an exceptional wine list. This is where local winemakers like to go to celebrate special occasions, or to take their best customers for dinner, or simply to hang out with their colleagues. Some of these restaurants host winemaker's dinners, where a special prix fixe meal may showcase the wines from a particular winery or region.

Wine-friendly restaurants have excellent wine lists — not necessarily long lists, but thoughtful ones. A good wine list features an interesting selection of wines by the glass, and it may even suggest interesting pairings with dishes on the menu. The staff has been trained in basic wine knowledge, so that any waiter can answer questions and make intelligent suggestions about wine selections. In other words, whether they are upscale or homespun, expensive or moderately priced, what these restaurants have in common, is some connection to the wine region in which they are located — and, of course, they have excellent food and thoughtful service.

No attempt has been made to list all the fine restaurants in a region, nor have I attempted to compile a comprehensive guide to the many pleasant inns and bed and breakfasts in each area. I offer only an occasional description of places that strike my fancy. The unifying principle is that they are all wine-related: a cozy bed and breakfast in a winery, for example, or an attractive inn located within easy driving distance of several wineries.

ABOUT THE RATINGS

This book offers a simple rating system that ranks the overall quality of the wines from each winery evaluated on a scale of one to five. One bottle indicates that at least some of the wines are decent and well made (occasionally, production of quality wine may be too limited to warrant more than one bottle). Two bottles indicates above average wine. Three bottles means the wines are well worth seeking out, while four bottles indicates overall superiority. The rare five-bottle wineries are the vey best in the East. Because this is an entirely subjective rating system reflecting only my own palate and points of view, and because the quality of wine in any given winery is constantly influenced by factors such as changes in personnel, equipment, individual vintages, and so forth, I urge readers to use this as a very general guide rather than an unimpeachable assessment of the wines. Your own taste buds will always be the best guide to what you like.

Wineries of the Eastern States

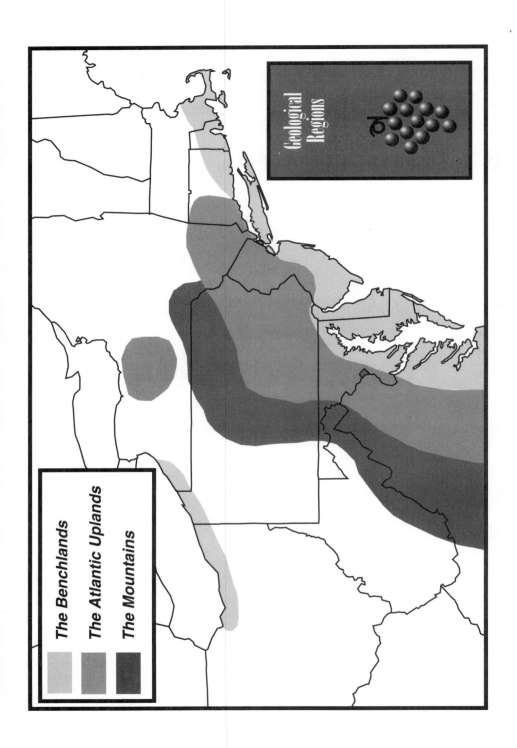

Geological Regions

The Benchlands

The Atlantic Uplands

The Mountains

INTRODUCTION

History, Grapes, and Marketing

Before we begin our tour, a few preliminaries are in order — some history, plus a few words about the grapes themselves and about marketing eastern wines.

HISTORY

From Peach Wine to Pinot Noir, from Scuppernong to Sauvignon Blanc, every state in the union produces wine of one sort or another. This is not a 20th-century trend, either. The Jamestown colonists started vinifying local grapes as soon as they got here, and we've been trying to make decent table wine ever since.

The colonists had no lack of native fruit to work with. In A.D. 1000, the Norse explorer Leif Eriksson was so impressed by the riot of grape vines he saw cascading from the trees in North America that he dubbed the place "Vinland." In fact, more grape varieties grow naturally between the Atlantic coast and the Rocky Mountains than in any other place on earth.

The problem, from the early settler's thirsty point of view, was that the fermented juice of native grapes had a powerful, musky smell and a stronger, more aggressive flavor than the more refined wines they were used to. Had the European settlers simply acquired a taste for wine made from grapes in their adopted land, they wouldn't have spent the next 350 years trying to coax European vines into growing in the harsh conditions of the New World.

The English monarchy, and eventually the individual states, hoped to establish a viticultural industry in the New World. Both invested heavily in the hope of reaping a substantial economic return. European vine cuttings were first imported to Virginia about 1619. From then on, determined viticulturists all along the Atlantic seaboard imported vines from every major wine-producing region in Europe.

For reasons that were not understood at the time, these vines always died. But hope is part of the job description of a winemaker and the trials continued. French *vignerons* were imported to Virginia as consultants, French Huguenot exiles came to the Carolinas, and German winemakers immigrated to Pennsylvania. But none of these experts could get *Vitis vinifera* to grow in the New World.

THE RAVAGES OF DISEASE

While they never gave up trying, European vineyard specialists were forced to acknowledge that European vines would not do well in the new country. Those that didn't die in the freezing winters would inevitably be killed off by American diseases against which they had no inherent immunity. Native American grapes, by contrast, were resistant to Pierce's disease, black rot, phylloxera, and a variety of mildews and other fungal problems.

Of all the problems besetting the American vinifera wine industry, phylloxera was its ruin. This minuscule, yellow louse attacks vines by sucking the life out of the plant through its roots. California's vinifera-based wine industry, which had been thriving in the 19th century, was decimated by phylloxera. To make matters worse, it was inadvertently imported into France on the roots of American vines around 1860. There, phylloxera spread like the plague it was, almost wiping out most of the major wine-producing regions of France. In fact, few winemaking regions in the world escaped. The insect invaded the vineyards of Russia, South Africa, Australia, and New Zealand, as well as those of other European countries.

Finally, in the late 1800s, it was discovered that native American vines were resistant to phylloxera. Eventually, grafting of vinifera vines onto native American rootstock became the established method of combatting phylloxera. Today, most of the world's grape vines are growing on native American roots.

Even after the threat of phylloxera diminished, growing vinifera vines remained an extraordinary challenge in the eastern states, although they flourished in Calfornia's mild climate. In the search for hardy grapes that would also produce palatable wines, viticulturists in the East turned to French-American hybrids. These new strains, developed in France after the phylloxera devastation, are American vine species crossed with European vinifera vines. They are a more disease-resistant variety than vinifera, while their fruit is lest pungently flavored than native American grapes. Thanks to these hybrids, the eastern wine industry finally began to grow. Leading production centers developed around Lake Erie, in Missouri and Ohio, and in New York's Finger Lakes region.

By 1900, the future looked good. As Leon D. Adams wrote in *The Wines of America*, "winegrowing was a full-grown, proud American industry. The brands of leading California, New York, Ohio, Missouri, and New Jersey wineries were competing with European vintages on many of the best restaurant wine lists."

PROHIBITION

Just when the wine industry was reaching maturity, however, a disaster far more deadly than disease or a climactic catastrophe struck, as America headed into Prohibition. In 1919, 55 million gallons of wine were produced in the United States; by 1925 the figure had dropped to barely 3.5 million gallons.

It is hard to imagine how rapidly this new calamity advanced, but the seeds of destruction had been gathering for almost a hundred years. Temperance societies and religious organizations lobbied Congress and terrorized the American public into accepting Prohibition. At first, local communities and cities went "dry"; then, in 1851, Maine became the first state to declare itself alcohol free. In 1920, the 18th Amendment to the Constitution of the United States, prohibiting the manufacture, sale, transportation, or importation of alcoholic beverages, was passed. Intoxicating liquor, as defined by Congress, was any beverage that contained .5% alcohol, which included all wine and beer. Some uses of wine were still permitted: for religious ceremonies, for medicinal purposes, for food flavoring, and for other non-beverage purposes.

Abuse of the law was rampant, however, and enforcement virtually impossible. In 1933, the 21st Amendment, repealing the 18th, was ratified. But, as *The Oxford Companion to Wine*, edited by Jancis Robinson, observes, "Unfortunately, the [21st] Amendment left to the separate states the entire regulation of the liquor traffic within their borders, with the result that the US liquor laws, including local and state prohibitions, remain a crazy quilt of inconsistent and arbitrary rules, another lastingly destructive effect of national prohibition. . . . Liquor — wine very much included — continues to be an object of punitive taxation, of moral disapproval, and of obstructive legislation in the United States today."

During the thirteen years of Prohibition, thousands of wineries across the nation went out of business. No one in the wine industry received any compensation for their losses. In addition to the personal and financial tragedy for people involved, the economic loss to local communities and to entire states was disastrous.

California ventured forward on the road to recovery immediately after Repeal, thanks in part to a more enlightened government than most states. But in the East, the wine industry lay in a coma for nearly half a century until the 1960s and 1970s, when it finally began to emerge from its long slumber and reinvent itself. While hardly the "Vinland" that dazzled Leif Eriksson, the wine growing regions of the eastern United States today are beginning to prosper again. Most of us would even consider much of the wine produced in the East to be above average in quality. And, once in a while, a truly great wine emerges.

FROM VINEYARD TO TABLE

Numerous factors affect the production of wines and our enjoyment of them. In this section, I will describe the various grape types used for wines in America and the challenges of marketing eastern wines. In the appendix, I have also included information about how wine is made, how to know when wine is ready to drink, and how to taste wine in a winery.

GRAPE TYPES

Vinifera: The world's most common wine grape comes from the vine species called *Vitis vinifera*, a native of Europe and West Asia. There are approximately 10,000 varieties of vinifera, which include Chardonnay, Sauvignon Blanc, Riesling, Pinot Noir, Cabernet Sauvignon, Merlot, and all the other grapes that are used to make traditional European wines.

Labrusca and rotundifolia: Of the many grape varieties that are native to America, only two are still used for winemaking in any quantity.

- *Vitis labrusca*, found in the northeastern United States, produces intensely aromatic grapes with a pronounced flavor that is often described as "foxy." Grape juice and raw Concord grapes have a typical foxy smell, which scientists attribute either to a component called *methyl anthranilate*, or to *o-amino acetophenone*. Whatever its cause, "foxiness" is seldom a complimentary term when applied to wine.

   The Concord, from which grape juice and many sweet, kosher wines are made, is the most widely planted labrusca grape, and the most common grape in the United States after the Thompson seedless table grape. Catawba, another well known labrusca, was for many years the leading wine grape in America. It is still used today, especially to make sparkling wines that have a pronounced, grapey flavor. Longfellow described this wine as "dulcet, delicious, and dreamy." Todays wine buff might be more inclined to characterize it as "foxy, funky, and forgettable."
- *Vitis rotundifolia*, a native of the southern states, produces the Scuppernong grape, which yields a sweet, musky wine that is still popular in the South.

Hybrids: French-American hybrid grapes are a cross between two grape varieties, usually vinifera and labrusca. The earliest vinifera vine cuttings imported from Europe sometimes survived here for a few years. During that time a natural hybridization took place by exchange pollination between the imported vines and local American species. The earliest offspring of these crosses, first noticed in the mid-18th century in Pennsylvania, became known as the Alexander, and it was the basis for the first commercially successful winery in North America.

In the early 1800s, many more of these accidental crossings were discovered, and by the middle of the century, controlled hybridization began in America. By the late 19th and early 20th century, after the devastation of the French vineyards by phylloxera, French hybridizers developed a host of hardy, flavorful grapes — Seyval and Vidal Blanc, Chambourcin, Baco, and Rayon d'Or among others. For many years these vines were planted all over France, but since 1955, French planting regulations have discouraged vine varieties that are associated with inferior wines, including many of the hybrids. While hybrid plantings have been phased out throughout most of France, they have remained popular in certain regions of the U.S.

In the 1930s, a hobbyist winemaker named Philip Wagner began experimenting with French-American hybrids in his vineyard in Maryland. At the time, it seemed unlikely that vinifera grapes could ever be grown in the eastern states, while the flavor of labrusca grapes would never be accepted. The better hybrids that Wagner helped develop and popularize seemed an exciting alternative.

When the eastern wine industry began its revival in the 1960s, hybrids were the principle grapes planted. Today, however, many wine producers are ripping out hybrid vines and replacing them with vinifera, while most new vineyards are planted exclusively with vinifera grapes. The switch is due to a number of factors, including the evolution of hardier vinifera vines, and the use of more advanced technology in combatting disease. New understanding about vineyard management — including new forms of trellising and pruning — also helps to keep the vines healthy. The fact that winters have generally been milder for the past few years has been another factor in increased vinifera plantings. Furthermore, like their French cousins, most contemporary vintners believe vinifera grapes make the best wines. Why work with mediocre grapes, they argue, when vinifera grapes have proven to be the best for winemaking?

On the other hand, not all wineries have rushed to raise Chardonnay, Pinot Noir, Sauvignon Blanc, Merlot, and other European grapes. Many people believe that the best wines made from superior hybridized grapes, such as Seyval and Vidal Blanc, can hold their own. They further insist that wine made from hybrid grapes has a unique American flavor, with as much varietal appeal as any other wine. Finally, they worry that the European vines will not survive over the long haul, pointing out that history is not on the side of vinifera in the East.

From an economic standpoint, however, vinifera has the edge. No matter how good the wine from hybridized grapes might be, marketing them is an uphill challenge. Skeptics wonder how, in a world awash in wine, the consumer can be persuaded to buy a bottle of unknown Baco over a similarly priced Merlot, or an obscure Aurora over a reliable Chardonnay. In addition, wines from vinifera grapes bring higher prices.

Many viticulturists in the eastern states hedge their bets, planting both vinifera and hybrids. In many ways this diversity is fortunate for consumers, who can taste and test their way through a wide range of wines, from simple country hybrids — many of which, in spirit and sometimes in palate, resemble some of France's regional *vin du pays* — to mid-range, moderately priced wines, all the way up to beautifully-crafted examples of premium wines made from both hybrids and the world's noblest grapes.

MARKETING WINE

It's a challenge of Sisyphean proportions to market wine made in the East. The first obvious difficulty is promoting an unknown product. The relatively small production of eastern wineries, ranging from a few hundred cases to a couple of thousand, is another. Add to this a complex web of licensing, distribution, taxation, and retail regulations, and one begins to understand why growing grapes is considered the *easy* part of winemaking! The problem is compounded when a winery sells and transports its wines from one state to another. As one New England winemaker described the convoluted logistics of interstate wine distribution, "If your hat blows off in Rhode Island and lands in Connecticut, you have to apply for a license to go get it."

For all these reasons, most eastern wine is sold in the state where it's produced. All eastern wineries sell their own wine, and for many, the wine is only available through the winery. Many regional wines are available in local restaurants, while a handful of the most successful wineries such as Bedell, Chaddsford, and Sakonnet, for example, may be featured on wine lists throughout their own state. The biggest producers, such as Rhode Island's Sakonnet Vineyards or Virginia's Williamsburg, are served in a few fine restaurants across the country. Several audacious wineries, such as Long Island's Palmer, have even begun to crack the European market.

PART ONE

The Benchlands

I. Southeastern New England

Connecticut
Massachusetts
Rhode Island

II. Long Island

North Fork
South Fork

III. Southeastern New Jersey and Coastal Virginia

Southeastern New Jersey
Coastal Virginia

IV. Lake Erie Region

New York
Pennsylvania
Ohio
Island Wineries

PART ONE

The Benchlands

Marguerite Thomas

Vines at Sylvin Farms, Germania, New Jersey, await the coming of spring.

The viticultural region of the eastern Benchlands includes southeastern Massachusetts and the coastal sections of Rhode Island, Connecticut, Long Island, New Jersey, and Virginia. This bench of sand, sediment, and stone was formed by the debris left behind by the massive melting glacier that drifted across the land tens of thousands of years ago. Benchland soils are typically low in most trace minerals except silica. The soil in some areas, such as parts of Long Island, may be gravelly.

The Benchlands tend to have moderate weather due to the influence of the Atlantic Ocean and Long Island Sound. The effect of this relatively mild climate was demonstrated most recently in 1994, when a particularly severe winter cut a wide swath inland, killing vines from the Finger Lakes down through Pennsylvania and northern Virginia, but leaving most of the coastal area unscathed.

Because a warmer climate leads to riper grapes than in colder interior sections of the Northeast, wine from the Benchlands is frequently characterized by a more pronounced color and flavor, and a softer texture. It is often slightly lower in acidity than wine from cooler regions. At its best, this wine will be full bodied and luscious. With some exceptions, it is best consumed young.

SOUTHEASTERN NEW ENGLAND

Tempered by the jet stream and situated just above Latitude 40 (making it slightly more southerly than France), New England ought to have reliable, moderate weather — but it doesn't. Mark Twain wrote about New England's weather: "In the spring, I have counted 136 different kinds of weather inside of 24 hours." Most vintners in this part of the world know exactly what he meant.

And yet, despite winter freezes, schizophrenic springs, steamy summer heat, and vine-flattening hurricanes, people have been making wine here since 1632, when the first vineyard was planted on Governor's Island in Boston Harbor. For those blessed with enough cash and a determined Yankee spirit, the odds in favor of producing wine sometimes outweigh the risks. An obsessive desire to succeed certainly helps. As Bob Russell, owner of Massachusetts's Westport Rivers winery puts it, "Anyone going into the wine business has to do it because they love it — because they have a dream, a passion."

The land beside the coast, protected as it is by the Atlantic, has proven to be the most suitable place for growing vinifera grapes in New England. The Chardonnay grape that is harder to grow further inland does well here due to a relatively long growing season — about 190 days, compared to the average of 145 days in other parts of New England. Other white wine grapes, especially Seyval and Vidal Blanc, also thrive along the coast.

While white wine predominates, New England does produce some above-average red wines too, particularly Pinot Noir. Only a handful of commercial wineries are operating in southeastern New England now, but as this is definitely one of the most promising viticultural regions in the eastern United States, others will surely follow.

Coastal New England is one of the country's great travel destinations, filled with charming villages and historic houses, antique stores and art galleries, picturesque farmland undulating down to the sea, colorful harbors and ports, wildlife refuges, woodlands, and beaches. All this and wine too — New England is truly blessed.

CONNECTICUT

CHAMARD VINEYARDS
Rating: 🍷🍷🍷
203-664-0299.
115 Cow Hill Road,
   Clinton, CT.
Directions: From US I-95
   take exit 63 to Rte. 81

Chamard's owner, William Chaney, is also chairman of the board and C.E.O. of Tiffany & Co. In the mid-1980s Chaney began searching New England for a place to plant a vineyard when, by a stroke of luck, he found a 40-acre farm for sale in Clinton, Connecticut, the same coastal community

north. Just past Morgan High School, turn left onto Walnut Hill Road, which will merge into Cow Hill Rd. after $^8/_{10}$ mile. The winery is on the left.
Owner: William Chaney.
Open: Year-round, Wed.–Sat., 11 AM–4 PM.
Price Range of Wines: $8.99 for Chardonnay to $12.99 for Cabernet Sauvignon.

where he owned a weekend house. Now the Kansas-born Chaney spends weekends and vacations in the vineyards or in the winery working alongside winemaker and general manager Larry McCulloch who, after training as a horticulturist, learned winemaking at Benmarl, a Hudson River winery. Both men share the strong belief that great wines come from great vineyards. "We've proven that if you pick the right site and put your mind and money into it, you can make nice wine. It may not be easy, but it can be done," McCulloch insists.

Chamard's exceptional recent Chardonnays have a concentration of fruitiness balanced by high levels of acidity and a pronounced mineral aftertaste. Very fine Cabernet Sauvignon, Pinot Noir, and Merlot are also produced here in limited amounts. Chamard Vineyard's total production is 6,000 cases.

Chamard's 20 acres of vines are edged by classic New England stone walls that undulate picturesquely across the land. There are no picnic facilities, but Chamard is a short drive from a number of New England seaside villages such as Branford, Madison, and Guilford, each of which has a village green that is an irresistible picnic spot.

STONINGTON VINEYARDS
Rating: 👤👤
860-535-1222.
Taugwonk Road, Stonington, CT.
Directions: Heading east on Rte. I-95 take exit 91. Turn left on Taugwonk Rd. and follow signs to the winery.
Owners: Happy and Nick Smith.
Open: Daily 11 AM–5 PM.
Price Range of Wines: $6.99 for Seaport White and Seaport Blush to $14.99 for Pinot Noir.
Special Features: Picnic facilities.
Special Events: Annual food and wine festival.

Stonington Vineyards is set in the hills a few miles inland from the borough of Stonington. Nick Smith, who arrived in the wine world via international banking, believes strongly in maintaining the individual character of regional wines. While 50% of his grapes are grown on the Stonington property, the rest are purchased from local vineyards, including Long Island, which is visible just across Long Island Sound.

Under the supervision of winemaker Mike McAndrew, the wines at Stonington Vineyards are improving year after year. The Chardonnay sometimes has a beguiling aroma of jasmine. The Pinot Noir is light and clean tasting. I am particularly partial to the Rosé of Pinot Noir, which should not be confused with a blush wine. This wine may be pink, but it is nice and dry, with a hint of rose petals in the nose and tannins in the mouth — all in all a fine partner for summer fare such as grilled vegetables or salade Niçoise. Seaport White is a user-friendly blend of Chardonnay, Vidal, and Seyval, which Smith describes as, "a real New England wine, great with scallops and lobster."

Stonington's production is currently at about 7,000 cases. Stonington Borough is a lovely seaport village, with many fine historic houses, and an outstanding collection of antique shops, art and craft galleries, and restaurants. Mystic Seaport Aquarium, one of the best in the East, and Mystic Seaport are a 15 minute drive from Stonington.

MASSACHUSETTS

WESTPORT RIVERS VINEYARD & WINERY

Rating: 🍷🍷🍷
508-636-3423.
417 Hixbridge Road, Westport, MA.
Directions: From Rte. 199 take Rte. 88 south to Hixbridge Rd. Turn left to winery.
Owners: Bob and Carol Russell.
Open: Apr. through Dec., noon–5 PM. Tours on Sat. and Sun. in winter by appointment.
Price Range of Wines: $8.50 for Westport White to $20 for sparkling wine.
Special Features: Picnic area, art gallery.
Special Events: New England Spring Picnics, Annual Sparkling Wine Independence Day Gala, other seasonal events.

Set on an old Massachusetts farm, on a spit of land facing Rhode Island, Westport Rivers is a family run winery. Almost two decades ago, Bob Russell decided to leave the security of his job as a metallurgical engineer for the uncertainty of operating a winery. The decision was based partly on the Russells desire to find an interest and occupation where "we could grow old together." The Russells were also influenced by long discussions with Carol's father, who had owned Germania Wine Cellars in Hammondsport, New York. "With my father's memories, our love of food and wine, our common concern for environmental issues, and a long-standing desire to preserve working agricultural land, a vineyard and winery was an obvious choice," explained Carol.

The Russells could have gone anywhere — California, Oregon, Australia — but they opted for this corner of the world for one simple reason: "We loved the New England landscape." By 1982 the Russells had purchased a farm and were planting Chardonnay vines. Their son, Bill, apprenticed at various wineries, including Napa's Frog's Leap, before joining the business as winemaker. Another son, Rob, manages the vineyard.

Ninety-two percent of Westport River's wine is made from grapes that are estate-grown (raised on their own property). With 56 acres of vineyards, Westport Rivers has the largest number of vinifera grapevines planted in New England. The remaining 8% are imported from Long Island. All of the wine is made from vinifera grapes and all of it is excellent, from the Gold Label Chardonnay to the Westport White, an off-dry (i.e. somewhat sweet) blend of Chardonnay, Riesling, and Pinot Blanc. About 8,500 cases are produced each year, but the ultimate goal is 12,000.

Westport Rivers is the only New England winery to produce a sparkling wine made from vinifera grapes that uses traditional French Champagne vinification techniques. This is a charming wine, with fruity flavors, a bracing acidity, and tiny, persistent bubbles.

Westport's setting, deep in the picturesque farmland, is lovely. The Russells' commitment to the environment remains strong: from 1993 on, a portion of the profits from every bottle of wine has been donated to an organization dedicated to the preservation of farmland in Massachusetts.

RHODE ISLAND

SAKONNET VINEYARDS
Rating: 🍷🍷🍷🍷
401-635-8486.
162 West Main Road (Route 77), Little Compton, RI.
Directions: From US I-195 take Rte. 24 south and continue to the Tiverton–Little Compton/ Rte. 77 exit. Go south on Rte. 77 through a traffic light at Tiverton Four Corners. Sakonnet is 3 miles from this junction on the left.
Owners: Susan and Earl Samson.
Open: Daily, June to Oct., 10 AM–6 PM; Nov. to May, 11 AM–5 PM.
Price Range of Wines: $6.75 for blended wines; $8.95 for Vidal; $17.50 for an Estate Pinot Noir.
Special Features: Picnic facilities overlooking the vineyards.
Special Events: Cooking classes, food and wine events throughout the year.

Sakonnet Vineyards is ideally situated on one of the handful of Rhode Island peninsulas poking out into Narragansett Bay. Established in 1975, Sakonnet is now New England's largest winery, with an annual production of 30,000 cases. Owners Susan and Earl Samson came to the wine business from backgrounds far removed from anything resembling agriculture — she from the Broadway theater, he from the world of investments and capital venture — but they have embraced Sakonnet Vineyards as a way of life as much as a commercial undertaking. Winemaker John Sotelo came to Sakonnet from Iron Horse Vineyards in Sonoma in 1994, while vineyard manager Joetta Kirk has been here for more than 17 years. Most of the winery's grapes are from Sakonnet's own 37-acre vineyard, although some additional grapes are purchased, mostly from local vineyards.

Particularly outstanding among Sakonnet's excellent wines is the rich and satisfying Estate Chardonnay, which is a pleasant accompaniment to summer foods, the Gewürztraminer, with a powerful, floral aroma (it's a real winner with smoked salmon), and the Vidal Blanc, which has flavors reminiscent of ripe peaches and melons, but with enough acidity to make it a fine accompaniment to shrimp, oysters, and other shellfish. Sakonnet also produces a few inexpensive, agreeable, lightweight wines made from blends of various grapes. These include Spinnaker White, America's Cup Red, and Eye of the Storm, a fruity blush named after a recent hurricane that devastated much of the surrounding area while sparing the Sakonnet vineyards.

This winery is in a particularly attractive spot, and Little Compton is a charming, and attractive New England village. Swimming beaches, fishing, and historic attractions are nearby.

Profile: Joetta Kirk

Joetta Kirk never set out to become a vineyard manager. On the contrary, her career path began evolving in a perfectly ordinary, conventional way. First she was a hairdresser, then a salesperson in a shop, followed by a stint in an advertising agency. Along the way she fell in love, got married . . . and got divorced.

At the time of the divorce, she was living in a cottage on an estate in rural Massachusetts, where she agreed to do groundswork in exchange for rent. Her fate was sealed as she embarked on her lifelong love affair with agriculture.

Characteristically, Joetta first learned everything she could about managing an agricultural property, from property management to equipment maintenance. Then, on a whim, she contacted Jim and Lolly Mitchell, the original owners of Rhode Island's Sakonnet Vineyards, after reading an article about their winery. The Mitchells, who happened to be looking for someone who knew how to operate a tractor, invited her to lunch, and the rest, as they say, is history.

Joetta Kirk became not just Sakonnet's vineyard manager, but also one of the most respected authorities on cool-climate vineyards, especially those in the Atlantic coastal states. For almost two decades she literally spent her life in the vineyards, habitually putting in seven-day weeks. "It was stupid and crazy," she sighed, "but I needed to learn a lot. And I *did* learn a lot, and I also witnessed many extraordinary changes during that time." What are some of these changes?

"One is that the technology of growing grapes in marginal regions has advanced significantly in the last ten years," Joetta explained. "The difference between the early 1980s and the 1990s is dramatic. Take the advancement of clonal selection: we've found that the most popular Chardonnay clone in California isn't that good here. The clone that's right for us is called Colmar, from France.

"Then there is the issue of canopy management that I first heard about at an international symposium in New Zealand in 1988. (Canopy management refers to pruning and trellising techniques that allow sunlight to reach all parts of the vine.) If some parts of the vine are shaded, it's defeating itself. You want the plant to photosynthesize properly, and we now know you have to supply sunlight to the leaves, the shoots, and the fruit. You should not allow the vines to droop to the ground."

Although Joetta talks about building more of a personal life after all these years of devotion to the vine, it is clear that the vineyard still enthralls her. "I can't imagine another crop that would be as fascinating as vines," she confessed. "A vineyard is a controlled environment that wants to run amok. There's an emotional bond there. It's a contest between grower and vine and you wonder who's going to win; who's going to be happy. Of course, I want both to win." Joetta mentioned another worker at Sakonnet who trims the hedges around the vineyard. "He comes in sometimes to tell me the vines look happy. So we go out and stand there admiring them. And you know, they *do* look happy."

OTHER SOUTHERN NEW ENGLAND WINERIES

DIAMOND HILL VINEYARDS (800-752-2505, 3145 Diamond Hill Road, Cumberland, RI). This winery specializes in fruit wines, but it does have a 4$^{1}/_{2}$ acre vineyard from which an exceptionally good Pinot Noir wine is produced in limited amounts (about 300 cases annually). When the weather is too cool to make red wine, owners Clara and Peter Berntson turn out a dry, crisp Pinot Noir Blanc — a white that would be a fine match for local seafood.

MELLEA VINEYARD (508-943-6527, 108 Old Southbridge Rd., Dudley, MA) is too far inland to be considered part of the coastal region, but from the traveler's point of view it makes sense to list this Massachusetts winery here. Just 15 minutes from historic Old Sturbridge Village, Mellea produces a variety of wines from vinifera and hybrid grapes that range from dry to sweet.

NANTUCKET VINEYARD (508-228-9235, Bartlett Farm Road, Nantucket, MA). Nantucket is a particularly challenging place to grow vines as it is an island, unprotected from the elements by a land mass. Lacking the extra boost of heat given off by the land in places such as Rhode Island and Connecticut, the grapes at Nantucket Vineyard have a hard time ripening fully. Nevertheless about 2,500 cases of wine, from the estate's own vineyard, are produced here.

RESTAURANTS AND LODGING

New England's greatest gift to gastronomy is its seafood. From chowders to stuffed clams, steamed lobsters to codfish cakes, broiled scallops to oysters on the half shell, this is died-and-gone-to-heaven dining for those of us who love fish. One of the best things about this bounty of seafood is that it is the perfect mate for the crisp, dry, high-acid white wines of the region. There are still active fishing ports all along the New England coast and at least 50 aquaculturists who raise oysters and other shellfish in ponds and inlets off the shore.

With its proximity to the vast assortment of accommodations and eateries throughout the area, especially in Newport and Providence, visitors to the northern section of New England's wine country will never lack for restaurants or places to spend the night. Two restaurants should be singled out for special mention in Providence.

RESTAURANTS

Providence, RI

AL FORNO
401-273-9760.
577 South Main Street,
   Providence, RI.
Price: Moderate–Expensive.

A contemporary Italian-style restaurant, owned by George Germon and Johanne Killeen, Al Forno is, quite simply, one of the best places to eat in America. Starters include individual grilled pizzas, garlic salad, crostini with prosciutto and honey, or one of the pasta dishes. The entrees present an agonizing choice — everything is tempting! Grilled portobello mushrooms with mashed potatoes and roasted sugar snap peas, is an outstanding vegetarian choice. The clam roast comes with an incendiary spicy sausage. The grilled lamb steak with garlic potato salad and mixed greens gets raves as well. The desserts are equally seductive — fresh fig and gooseberry tarte tatin is one example, another is a mint-chocolate chunk ice cream sandwich. The wine list presents a further embarrassment of riches. It contains 16 Champagne and sparkling wine choices that range from Taittinger's Comptes de Champagne Rosé ($150) to Nino Franco Prosecco "Rustico" ($22). Predictably, there's a strong Italian bias running a long gamut from Gaja to Jermann to Ceretto. There are also interesting French and American selections, including a couple from Rhode Island's own Sakonnet Vineyards.

**THE BLUE POINT
   OYSTER BAR AND
   RESTAURANT**
401-272-6145.
99 North Main Street,
   Providence, RI.
Price: Moderate–Expensive.

The Blue Point Oyster Bar is noted not only for the wonderful seafood items on its menu, but also for one of the most remarkable wine lists in this part of the country. Although it's a tiny, 45-seat restaurant, there are over 3,000 bottles in the cellar. The extensive list of wines includes selections by the glass and by the half-glass, including Rhode Island's own Sakonnet Vineyards.

LODGING

Rhode Island

THE ROOST (BED &
   BREAKFAST)
401-635-8486.
162 West Main Road (Rte.
   77), Little Compton, RI.
Price: Moderate.

Located in the original farmhouse on the property of Sakonnet Vineyards, The Roost has three nicely furnished bedrooms, all newly renovated, and each with its own bath.

Connecticut

Old Lyme, a small village about half way between Stonington and Chamard Vineyards, has two attractive inns, both with reasonably good restaurants.

THE OLD LYME INN
860-434-2600.
85 Lyme Street, Old Lyme, CT.
Price: Expensive.

This large and elegant restaurant, located on the main floor of a handsome colonial mansion, has guestrooms upstairs in the main building, as well as in an adjacent carriage house. The wine list includes Connecticut wines.

THE BEE AND THISTLE INN
860-434-1667 or 800-622-4946.
100 Lyme Street, Old Lyme, CT.
Price: Moderate–Expensive.

On grounds that reach to the Lieutenant River, this charming country inn with 11 guestrooms and a cottage, wins numerous awards for its romantic atmosphere and its cuisine. There's entertainment on the weekends. Connecticut wines are featured on the wine list.

Oysters

New England's commercial fishing fleet is still productive, and so are a new breed of farmer: aquaculturists, or farmers of the sea, who raise fish and shellfish in inlets and salt ponds near the shore. While most of the local seafood is well suited to eastern wines, there is nothing quite so delicious as the taste of sweet and briny oysters fresh from the sea accompanied by one of the lively white wines from the Atlantic coastal regions.

Like grapes, the flavor of oysters varies tremendously, depending on where they are raised. No one yet understands all the factors that contribute to this variation in flavor, but it is safe to assume that the degree of salinity, as well as the fluctuations in water temperature may affect both the oysters and the microscopic algae, called phytoplankton, they feed on.

While the oysters from different locals have individual flavors, they all — except for the French Belon oyster that one East Coast farmer is beginning to experiment with — originate from the same oyster family. Whether they are called Bluepoint, Peconic Bay, Wellfleet, Fishers Island, or Cotuit, virtually all oysters raised on the East Coast are grown from the seed of the American oyster.

CUTTYHUNK SHELLFISH FARMS (508-636-2072, Cuttyhunk Island, MA. Open: May through October.)

One of the most notable oyster farms is located just off the coast of Massachusetts, not far from Westport Rivers winery. Oyster farms, like vineyards, are vulnerable to weather patterns, explains owner Seth Garfield, "We are still recovering from Hurricane Bob, which hit two years ago. It wiped out not only all of our oysters, but all the hatcheries as well." In addition to oysters, Cuttyhunk also harvests wild quahog clams. The plan is to gradually begin cultivating these clams as they become less available in the wild. Cuttyhunk oysters may be enjoyed in many East Coast restaurants, from Boston to New York. Visitors are welcome at the farm. A ferry travels to the island from New Bedford.

→

MOONSTONE OYSTERS (401-783-3360, Narragansett, RI. Open: By appointment only.)

Moonstone supplies its trademarked oysters to some of the best restaurants in the East, from the Oyster Bar in New York's Grand Central Station to Providence's Bluepoint Oyster Bar and Restaurant. Both native species and Belon oysters, are raised in coastal salt ponds at Moonstone; scallops are grown as well.

FISHERS ISLAND (516-788-7889)

Fishers Island oysters are raised in nets off the harbor bottom on Fishers Island (NY), a private island nestled between Connecticut and Long Island in Long Island Sound. Ninety percent of the oysters go to restaurants in Manhattan, while the rest are reserved for other East Coast restaurants, including the Old Lyme Inn. Not open to the public.

LONG ISLAND

Long Island is a 120-mile-long bed of gravel and silt left behind by a glacier sliding in slow motion over the land some 10,000 years ago. Looking at the flat and almost treeless land now, it is hard to believe that when the first Europeans arrived, it was thickly forested and inhabited by bears and snakes. Fields, lying beyond the sandy beaches, were tilled and planted in corn by the Native Americans living there.

Like the original inhabitants, the newcomers found that because of its well-drained soil and temperate climate, Long Island was a good place to grow a variety of crops. Many of the early settlers raised table grapes on arbors near their houses, and in the 1950s, John Wickham planted the first experimental vinifera grapes on his farm in Cutchogue, on Long Island's eastern North Fork. Rather than attempt to make wine, he sold the grapes at his farm stand.

Today, fourteen of Long Island's eighteen wineries are on the North Fork, a 159-square mile band of well-drained soil. Surrounded on three sides by water, with the moderating Gulf Stream paralleling the island some 50 miles offshore, this region has the longest, coolest growing season of any viticultural region in the Northeast. Because the water cools down slowly in the winter, reflecting heat back onto the land, the severe freezes that threaten other regions are mostly unknown here. In the summer, the water warms up gradually, keeping temperatures from soaring disastrously.

The North Fork is the sunniest part of New York state, with at least 210 growing days per season (this compares with 150 days in the Finger Lakes). This long and sunny season allows vinifera grapes — whose ripeness is often unpredictable from year to year in other areas in the Northeast — to ripen consistently here. Furthermore, the constant sea breezes that blow across the vineyards discourage the formation of molds and mildew on the grapes.

This is not to say that the area is trouble-free. In addition to the usual vagaries of weather and pests that threaten viticulture everywhere, Long Island's vineyards are particularly susceptible to damage from wind and hurricanes, as well as from great flocks of birds, who love nothing better than to dine on grapes.

The first commercial vineyard was planted by Alex and Louisa Hargrave in 1972. There were four more by 1980, when the first big flush of vineyard planting on Long Island began in earnest. During the economic slump of the late '80s things slowed down, but today, with eighteen wineries operating on Long Island and more about to open, the boom may be back.

Virtually all of the grapes grown on Long Island are vinifera. In addition to white grapes, such as Chardonnay and Gewürztraminer, red wine grapes also perform consistently better than they do farther north.

The remarkable improvement in Long Island wines over the past few years can be explained by the increased age of the vines, as well as by better vineyard management that allows the grapes to ripen more completely on the vine. It seems likely that Long Island wines will continue to improve — experts say the newly released 1993 vintage is the best to date.

Long Island wines are generally more intense in color and flavor than those from New York's Finger Lakes, but they are more delicate and restrained than wines from California. Critics agree that some of the Long Island Chardonnays are as good as any in the world, and interest in the reds is also increasing. "I think we'll be known first for our Merlot," said winemaker Kip Bedell. "The grape ripens just after Chardonnay, and it is our most consistent producer. Eventually, I think we'll be known for our Cabernet Sauvignon and Cabernet Franc too. In good years we already make world class red wines."

Long Island wines, with an average price of $10 per bottle, are the most expensive in the East, rivaling California's premium wines. Long Island produces 2% of New York State's total wine output, but 90% of its high-end wine. With the added bonus of its proximity to New York City — the most sophisticated and largest per-capita wine consumption center in the East — Long Island has a unique marketing advantage. Long Island sells about 10% of its crop each year to other wineries, mostly in New York State, New Jersey, and New England.

Long Island's wine country is approximately a two-hour drive from Manhattan, and an hour and a half by ferry from Connecticut. Most of Long Island's wineries are located on the North Fork, along a 35-mile-long strip of land that is scarcely five miles wide. The drive to the South Fork wineries will take approximately three hours from Manhattan. They can be reached from the North Fork by driving through Riverhead or by taking the ferries that connect to Shelter Island.

NORTH FORK

BEDELL CELLARS
Rating: 🍷🍷🍷🍷🍷
516-734-7537.
Main Road (Route 25), Cutchogue, NY .
Directions: From I-495, take exit 73 in Riverhead, continue east on Old Country Road (Rte. 58) to Rte. 25. Continue east to winery.
Owners: Kip and Susan Bedell.
Open: Daily 11 AM–5 PM.
Price Range of Wines: $6.99 for Cygnet to $24 for Eis.

Bedell is housed in a turn-of-the-century potato barn which has been embellished in an understated fashion with stained glass windows and a small tasting bar. There are 30 acres of fields planted with grapes, and the winery bottles 6,200 cases annually. Bedell wine labels are easily recognized by the stylized pair of swans on a black and white background. "We wanted to represent some of Long Island's marine bird life on the label," explains owner-winemaker Kip Bedell.

The most popular Bedell wine, called Cygnet, is an alluring blend dominated by Riesling and Gewürztraminer grapes. "It's as close to a blush

Kip Bedell

It was a slow journey from running a fuel oil business to opening a winery, but John (Kip) Bedell inched along his chosen path patiently. After buying a potato farm in Cutchogue in 1980, Kip, and his wife, Susan, spent the next ten years commuting from their home in Garden City to Long Island's North Fork. Gradually they began planting grapes and tending the vineyard. When he arrived on the North Fork, there were only four other pioneering wineries — Hargrave, Lenz, Pindar, and Peconic Bay. Barely aware of what the others were doing, each invented his own rules for growing grapes and turning out wine, learning by trial and error what would work in this unique environment.

Kip Bedell made his first wines in 1989. He had, as it turned out, selected the perfect site for a vineyard. He also seemed to be gifted with an unusually fine palate and a talent for creating superior wine. "Nobody — nobody — is more gifted," said *The New York Times* writer Howard G. Goldberg in *Fine Wine Folio.*

In 1990, after ten years of juggling winemaking, working the vineyard, and marketing his wines with the family fuel oil business, he sold the oil company. He and Susan moved to Cutchogue and he became a full-time winemaker. "I'm still in a business that depends on the weather. And I'm still just pumping liquid from one container to another," he jokes, "but at least now I can drink the product."

Kip Bedell is a winemakers' winemaker, a widely respected technician and experienced vintner who others turn to for inspiration and advice. He also makes some of the best wines in the region. "There's no doubt that some of our earlier wines weren't great," he acknowledges now. "Our vines were young and we made some mistakes. We're still fine-tuning some of our viticultural practices, but there's been a great improvement over the past five years."

The future looks rosy from Kip Bedell's perspective. "We're sitting next to the biggest market in the world, which we've only just begun to tap," he explains, cocking his head in the direction of New York City. In fact, the market is already beginning to respond. Bedell wines are sold in several Manhattan stores and in many of the city's finest restaurants. Dressed in jeans and high rubber boots, the typical uniform of a winemaker, Kip was working in the cellar while he mused about wine. "The Long Island style is just beginning to evolve. We'll be able to define it better when our region gets a little more time under its belt." He paused for a moment to adjust a hose attached to a large stainless steel tank filled with Chardonnay. Then he looked back up with a smile. "We're poised right on the edge of a very exciting time."

Marguerite Thomas

wine as we'll ever get here," says Kip, but this luscious and somewhat sweet wine is far more complex and classy than any blush could hope to be. The Reserve Chardonnay is soft and elegant with discreet, rather than overbearing, vanilla flavors picked up from oak barrels and malolactic fermentation. Main Road Red, an 80% Cabernet Sauvignon/20% Merlot blend, is an easy-drinking wine that is terrific with informal foods, from picnics to pastas. This is a particularly good wine to serve with chili, according to Kip.The label on this wine depicts the old red '51 Ford pickup that has been put out to pasture next to the winery. Bedell's Merlot and Cabernet Sauvignon are excellent, as is Eis, a Riesling dessert wine.

Peter Gristina, manager, Gristina Vineyards.

Marguerite Thomas

GRISTINA VINEYARDS
Rating: ▸▸▸
516-734-7089.
Main Road (Route 25),
   Cutchogue, NY.
Directions: From I-495, take
   exit 73 in Riverhead,
   continue east on Old
   Country Road (Rte. 58) to
   Rte. 25. Continue east to
   winery.
Owners: Carole Gristina
   and Jerry Gristina, M.D.
Open: Daily 11 AM–5 PM.
Price Range of Wines: $8.99
   for Rosé to $19.99 for
   Pinot Noir. The average
   price is $13.99.
Special Features: Picnics
   may be enjoyed on the
   deck overlooking the
   vineyards.

Before the Gristinas purchased their property, it was a kosher wheat farm, at least until the rabbi got too old to oversee the crops. Now it is a modern vineyard and state-of-the-art winery, owned by Carole Gristina and Jerry Gristina, M.D., a physical medicine specialist.

The Gristinas' oldest son, Peter, manages the business and vineyards. Coming from a family who respects and understands wine (his parents have a 5,000 bottle cellar), Peter grew up with a keen interest in the subject. When they purchased the Long Island property in 1983 it seemed natural that he would come to work here, especially after apprenticing with local growers Dave and Steve Mudd, who taught him how to plant, grow, and prune vines.

Gristina is one of the few Long Island wineries to produce a consistently fine Pinot Noir. The grapes come from a tiny parcel of land and the total pro-

Special Events: Gristina hosts seminars and other popular events all year. They range from a Bud Break Renaissance Festival in May, to a Chestnuts on an Open Fire afternoon in December.

duction is limited to about 140 cases. "I didn't think we could get the grape to do well here since so many others had failed with it, but my father wanted to plant Pinot Noir because we are Burgundy fanatics," Peter explained. "He insisted, I resisted. But, in the end, he was right."

Gristina also makes a barrel-fermented, oak-aged Chardonnay, a Merlot with a touch of Cabernet Sauvignon added for backbone, a well-rounded Cabernet Sauvignon with complex aromas, and a fine, perky Rosé of Cabernet Sauvignon. The annual production is around 8,000 cases. At the back of the tasting room, huge windows look down into the cellar, giving visitors a good view of the tanks and other winery apparatus.

Louisa Hargarve, Hargrave Vineyard.

Marguerite Thomas

HARGRAVE VINEYARD
Rating: 👤👤👤
516-734-5111.
Sound Avenue (Route 48), Cutchogue, NY.
Directions: From I-495, take exit 73 in Riverhead, continue east on Old Country Road (Rte. 58) to Rte. 25. Continue east to Cutchogue. Rte. 48 is just north of Rte. 25 and paralleling it.
Owners: Louisa and Alex Hargrave.
Open:May through Dec., daily, 11 AM–5 PM.

Hargrave was the first commercial vineyard and winery on Long Island. Like many American vintners, Louisa and Alex Hargrave did not set out to be winemakers. Louisa had graduated from Smith College and Alex was getting his degree in Chinese from Harvard. They lived in Boston and drank great French wines while contemplating a scholarly life. But then Alex was sidelined by back surgery. After a period of recuperation in New York's Finger Lakes region and California, the couple gradually became more interested in winemaking than in academia. After searching up and down both coasts for an appropriate spot to make the French-style wines they

Price Range of Wines: $5.99 for Dune Blanc, a Pinot Blanc/Chardonnay blend, to $30 for the limited '93 Pinot Noir.

Special Features: Tiffany stained glass window in winery.

Special Events: Art shows, concerts, and wine seminars.

loved, they heard about John Wickham, a farmer who was raising a small, experimental plot of vinifera grapes in Cutchogue. If he could do it on a modest scale, they reasoned, why shouldn't they succeed on a larger one?

They planted their first vines in 1973. "We were here eight years before anyone else came," said Louisa. "At that time we weren't thinking in terms of this becoming a viticultural region someday. One reason we came here is that it was a farm community, so we knew we could get tractor parts," she added ironically.

Today the Hargraves own 84 acres, of which about 40 are planted. They produce 8,000 to 10,000 cases a year, depending on the vintage, which includes a mellifluous Chardonnay and a good Pinot Noir. The handsome winery which, like so many others in the region began its life as a potato and hay barn, looks now as if it's on the way to becoming a wine museum. Among the objects on display are a Greek amphora from 209 B.C. and a spectacular Tiffany stained glass window. The latticework label for Hargrave Reserve wines is a work of art itself. "It's the world's only laser-cut wine label," explains Louisa.

LENZ WINERY

Rating: 🍷🍷🍷🍷

516-734-6010 or 800-974-9899 (NY State only); fax 516-734-6069.

Main Road (Route 25), Peconic, NY.

Directions: From I-495, take exit 73 in Riverhead, continue east on Old Country Road (Rte. 58) to Rte. 25. Continue east to winery.

Owners: Peter and Deborah Carroll.

Open: Mon.–Fri., 11 AM– 5 PM; weekends 11 AM– 6 PM.

Price Range of Wines: $9.99 for White Label Chardonnay to $19.00 for sparkling wine.

Winemaker Eric Fry got his start in California at the Robert Mondavi and Jordan wineries under the tutelage of the legendary André Tchelistcheff. Following a stint in Australia, he made his way to the Vinifera Wine Cellars in New York's Finger Lakes region and then to Westport Rivers in Massachusetts, settling finally at Lenz in 1989.

When asked to compare wines from the warmer regions of California and Australia to the cooler eastern United States, the peripatetic winemaker mentions the lower sugar content of the eastern wines and their lower alcohol content (12% versus 14%.) He comments on the fact that the flavors and acid structure of the grapes are different. But he says the biggest surprise, when he first arrived in the East, was the amount of acidity in the wine. "What's the drug of choice for eastern winemakers?" he asks with a smile. "Acid. First it shocked me. Then I began to get used to it. Now, I want more and more of it all the time, like any true junkie. One advantage of acidity is that it adds to wine's compatibility with food."

With a Viking-like beard and a mane of russet curls, Fry is not the type of winemaker to coddle his grapes. His approach is to let them ripen in the vineyard to a maximum degree and then "mash the hell out of them to extract every bit of color and flavor." The result is red wines that do indeed have good color and flavor intensity, including a funky, Burgundy-style Pinot Noir and a rich Cabernet Sauvignon characterized by cherry flavors and a pleasant, long finish. Lenz Chardonnays tend to be well rounded, with layers of peach and pear flavors along with a hint of spiciness on the palate. Fry has been experimenting with Pinot Blanc, turning out the kind of fragrant, high-acid wine found in Alsace. Lenz sparkling wines, a passion for Fry, are crisp and elegant. Aiming for an annual production of 10,000 cases, Lenz currently produces about 8,500. The tasting room is in a typical converted Long Island potato barn.

Winemaker Don Klack in the Palmer Vineyards tasting room.

Marguerite Thomas

PALMER VINEYARDS

Rating: 🍷🍷🍷🍷
516-722-4080;
   fax 516-722-5364.
Sound Avenue (Route 48),
   Aquebogue, NY.
Directions: From I-495, take exit 73 in Riverhead, continue east on Old Country Road (Rte. 58) to Rte. 25. Continue east to Aquebogue. Rte. 48 is just north of Rte. 25 and paralleling it.
Owner: Robert Palmer.
Open: Apr. through Oct., daily, 11 AM–6 PM; Nov. through Mar., 11 AM–5 PM.

Palmer has two things that every winery needs: an excellent winemaker and a marketing genius. Owner Robert Palmer, who, in virtually every article written about him, is described as "bearlike," also owns a Manhattan-based radio and TV advertising agency. Dan Kleck, the winemaker, is a Hollywood-handsome guy. The two are a great team.

Their efforts have paid off in a number of ways. In terms of distribution, Palmer is considered one of the giants of the East, for the wine is available in stores and restaurants in 16 states as well as in England, Germany, Switzerland, Scandinavia, and Canada, and it is also served on American Airlines. In every other way as well, Palmer seems larger than life. The tasting room is designed like an

Price Range of Wines: $7.99 for Blush Wine to $14.99 for the Barrel Fermented Chardonnay.

Special Features: Outdoor picnic area; pub-style tasting room.

Special Events: Annual Yard Sale (wine bargains), Harvest Festival, 4th of July Hot Dog Event, Memorial Day Celebration, all with music on the deck.

English pub, with several Victorian booths that were once part of a pub in England. Palmer's production, at 15,000 cases, is sizeable compared to other wineries in the region, and the 50-acre vineyard is bigger than most. Even the wines are fuller-bodied and bolder-flavored than the average eastern libation.

Palmer's barrel-fermented Chardonnay exhibits complex fruit and vanilla aromas and the Cabernet Franc has some of the berrylike qualities of the Chinon reds that Dan Kleck admires. When asked if he thinks Long Island wines have any particular distinguishing characteristics, Dan describes a whiff of citrus, a lemony flavor that he believes is imparted by the distinctive Long Island soils. "It's also said that there's a hint of salt air in our wines," he adds, emphasizing that the ocean air affects not just flavor, but also moderates temperature and humidity levels.

It sounds as if it's an ideal spot for a vineyard, right? Not quite. "We're right in the middle of the North-South flyway pattern of migratory birds," sighs Dan, "which means that for 50 acres of vines, 50 acres of birdnetting are required. And we're also in the hurricane path. We put the weather channel on in late August and it stays on until October." When there's no hurricane afoot, visitors can take advantage of Palmer's outdoor picnic area.

PAUMANOK VINEYARDS

Rating: 👤👤

516-722-8800; fax 516-722-5110.

Main Road (Route 25), Aquebogue, NY.

Directions: From I-495, take exit 73 in Riverhead, continue east on Old Country Road (Rte. 58) to Rte. 25. Continue east to Aquebogue.

Owners: Charles and Ursula Massoud.

Open: Daily 11 AM–6 PM.

Price Range of Wines: $7.99 for Riesling to $26 for a half bottle of the rare late harvest Sauvignon Blanc.

Special Features: Picnic tables on the deck overlooking the vineyards.

Paumanok (this was Long Island's native name) is owned by Charles and Ursula Massoud, who sell grapes from their 50-acre vineyard to other wineries, and produce about 5,000 cases of wine at their own facility. Lebanese-born Charles says that he woke up one day and realized that he would never become the president of IBM, where he was an executive. Determined to start looking for something else that would provide an interesting and creative outlet for his interests and skills — and influenced, perhaps, by the fact that Ursula's family has been in the wine business in Germany for several generations — the Massouds elected to settle on Long Island's North Fork, where they began planting vines in 1983. Charles left IBM in 1992.

Charles feels that the vines are now mature enough to make exceptional wines, and indeed most of the wines at Paumanok prove him right. The Chardonnays range from a light and delicate style that goes well with shellfish, to bigger fla-

Special Events: Sunset at
the Vineyard (music,
gourmet dishes from
local restaurants, wine
tastings), classical music,
jazz concerts, Harvest
Festival, Christmas music
and wine tasting.

vored barrel-fermented wine that's a fine match for the native bluefish Long Islanders love in summer. Paumanok also makes a good Riesling with honeyed flavors and a faint whiff of petrol that often characterizes this grape. The late harvest wines, including Chenin Blanc, Riesling, and especially the 1993 Sauvignon Blanc, are terrific. They might be served by themselves at the end of a special meal or with a simple dessert such as biscotti. "Don't swallow sweet wines too quickly," advised Charles. "Let them sit in your mouth for a moment while you look for the dried-fruit flavors."

*Pellegrini Vineyards,
Cutchogue, Long Island.*

Marguerite Thomas

PELLEGRINI VINEYARDS

Rating: 🍷🍷🍷🍷🍷
516-734-4111;
fax 516-734-4159.
Main Road (Route 25),
Cutchogue, NY.
Directions: From I-495, take
exit 73 in Riverhead,
continue east on Old
Country Road (Rte. 58) to
Rte. 25. Continue east to
winery.
Owners: Joyce and Bob
Pellegrini.
Open: Daily 11 AM–5 PM.
Price Range of Wines: $8.99
for Rosé to $13.99 for
Pinot Noir.

Pellegrini is across the street from the site of Fort Cutchogue, where some of Long Island's first European settlers lived in the 17th century. The communal farmland surrounding the fort was known as "Commonage," which is the name Pellegrini uses for a line of very good, easy-sipping, everyday wines. Pleasant as they are, however, the Commonage wines are not what this place is really about, for Pellegrini also produces some of Long Island's finest, most serious wines. The Vintner's Pride Chardonnay is lush, with a big burst of fresh pear flavor and enough acidity to make it a good food wine. The Cabernet Sauvignon is full-bodied, with hints of mint, cedar, and chocolate flavors, while the Merlot is chockablock full of fresh plum and berry tones. "If Bordeaux-style

Cabernet is the king of red wines," said Australian-born winemaker Russell Hearn, "Merlot is the queen. It's supple and soft, not as hard and closed as Cabernet." Another of Russ' winners is Finale, a lush dessert wine made in the German eiswien style from late-harvested Gewürztraminer and Sauvignon Blanc grapes that are frozen before pressing.

Pellegrini is owned by Joyce and Bob Pellegrini — she a retired teacher, he the owner of a successful New York graphic design business. Everything about this winery reflects the good taste of a superior designer, from the handsome, stylized wine labels to the modern, cathedral-like tasting room, where a few cafe tables and chairs provide a nice spot to relax and sip. The building itself, which opened in 1992, is the North Fork's most spectacular winery, designed by local architects Samuels and Steelman. It is built around a grassy courtyard flanked by white columns. The cellars lie beneath. Outdoor balconies allow visitors to look down into the tankroom, where 5,000 cases of wine are processed each year.

PINDAR VINEYARDS

Rating: 🍷🍷🍷
516-734-6200.
Main Road (Route 25), Peconic, NY.
Directions: From I-495, take exit 73 in Riverhead, continue east on Old Country Road (Rte. 58) to Rte. 25. Continue east to winery.
Owner: Dr. Herodotus Damianos.
Open: Daily 11 AM–6 PM.

As one might expect from a place named after a Greek poet, Pindar is of heroic proportions. It has a larger production, with about 50,000 cases, and more land, with 400 acres, than any other winery on Long Island. Even the number of people its picnic pavilion can accommodate (three hundred), is larger than other wineries.

Founded in 1979 by Dr. Herodotus Damianos, a physician of Greek descent, who is affiliated with several Long Island hospitals, Pindar outdoes its neighbors in other ways as well. The variety of

Price Range of Wines: $6.99 for simple blended wines, such as Long Island Winter White, to $27 for the rare Cuvée Rare sparkling wine.

Special Events: Food and wine pairings, such as red wine and chocolate desserts in February, Riesling and Irish soda bread in March.

grapes planted is greater: 14 in all, including the standard Chardonnay, Cabernet, and Merlot, as well as unusual varieties such as Malbec, Viognier, and Pinot Meunier.

Pindar produces 18 different wines, including Mythology, Long Island's first blended red wine. Among the winery's fine sparkling wines, Cuvée Rare is particularly outstanding — dry, yet full of rich, pleasing, yeasty flavors. This elegant sparkler is the only wine in the East (perhaps in the nation) made from 100% Pinot Meunier grapes, one of the traditional varietals used in France as a Champagne blending grape.

Winemaker Mark Friszolowski, a Long Island native, has been at Pindar since 1994. He is also the winemaker at Duck Walk Vineyards on the South Fork, a winery recently acquired by Dr. Damianos.

SOUTH FORK

SAGPOND VINEYARDS

DOMAINE WOLFFER
CHARDONNAY RESERVE

The Hamptons, Long Island
1993

CELLARED AND BOTTLED BY SAGPOND VINEYARDS ∞ SAGAPONACK ∞ NEW YORK
750 MILLILITERS ∞ ALCOHOL 12.5% BY VOLUME

SAGPOND VINEYARDS
Rating: 🍷🍷🍷
516-537-5106;
    fax 516-537-5107.
Sagg Road, Sagaponack, NY.
Owner: Christian Wolffer.
Directions: From I-495, take exit 70 in Manorville. Travel south to Rte. 27. Take Rte. 27 east to Bridgehampton. At the

One of the newest Long Island wineries, Sagpond is on the South Fork, where conditions for growing grapes are more challenging than on the North Fork: it's flatter and siltier, with somewhat cooler temperatures — there are 195 sunny growing days as compared to 210 — and there's more fog and wind. If any of this deters Christian Wolffer, he doesn't show it, but raising grapes wasn't really what he had in mind when he first moved out here in 1977.

first traffic light after leaving Bridgehampton, turn left onto Sagg Road. The winery is $1/4$ mile on the right.

Open: June through mid-Sept., daily, 11 AM–6 PM; mid-Sept. through Dec., daily, 11 AM–5 PM; Jan. through May call for hours.

Price Range of Wines: $8.99 for a sophisticated, European-style Rosé to $14.99 for the Reserve Chardonnay.

Special Features: In 1995, the tasting room was in a small shed, but new facilities (and probably a picnic site as well) are under construction.

When Christian Wolffer purchased his 14-acre potato farm, his goal was to create a horse farm, which now includes a 13-acre Grand Prix jumping ring. This enterprise has helped make equestrian pursuits one of the Hampton's hottest hobbies. He also built a nursery, but when hurricane Gloria blew down all the trees in 1988, he decided to plant a vineyard instead. The first wines were released in 1992.

Christian Wolffer left his native Hamburg, Germany, and made his fortune in real estate and venture capital investments in South America and Canada. He still travels more than 200,000 miles a year, while remaining deeply involved in his Long Island projects. When a writer once asked him how he managed to keep up the pace, Christian answered, "I drink a lot of wine and ride a lot."

The South Fork's climate doesn't worry Sagpond's German-born winemaker, Roman Roth, any more than it does his boss. "We are the latest on Long Island to harvest," he explained, "so we get nice, ripe fruit with more delicate flavors and excellent acidity." Roman's goal is "to make wine for food. The whole structure of wine is meant to accompany food."

The first wines released by Sagpond show that the winery can take its place with the best. The 1992 Domaine Wolffer Chardonnay, 100% oak aged with 100% malolactic fermentation, is a clean and elegant wine. The Pinot Noir and Merlot, which I tasted out of the barrel as they hadn't been bottled yet, are fruity and full of flavor, showing great promise of evolving into rich and complex wines. The reds are all unfiltered and unfined. The current production is about 6,500 cases.

OTHER LONG ISLAND WINERIES

BIDWELL VINEYARDS (516-734-6763, Route 48, Cutchogue) makes a popular Riesling.

JAMESPORT WINERY (516-722-5256, Main Road, Jamesport) has a new winemaker, Richard Olsen-Harbich, and is now moving toward a very promising new product.

MATTITUCK HILLS WINERY (516-298-9150, 4250 Bergen Ave., Mattituck) produces Chardonnay, Cabernet Sauvignon, and Merlot.

PECONIC BAY VINEYARDS (516-734-7361, Main Road, Route 25, Cutchogue). Ray Blum was one of the earliest North Fork vintners. Today he is particularly well-known for his Cabernet Sauvignon, Merlot, Chardonnay, and dry Riesling. He also makes a late harvest Riesling that's perfect with desserts.

PUGLIESE VINEYARDS (516-734-4057, Main Road, Route 25, Cutchogue) produces an excellent sparkling wine.

BRIDGEHAMPTON WINERY (516-537-3155, Bridgehampton), on the South Fork, was recently purchased by the Carroll's of Lenz Winery and released its first wines bearing the imprint of skilled winemaker Eric Fry in 1995.

DUCK WALK VINEYARDS (516-726-7555, 231 Montauk Hwy., Route 27, Water Mill) has had a checkered history. First known as Le Rève, then as Southampton Winery, it is now owned by Dr. Herodotus Damianos, also the owner of the North Fork's Pindar Vineyards. The future looks bright as winemaker Mark Friszolowski's first vintages are being released. The Chardonnay and Pinot Gris are particularly promising, and the sparkling Pinot Meunier may rival Pindar's own outstanding Cuvée Rare. A late harvest Gewürztraminer, named Aphrodite, should also be a winner. Mark Friszolowski is excited about a low-lying spot in the vineyard where he hopes his planting of Muscat grapes will attract the botrytis organism that produces the distinctive flavor of the fine dessert Sauternes of France. The winery is housed in a dramatic brick chateaulike structure, which is well worth a visit itself.

RESTAURANTS AND LODGING

RESTAURANTS

The North Fork

ALDO'S RESTAURANT
516-477-1699.
105 Front Street, Greenport, NY.
Open: Daily in summer 7:30 AM–10 PM; winter 9 AM–6 PM plus dinner Fri., Sat., and Sun. to 9:30 PM.

This tiny, informal bistro is a favorite of residents of the North Fork. Owner Aldo Maiorana, who was born in Sicily and raised in France, is a true perfectionist who makes everything from scratch — and I mean *everything*, from roasting his own coffee beans to baking his own biscotti. It's BYOB, so be sure to pick up a bottle or two from one of the North Fork wine producers.

Price: Inexpensive to
    moderate

Resist Aldo's tempting desserts in favor of those
outstanding biscotti, enjoyed Italian/Long Island-
style, with a dessert wine such as Paumanok's late
harvest wines, or a Pellegrini or Bedell eiswien.
Aldo's takeout goodies make excellent picnic fare.

*The Jamesport Country
Kitchen in Jamesport,
New York, features a wide
variety of local wines.*

Marguerite Thomas

**JAMESPORT COUNTRY
KITCHEN**
516-722-3537.
Main Road (Route 25),
    Jamesport, NY.
Price: Inexpensive to
    moderate.

This small, casual and homey restaurant has 57
different, reasonably priced, local wines on the
wine list. On any given day, two or more of the
region's winemakers can be spotted having lunch
here. One day, stalling for time because I couldn't
make up my mind what to order, I asked the waitress what the winemakers usually eat. Without
hesitation, she answered, "The salmon cake or one
of the pastas." I ordered the salmon cake, which was delicious, and later tested
the waitress's credibility by asking winemaker Dan Kleck what he had eaten.
"The pasta special," he said. "I usually have that or the salmon cake."

**ROSS' NORTH FORK
RESTAURANT**
516-765-2111.
Route 48, Southold.
Open: Daily except
    Mondays, from mid-Feb.
    through Dec.; closed Jan.
    through mid-Feb.
Price: Inexpensive–
    Expensive.

Ross' is another favorite dining spot for Long
Island winemakers, and no wonder. At the
entrance, a floor-to-ceiling wine cabinet holds a
fine collection of vintage Long Island wines, as well
as current ones. The setting is elegant and refined.
Local winemakers, who meet here informally once
a month to taste wines and to catch up on what the
others are doing, each bring a bottle of wine from

anywhere *but* Long Island. They taste the wines blind and discuss them. "It's a great excersize," enthuses Kip Bedell, who tries never to miss these get-togethers. "Ross' food is special," says Louisa Hargrave. "He doesn't drizzle it with fancy herbed oils like a New York restaurant, but he's a fanatic for freshness, offering great seafood, and sweet corn guaranteed to be only a few hours from the field. Furthermore, Ross is the only one who has back vintages of local wines."

The South Fork

Restaurants abound in the Hamptons, ranging from chic to bleak in decor and cuisine.

At Bobby Van's: Roman Roth, Sagpond's winemaker, with Sagpond owner Christian Wolffer.

Marguerite Thomas

BOBBY VAN'S
516-537-0590.
Main Street,
   Bridgehampton, NY.
Open: Daily year-round.
Price: Inexpensive–
   Expensive.

This attractive, airy eatery in Bridgehampton is a current favorite, with my own informal poll showing that the steak sandwich is particularly popular among the winemaking crowd. This is a rare treat (or medium-rare if you prefer) topped by a fine sauce heaped with fresh mushrooms. You'd normally think of red wine with this but, surprisingly, it tastes wonderful with the Sagpond Chardonnay that is on the restaurant's wine list.

Other spots that are popular with vintners include **95 SCHOOL STREET**, in Bridgehampton and **CAFE MAX** in East Hampton, both of which serve Long Island wines.

LODGING

Shelter Island

RAM'S HEAD INN
516-749-9959;
  fax 516-749-0059.
Ram Island, Shelter Island,
  NY.
Open: Year-round.
Price: Inexpensive–Very
  Expensive.
Directions: A ferry leaves
  for Shelter Island from
  Greenport on the North
  Fork and from North
  Haven on the South Fork.
  Once on Shelter Island,
  follow signs to Ram
  Island.

Located halfway between the two forks of eastern Long Island, Shelter Island was so named because it was a haven for Quakers during the New England persecutions at the end of the 17th century, and because it's sheltered from the ocean's fury by the two forks. Lovely and romantic, Ram's Head Inn stands in stately splendor atop a bluff overlooking the water. With 17 brightly furnished rooms, Oriental rugs, fireplaces, wicker furniture on the porch, tennis courts, and pristine lawns, it's like a marriage between Jane Eyre and Ralph Lauren. Ram's Head Inn also has a fine restaurant, where Long Island wine tastings are often held.

The South Fork

THE MAIDSTONE ARMS
516-324-5006;
  fax 516-324-5037.
207 Main Street, East
  Hampton, NY.
Open: Year-round.
Price: Expensive–Very
  Expensive.

This charming place has been the "in" inn for many generations. The original Maidstone Arms was built in 1750, but it was destroyed by fire in the 1930s. Rebuilt to resemble the original, and recently refurbished, this hotel personifies comfortable country elegance. It has 16 rooms and three private cottages, as well as a very good restaurant where Long Island wines are served.

SOUTHEASTERN NEW JERSEY AND COASTAL VIRGINIA

Farther to the south, along New Jersey's southeastern coast and in coastal Virginia, are two other Benchland regions that are definitely worth a visit. The wineries range in size from small to very large.

BH77-5

BERKSHIRE HOUSE PUBLISHERS

480 Pleasant Street, Suite #5

Lee, MA 01238

Berkshire House Publishers

GREAT DESTINATIONS GUIDES....COOKBOOKS....THE BERKSHIRES....SHAKER CRAFTS....AMERICANA

We hope you enjoy this Berkshire House title! To help us make this book even better, please take a moment to give us your thoughts.

name _____

address _____

city, state, & zipcode _____ (if you like, add your daytime telephone number)

YOUR COMMENTS
ON THIS TITLE: _____

We'd also be grateful if you could let us know how you found this book.
Please check where you heard of the book, and write in where you got it.

☐ advertisement   ☐ radio   bookstore _____
☐ review   ☐ browsing
☐ friend   ☐ book club/catalog   other source _____
☐ television   ☐ other:

SOUTHEASTERN NEW JERSEY

Because New Jersey is such a productive agricultural area, it is nicknamed the Garden State. Today, a lot of New Jersey's commercial gardening is in the form of vineyards, just as it was in the mid-1700s when wine-producing grapes were cultivated in New Jersey for the British Empire. Those early efforts were so successful that in 1767, two New Jersey vintners were praised by London's Royal Society of Arts for producing the first bottles of quality wine from the Colonies. After early triumphs, however, things went downhill. First American vine diseases and then Prohibition brought the state's wine industry to a virtual standstill.

Today, wines are once again being produced in New Jersey. There are two separate viticultural regions, one in the north, in Warren and Hunterdon counties, the other south and west of Atlantic City. The northern section is in the Uplands country of rolling hills with limestone, clay, and shale soils. Southern Atlantic County, considered a Benchlands region, is a flat terrain, with sandy soils and a maritime climate. Set in the Pine Barrens, the strange landscape features mile after mile of short, stiff pine trees carpeting the countryside like bristles on a hairbrush. There isn't a whole lot to distract one in terms of sightseeing or shopping along Routes 30 and 40, where most of the wineries are located, and there are few places to eat or sleep. That this region is so ungentrified is surprising considering how close it is to major urban centers.

New Jersey wines are made from both vinifera and hybrid grapes. While the wine industry is not as advanced as on Long Island, this is a promising region that will undoubtedly develop further in the near future.

AMALTHEA CELLARS
Rating: 🍶
609-768-8585.
267 Hayes Mill Road, Atco, NJ.
Owners: Louis and Gini Caracciolo.
Directions: From the NJ Turnpike take exit 4. Take Rte. 73 south to Atco RR station; stay in the right lane and take the exit for Rte. 30 east. Go 2 miles to the first right after Atco Lake. Travel 1 mile to the winery on the right.
Open: Open varied hours; call for specific times.
Price Range of Wines: $8 for Chelois to $14 for Chardonnay.

Amalthea is named for one of the moons of Jupiter. So is Metis, a blush wine made here from Chancellor grapes, and the winery's logo features grapes and a mandala. Does this take you back to the days of patchouli oil, love-ins, Joplin, and Hendrix? The *esprit* here may be from the 1960s, but the wine is definitely for the 1990s.

Amalthea specializes in dry, red table wines that are aged in barrels longer than the average American wines. Owners Louis and Gini Caracciolo produce 25,000 cases annually from their 28-acre vineyard, where both vinifera and hybrid grapes are grown.

BALIC WINERY

Rating: 🍷
609-625-2166.
Route 40, Mays Landing, NJ.
Directions: From the Garden State Pkwy., take exit 37 to Rte. 40.
Owner: Salvo Balic.
Open: Mon.–Sat., 9:30 AM–5:30 PM; Sun. 10:30 AM–5 PM; closed Sundays Nov. and Dec.
Price Range of Wines: $5.50 for Country Red to $8.50 for Chardonnay.

Salvo Balic, a native of the former Yugoslavia, became one of New Jersey's vinous pioneers when he established this winery in 1974. It's a modest place that produces inexpensive wines, among them a decent Chardonnay and several wines made from Chancellor and other hybrid grapes. This is a good spot to stop for a picnic on the way to Atlantic City.

Marguerite Thomas

Gardens of the historic Renault Winery, Egg Harbor, New Jersey.

RENAULT WINERY

Rating: 🍷
609-965-2111.
72 N. Bremen Avenue, Egg Harbor City, Galloway Township, NJ.
Directions: From the Garden State Pkwy. take the parkway service exit at mile market #41. Go to the north end of service area and follow the signs to Jimmy Leeds Rd. At the traffic light turn left, then bear right at the

Not only is this New Jersey's oldest winery, it's also the longest continuously operating winery with its own vineyard in America. It's worth a visit for its historical importance alone.

Renault Winery was founded by Louis Nicholas Renault, a French Champagne maker, who came to the United States in 1855 to establish a vineyard that would be free of the phylloxera organism that was destroying European vineyards. First he went to California, but he found the vines were ravaged by phylloxera there also. Then Renault learned about phylloxera-resistant native American labrusca grapes.

fork and continue on Rte. 561 to Bremen Ave. Turn right onto Breman and go 1¹/₂ miles to the winery.

Owner: Joseph P. Milza.

Open: Mon.–Sat., 10 AM–5 PM; Sun. 12 PM–5 PM.

Price Range of Wines: $4.99 for Pink Lady to $12.50 for Chardonnay; the popular Blueberry Champagne is $8.99.

Special Features: Several restaurants on property; picnic areas; enormous gift shop.

He traveled to New Jersey, where labrusca was thriving. Finding a climate and soil that reminded him of France, he settled outside of Egg Harbor and established his own vineyard. By 1870 he was producing Concord grape "champagne" and before long he had become the largest distributor of sparkling wine in the nation. Egg Harbor (so named because of the nesting sea birds) also became known as "the wine city."

Louis Renault died in 1913 at the age of 91. New owner John D'Agostino continued to operate the winery even during Prohibition by obtaining a government permit that allowed him to make Renault Wine Tonic, a product that contained 22% alcohol and was sold in drugstores throughout the nation.

After Repeal, Renault began blending its New Jersey fruit with grapes imported from California, to create an immensely popular sparkling wine. In 1948, Maria D'Agostino took over the winery following her brother's death. It was Maria who built the chateaulike structure, and it is her collection of wine glasses that today's visitors admire in the winery museum.

Under the direction of current owner Joseph P. Milza, who was formerly a newspaper owner and publisher, Renault is the New Jersey winery giant. Ninety of its 1,400 acres are planted in grapes, and it produces 125,000 cases of wine annually.

Renault makes what writer John Baxavanis has described as "a bewildering assortment of wines." The most popular selections include a Chardonnay, Pink Lady (a sweet rosé), and Blueberry Champagne. Although the sparkling wines are still especially popular, none of them will tempt a connoisseur. Nevertheless, Renault's historic importance is ample reason to pay the winery a visit.

Renault has dining facilities (see page 40) as well as picnic areas, and an enormous gift shop. A popular stop on the tour bus circuit, Renault receives 100,000 visitors a year.

SYLVIN FARMS

Rating: 🍇🍇
609-965-1548.
24 Vienna Avenue, Germania, NJ.

Directions: From the Garden State Pkwy., take exit 44. Bear right onto Moss Mill Rd. (Alt. 561) and travel 4.2 miles to Vienna Ave. Turn right in 800 ft. at winery entrance.

This is the most remarkable winery in New Jersey. Frank Salek is a civil engineer and college professor who teaches in upstate New Jersey, commuting down to his modest winery and vineyard on weekends. In general, weekend winemakers operate with a tremendous handicap in terms of time and energy, but Frank Salek is certainly doing something right. Maybe it's the vineyard's location. "Could be," Frank nods. "After all, we're on the highest point around." Incredulous, I stare across the flat vista of the Chardonnay section of

Marguerite Thomas

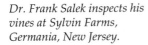

Dr. Frank Salek inspects his vines at Sylvin Farms, Germania, New Jersey.

Owners: Franklin and Sylvia Salek.
Open: By appointment only.
Price Range of Wines: $7 for Chardonnay and Sauvignon Blanc to $10 for Merlot and sparkling wines.
Special Features: Informal picnic area.

vineyard where we're standing. Well, okay, maybe the land does sort of swell up into a little mound toward the center. "Even the slightest rise makes a difference," Frank assures me. "And in this location the steady southwest winds permit the vines to dry off in summer, so we have less of a problem with fungal diseases."

Both the Atlantic Ocean and the Mullica River moderate the temperature, Frank explains, and he has learned, usually by hard experience, which grape varieties and clones will do well here. And yet, Dr. Salek is one of the few New Jersey vintners to raise only vinifera grapes, having decided that hybrids could be almost as much trouble to care for as the European species — and considerably more difficult to market.

Frank pockets his pruning shears and we abandon the frigid February vineyards for the relative comfort of the cellar. This is not one of those quaint cellars full of neatly stacked oak barrels and high-tech, computerized gizmos. It's a basement crammed full of stainless steel containers and a couple of old wooden barrels. I am not optimistic.

But as Frank starts drawing wine from these various receptacles and we begin tasting, I'm blown away. The Chardonnay is distinguished and golden; the Pinot Noir is redolent of fresh berries; the Cabernet Sauvignon has great flavor intensity; and the Merlot is juicy and ripe. How does Frank Salek *do* it? "Wine is made in the vineyard," he says modestly. "I decided a long time ago that you had to have good grapes to make good wine. When I couldn't find ones I liked, I decided to grow my own. Everyone thought I was really crazy." Today he owns about 40 acres of land, of which seven are planted, and his annual output ranges from 600 to 3,000 cases.

Nobody thinks he's crazy now. Frank Salek has become the guru for the

New Jersey winemakers, who admire his wines, respect what he's doing in his vineyard, and frequently turn to him for advice. Charlie Tomasello (Tomasello Winery) has even teamed up with Frank to make a sparkling Rkatzitelli, which won the 1993 Governor's Cup for the best New Jersey wine. Rkatzitelli is the most common wine grape in Russia and it's also grown in other parts of Eastern Europe. It appears to thrive in New Jersey as well.

Sylvin Farms has a small tasting room and an informal picnic area in a rural setting.

Tomasello Winery, Hammonton, New Jersey.

Marguerite Thomas

TOMASELLO WINERY
Rating: 🍷🍷
609-652-2320.
225 White Horse Pike, Hammonton, NJ.
Directions: From Atlantic City, take Rte. 30 west for 5 miles. White Horse Pike is just past mile marker #29. Follow the signs to the winery.
Owners: Charles and Joseph Tomasello.
Open: Open daily 11 AM–6 PM; July & Aug., 11 AM–9 PM.
Price Range of Wines: $8.50 for Steuben to $12 for Estate Chardonnay.
Special Features: Picnic facilities.

Tomasello Winery was established in 1933 by Frank Tomasello, a local farmer. It is run today by Frank's sons, Charles and Joseph, whose empire is expanding at an astonishing rate. With 86 acres of vines, Tomasello rivals Renault as New Jersey's biggest grape grower. An enormous assortment of wine is produced here from hybrids, including an excellent Chambourcin, a light, flavorful red that resembles Beaujolais in character. Wines from vinifera grapes are made as well. The Cabernet Sauvignon is particularly fine, with a nice balance between fruitiness, complex oak flavors, and restrained tannins. Tomasello is also one of the few wineries in the region to produce wine from Concord and Catawba grapes.

The vineyard and winery are actually only part of the Tomasello picture. There is also a Tomasello outlet store in Smithville, where wine tastings take place and gourmet food items are sold. It's a good place to stock up for a canoe trip or a picnic in the Pine Barrens. Tomasello is housed in a modern Mediterranean-style complex built around a courtyard. It includes a banquet room, a pleasant tasting room, and picnic facilities in addition to the winery operation itself.

RESTAURANTS AND LODGING

RENAULT GARDEN CAFE and RENAULT GOURMET RESTAURANT
609-965-2111.
72 N. Bremen Avenue, Egg Harbor City, Galloway Township, NJ.
Open: Garden Cafe open daily; Gourmet Restaurant open weekends only.
Price: Inexpensive– Expensive.

The Garden Cafe is an agreeable spot to enjoy a simple lunch and a glass of Renault wine. The Gourmet Restaurant is more formal. Other than this Renault duo, there are virtually no interesting restaurants in southern New Jersey, and no place to stay, except for an occasional motel, until you get to the charming inns and eateries of Cape May. Incidentally, the new Cape May Winery is scheduled to open in early 1996. Local vintners travel to Philadelphia, less than an hour away, for a good meal.

COASTAL VIRGINIA

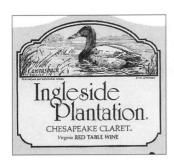

Two years after they landed in the New World, the settlers of Jamestown harvested, crushed, and fermented wild native grapes, to produce America's first grape wine. While the results left much to be desired, the yearning for palatable wine, and for an economically viable industry with which to slake the thirst of this large new market, was strong enough to lead to years of frustrating and futile endeavors.

European grapes were imported into the colonies, and all householders were required by law to plant grapevines. French grapegrowers were sent by the London headquarters of the Virginia Colony to assist in the development of a wine industry. By 1769, as the Revolutionary War dawned, the colonists were still trying to make a drinkable wine in Virginia. It wasn't until the late 20th century that science and technology advanced to the point where wine, at last, was produced in the coastal area of Virginia.

Ingleside Plantation Vineyards, located not far from Washington's birthplace on Virginia's Northern Neck.

Marguerite Thomas

**INGLESIDE
PLANTATION
VINEYARDS**
Rating: 🍷🍷
804-224-8687;
  fax 804-224-8573.
Route 638, Oak Grove, VA.
Directions: $2^1/2$ miles south
  of Oak Grove.
Owners: The Flemmer
  family.
Open: Mon.–Sat., 10 AM–
  5 PM; Sun. 12 PM–5 PM.
Price Range of Wines: $8
  for Popes Creek White to
  $16 for Cabernet
  Sauvignon Reserve.
Special Events: Jazz
  concerts in the courtyard.

L ocated on the northern neck of Virginia, a peninsula formed by the Rappahannock and Potomac Rivers where they empty into the Chesapeake Bay, this is a region filled with history. Both George Washington and Robert E. Lee were born here.

Ingleside Plantation Vineyards belongs to the Flemmer family, whose ancestor purchased the plantation in the late 1800s. The first vines were planted in 1960, and the winery began operation in 1980. When the original winemaker, Belgian-born Jacques Recht, retired recently, Tom Payette, a graduate of Virginia Polytechnical Institute, stepped in. This may mean that stylistic changes are in store for one of Virginia's oldest wineries. As both the wines and the tasting room could use some brightening up, one hopes that Tom Payette will reinvigorate Ingleside.

Ingleside has 50 acres planted in vines and produces up to 15,000 cases of wine annually. The wines are made from both vinifera and hybrid grapes. While several white wines are made here, reds are Ingleside's strength. The 1990 Cabernet Sauvignon, blended with some Merlot, has been winning prizes recently. The 100% Merlot is another winner, exhibiting good cherrylike flavors balanced by a hint of oak. The George Washington Colonial Red is one of the more interesting Ingleside products. It's a Chambourcin/Cabernet Sauvignon blend that is based on the wine used for Communion in Washington's day. Today it is sold to local Episcopal churches. It's a fairly sweet wine, said to make a nice aperitif when chilled.

Patrick Doffeler, owner of Williamsburg Winery, in the winery's museum of Colonial wine bottles.

Marguerite Thomas

WILLIAMSBURG WINERY

Rating: 🍷🍷🍷
804-229-0999.
2638 Lake Powell Road, Williamsburg, VA.
Directions: From Colonial Williamsburg take Rte. 31 toward Jamestown. Go left to Rte. 199, turn right onto Brookwood Lane, then turn left onto Lake Powell Road. The winery entrance will be on the left.
Owner: Patrick Doffeler.
Open: Daily 11 AM–5:30 PM.
Price Range of Wines: $6.50 for Governor's White to $21 for Gabriel Archer Reserve.
Special Features: Colonial wine bottles on display.
Special Events: December candlelight open-house in conjunction with Colonial Williamsburg.

Belgian-born Patrick Doffeler, who was a business executive in France and New York while working for Eastman Kodak and Phillip Morris, is the owner of Williamsburg Winery. "After living as a corporate mercenary for twenty years, my wife, Peggy, said, 'Now do something intelligent,'" recalls Patrick. His answer was to buy a farm in Williamsburg in 1983, that he converted into a vineyard and winery. Why wine? "Because it's the last consumer product that isn't standardized," Patrick explained. "There are too many variables in winemaking for it to ever become standardized." Why Virginia? "I first came to Williamsburg in 1951, when I was a high school student. The place stands for our history, for a century of enlightenment, for grace of architecture. It stands for searching for a way of doing things differently."

By nature, Patrick loves a challenge (one of his great passions is to race vintage automobiles), so embarking on a winemaking project in an area where others had floundered for 300 years was just the sort of thing that interested him. It was also intelligent, as it turns out, for Williamsburg Winery has achieved surprising success. Financially it has enjoyed small but solid sales growth and critically it has received awards and national attention, including praise from such respected writers as Robert Parker.

Williamsburg is the largest winery in Virginia, producing 50,000 cases annually, and it has the state's largest barrel cellar, with over 600 barrels. It is also Virginia's most aggressive marketer, having succeeded in placing its wines in restaurants from Vermont to Atlanta.

Williamsburg produces some terrific wines, all from vinifera grapes. Steve Warner, the winemaker, graduated from Fresno State University in California. Most of his wines have layers of complex flavors underneath full fruit tones, which leave a pleasing, long aftertaste at the back of the palate. The whites include Governor's White, Williamsburg's most popular wine, a good sipper made from Riesling and Vidal. John Adlum Chardonnay honors the foremost Virginia winemaker in Thomas Jefferson's day. Acte 12 of Sixteen-Nineteen Chardonnay is named after the law passed by the Virginia House of Burgess in 1619 requiring every householder to plant and maintain 10 vines.

The full-bodied Merlot has rich flavors of spice and fruit, and the Gabriel Archer Reserve, named for the co-captain of the Godspeed, which brought the first settlers to Jamestown in 1607, is a Bordeaux-style blend of Cabernet Sauvignon, Cabernet Franc, and Merlot. This wine is produced only in years when the fruit achieves an exceptional degree of ripeness.

There is an interesting collection of colonial wine bottles on display at the winery.

RESTAURANTS AND LODGING

THE TRELLIS RESTAURANT
804-229-8610.
Duke of Gloucester Street, Williamsburg, VA.
Price: Moderate–Expensive.

As befits its location in the heart of historic Colonial Williamsburg the Trellis serves food with a traditional American personality, but owner/chef Marcel Desaulniers puts a distinct, contemporary spin on it. Instead of the overcooked veggies most of us associate with traditional American cookery, Marcel is more apt to come up with a smoked vegetable stew to serve with skewers of duck breast, rabbit and fresh Surry sausage, a local product. Virginia ingredients are featured, including pork medallions garnished with fresh grapes, and country ham served over pumpkin fettucine. The Trellis offers a thoughtfully chosen and reasonably priced wine list that includes selections from Virginia.

THE LAKE ERIE REGION

Gary Woodbury of Woodbury Winery & Vineyards in Dunkirk, New York, tests the sugar content of his grapes.

Marguerite Thomas

Grapes, grapes all around, and lots of wine to drink! The Lake Erie region is the largest grape producing area in the nation outside of California. It starts just west of Niagara Falls and continues almost as far as the Ohio/Michigan border. It's literally awash in vines, mostly the dark-leaved American natives, which cover approximately 40,000 acres and span three states. Increasingly, European vinifera vines are replacing the stalwart natives in winemaking, but wine accounts for less than 10% of the grapes grown in this region; the rest go to the grape juice industry, which is based on Concord and other American labrusca grapes.

Although it isn't near the ocean, the area along the shores of Lake Erie has soil and climate reminiscent of the coastal regions. When the glaciers inched south during the Ice Age, the Canadian soil, rocks, and boulders they carried scooped out monstrous holes in the earth. Later, as temperatures warmed and the glaciers receded, the holes filled with glacial melt to form the Great Lakes.

A unique, narrow plateau of gravel and loam that is well-suited for grapevines, was left behind near Lake Erie. "Our vineyards are where a lake beach was located many, many years ago," explains Gary Woodbury, whose winery bears his family name. As the land rises beyond this plain — sometimes only a mile behind the lake — the soil becomes too heavy for vine roots to thrive.

The deep waters of the lake store warmth from the sun that is reflected back on the land, raising nearby temperatures in much the same way as the Atlantic Ocean keeps the coastal region temperate. Because of this combination of topography and weather patterns, and with 190 sunny growing days a year, the grape industry flourishes here. Chautauqua County, in the westernmost section of New York, for example, supplies almost 60% of the state's annual grape production.

In the 19th century, the Lake Erie region was an important wine center — in fact, at the turn of the century, Ohio was the largest wine-producing region in the nation. But Prohibition knocked out Lake Erie's wine industry. Only in the last few decades, has it finally begun to re-emerge as a serious player in the eastern wine market.

A handful of family-run wineries are still making the traditional, sweet wines their fathers and grandfathers made from labrusca grapes. "It's what the customers want," shrugged Ed Heineman, the fourth generation at Heineman Winery on Put-In-Bay Island in Ohio. "If you're brought up on native American grapes like the folks around here, that's what you prefer. And if you're a beginner, you like something sweet. But the more you drink, the more you'll probably move to drier wine," he acknowledged.

As more Americans are becoming familiar with wines from California and Europe, a new generation of winemaker is emerging in the Lake Erie region. They are knowledgeable winemakers who are willing to satisfy the demand for a drier, European-style wine. There's still work to be done, but some of the wines emerging from the Lake Erie region are as exciting as any in the East. This is especially true of the white wines, such as Riesling, Gewürztraminer, and Pinot Gris, and there seems to be a potential for certain reds, especially Cabernet Sauvignon, Cabernet Franc, and perhaps Pinot Noir.

"For today's wine tourist, no other district in America offers historic vineyards and colorful wineries in settings as uniquely spectacular as those that still operate along the shore and on the Wine Islands' of Lake Erie," wrote Leon Adams in *The Wines of America*.

The wineries, spread out almost in a straight line that parallels the lake, will be found along Routes 2 and 5, and they're easy to find. They tend to be clustered together, so it's possible to visit several in a day. One of the most unique and colorful experiences of wine-country touring awaits the visitor at the northwestern edge of Ohio, where one can island-hop from wineries to vineyards on the lake.

Even without the wineries, Lake Erie is a great travel destination. Boating, fishing (including ice fishing) and other water sports are a lure, and Niagara Falls is not far away. Cleveland's cultural attractions abound. The bounty of local farm stands and U-pick apple farms, plus the natural beauty of the region's many parks, such as Presque Isle Wilderness Area, offer additional scenic and recreational opportunities. Now that good wine can be factored into the equation, a sojourn to the Lake Erie region becomes irresistible.

NEW YORK

JOHNSON ESTATE WINES

Rating: 🍷
716-326-2191.
Route 20, Westfield, NY.
Directions: Two miles west of village.
Owners: The Johnson family.
Open: Daily, 10 AM–6 PM.
Price Range of Wines: $5.98 for blush to $12.50 for Chancellor.

The Johnson family has been growing grapes in this location for more than a century; they opened the winery in 1961. This makes Johnson the oldest estate winery in New York State, meaning that it grows all its grapes on its own property.

Johnson winery is a regional winery, producing quality wines from labrusca and French-American hybrids. It does not make wine from vinifera grapes. "With vinifera, you can only make good wine every few years in this area," said Mark. "We're interested in making good wine every year."

The Johnson wines include rosés, a blush, and white wines ranging from Blancs de Blancs Sec, a dry sparkling wine, to Liebestropfchen, "Little Love Drops," a rich, fruity dessert wine. The reds include an excellent barrel-aged Chancellor Noir that has the color of dark velvet and the taste of mixed berries. Sweet Dreams is a nectar made from late-harvested Vidal grapes.

There are no picnic facilities and no special events. "We just concentrate on making wine," explained Mark.

WOODBURY WINERY & VINEYARDS

Rating: 🍷
716-679-9463;
fax 716-679-9464.
3230 South Roberts Road, Dunkirk, NY.
Directions: From I-90, take Exit 59; turn left onto Rte. 60, then left onto Rte. 20, then right onto South Roberts Rd. Follow signs to the winery.
Owner: Gary Woodbury.
Open: Mon.–Sat., 10 AM–5 PM; Sun. noon–5 PM.
Price Range of Wines: $5.49 for Niagara to $12.99 for Cabernet Sauvignon aged in oak barrels.
Special Features: Picnic area.

I met Konstantin Frank in 1967," said Gary Woodbury, referring to the Finger Lakes vintner, who through his own success and powers of persuasion, inspired so many other easterners to plant vinifera grapes. "It's because of him that we stand here today and talk." It was the last day of summer, and Gary and I were strolling through the 2.3 acres of Chardonnay, Riesling, and Cabernet vines that he planted after that fateful meeting with Dr. Frank. Another 75 acres of hybrids and native American grapes had been planted by Gary's grandfather in 1915. Most of this crop is sold to the Welsh Company for grape juice. "When local 'experts' said you couldn't possibly grow vinifera grapes here, that was a challenge to me," smiles Gary, recalling that he sold his first bottle of vinifera wine on June 29, 1980.

He has never looked back. As we make our way through rows of vines, we pop a few golden Chardonnay grapes into our mouths, savoring the honeyed sweetness of their juice. Gary's hand-held device for measuring the fruit's sugar content confirms our impression of ripeness: the grapes range from 18 to 22.2 Brix, indicating that this vineyard is just about ready for harvesting.

Back at the winery, we taste Woodbury's Riesling and Chardonnay, a clear and crisp Seyval (Seyval's outstanding virtue, according to Gary, is consistency), and a sweet Niagara. "Just as a supermarket has to have sugar, a winery in New York State has to have a Niagara," observes Gary. Served over ice on a hot afternoon, Woodbury's Niagara makes a pleasant sipping wine.

Woodbury produces nine wines and has a production of 15,000 cases annually. "I try to keep it at a manageable level of confusion," said Gary wryly.

He is confident the Lake Erie region is on its way to success as vines and winemakers mature. "We think our own wines have been getting better as the vines age. Of course, we also got better at making it," he says.

Woodbury Winery offers a unique Adopt-A-Barrel program. Any individual or group can "adopt" a barrel full of wine that will remain in Woodbury's cellars for four years. At the end of that time, each "parent" will receive two cases of wine — and they can keep the barrel as well.

There are picnic tables under the apple trees, with a lake view. This would be a good place to celebrate the new addition of a barrel to your family.

PENNSYLVANIA

CONNEAUT CELLARS WINERY

Rating: 🍷
814-382-3999;
 fax 814-382-6151.
Route 322, Conneaut Lake, PA.
Directions: From I-79 take exit 36-B and follow signs to winery.
Owner: Phyllis Wolf.
Open: Daily 10 AM–6 PM, except Jan.–Mar. when closed Mon.
Price Range of Wines: $5.25 to $14.95.
Special Features: Picnic area.
Special Events: Open House the last weekend in April; Fall Picnic.

Conneaut Cellars has fashioned itself after a turn-of-the-century winery, with much of the work done by hand. "We are an old-fashioned winery," said winemaker Joel Wolf, whose mother, Phyllis owns Conneaut Cellars. "We have no high-speed automatic bottling lines, for example. We do all of that by hand."

Owning no vineyards of its own, Conneaut purchases its fruit from the Lake Erie region. It produces 5,500 cases of wine a year, including a Chardonnay and a Cabernet Sauvignon. Other dry vinifera and hybrid-based wines, and a sweet American native wine are made as well.

Conneaut is further from Lake Erie than the other Erie wineries (about 30 minutes from Markko Vineyard), but its outlook is tied to the region. "Our philosophy is to produce wine from our own region rather than to copy California or France or Austria," explained Joel. "For that reason we use only American oak, for example. We want to extract the best character from our region." Picnickers are welcome at Conneaut.

MAZZA VINEYARDS
Rating: 👤👤
814-725-8695.
11815 East Lake Road
(Route 5), North East,
PA.
Directions: 15 miles east of
Erie on Rte. 5.
Owner: Robert Mazza.
Open: July and Aug.,
Mon.–Sat., 9 AM–8 PM;
Sept. to June, Mon.–Sat.,
9 AM–5:30 PM; Sun. year-
round, 11 AM–4:30 PM.
Price Range of Wines: $5.95
to $15.95.
Special Features: Picnic
area.
Special Events: Dining in
the Vineyards (dinner
prepared by local
restaurants), limited
seating, by reservation
only.

Born in Italy, Robert Mazza came to the United States as a young child. He is thoroughly American, but with a hint of European aesthetic sensibility. The winery itself has a distinctly Mediterranean look compared to the rural wooden structures that predominate in this region. And the wines include European varietals such as Riesling, Chardonnay, and Cabernet as well as the locally-popular hybrids and American labruscas.

Robert and his brother Frank, started the winery in 1972, after their home-winemaking hobby esca-lated into a full-time occupation. Although Mazza grows four acres of Vidal Blanc, the bulk of their grapes is purchased from other Pennsylvania growers. Under the terms of the state's farm win-ery law, no out-of-state grapes may be used to make Pennsylvania wine. Mazza makes a delicious icewine from Vidal Blanc grapes. Unlike some ersatz versions of German eiswein, which are made from grapes frozen in a freezer, Mazza's grapes hang on the vine in the traditional way, usually until late December, by which time their juice has frozen into concentrated sweetness.

The Mazza's produce 12,000-15,000 cases of wine annually. A picnic pavilion looks towards the lake.

**PENN SHORE WINERY &
VINEYARDS**
Rating: 👤
814-725-8588.
10225 East Lake Road
(Route 5), North East, PA.

Founded as a co-op by local grape growers, the winery today has three owners. Robert Mazza, one of the owners, manages this winery, as well as his own. Gary Mosier, the winemaker at Mazza Vineyards, handles winemaking for Penn Shore as

Directions: 15 miles east of Erie on Rte. 5.

Owners: Robert Mazza and others.

Open: July and Aug., Mon.–Sat., 9 AM–8 PM; Sun. 11 AM–5 PM; Sept.–June, Mon.–Sat., 9 AM–5:30 PM; Sun. 11 AM– 5 PM.

Price Range of Wines: $5.40 for Kir and Dry Red to $8.75 for an oak-aged Chardonnay and $10.95 for a sparkling wine.

PRESQUE ISLE WINE CELLARS

Rating: 🍷🍷🍷
814-725-1314; fax 814-725-2092.

9440 Buffalo Road, North East, PA.

Directions: From the west on I-90, take exit 10 (Harborcreek), then go north on Rte. 531 to Rte. 20, then east on Rte. 20 for 3.8 miles. From the east take I-90 to exit 12 (North East), go west on Rte. 20 for 7 miles.

Owners: Doug and Marlene Moorehead.

Open:Year-round, Mon.–Sat., 8 AM–5 PM; Sun. during harvest only.

Price Range of Wines: $4.25 for Eastern Catawba to $9.40 for Merlot.

Special Features: Picnic tables in a charming setting beside a stream.

well. At this winery he produces a variety of wines that include several crisp, dry whites, such as Seyval and a Vignoles, and a dry red that he calls — Dry Red. The best-selling "Kir" is a sweet blend of Catawba and Seyval with a touch of cassis flavoring.

By the consensus of most of his colleagues, Doug Moorehead has been instrumental in encouraging people to gamble on vinifera grapes. He has also been a pivotal force in encouraging regional vintners to band together to market Lake Erie wines.

The Moorehead family has been growing grapes in this region for three generations. They own 160 acres of vineyards, with 130 acres planted in Concord and Niagara grapes that are sold to the Welch Juice Company. The remaining acres are planted in wine grapes, supplemented by fruit purchased from "two superb growers on Lake Erie," as Doug describes them.

Doug and his wife Marlene first made their mark as suppliers of juice and equipment to home and professional winemakers. This continues to account for about 97% of their winery business. But it is that remaining 3% — the wines — that will put Presque Isle on the map. Only 2,000 cases are produced now, from both hybrid and vinifera grapes.

Doug clearly believes the future lies with vinifera. "Hybrids are one good pathway," he says, adding that some day in the future, new hybrids may rival and even surpass vinifera. "But for now, anyone who wants to be on the national or world stage — and this is a possibility for our region — will have to do it with vinifera."

While Chardonnay and Cabernet Sauvignon are Presque Isle's best selling vinifera wines, Doug is excited about his Petite Sirah, despite the difficulties involved in producing it. "If we get 100 gallons a year from it we're lucky," he sighs. Why bother with such a problematic variety? "Because the wine is just *so* good," answers Doug. "Making it can be equated to the task of Sisyphus. But every time I get discouraged, I taste another bottle. . . ."

In general, Doug believes the region's future in red wine lies in Cabernet Sauvignon. He is cautiously optimistic about the prospects for Lake Erie's wine. "We've organized a quality control group. We're beginning to sort out which varieties we should be concentrating on. The dilettantes who got into the business in the 1980s have dropped out — most of the people now are serious about making wine."

One of the most important strengths of the region, says Doug, "is the great varietal fruit characteristics we get here." Indeed, his own wines live up to this description. From an elegant Riesling to a fine Cabernet Franc blended with small amounts of Petite Syrah, to a Cabernet Sauvignon with unusual depth of color and flavor, all are excellent.

Presque Isle's setting is as charming as its wines. There are picnic tables in the woods next to a small stream.

OHIO

CHALET DEBONNE VINEYARDS

Rating: 🍷
216-466-3485; 800-424-9463.
7734 Doty Road, Madison, OH.
Owners: Tony Debevc, Sr. and Jr. and their wives Rose and Beth.
Directions: From Cleveland, take I-90 east, turn south onto Rte. 528 to Griswold, turn left onto Emerson, and then right on Doty, follow signs to winery; from Erie, take I-90 west, turn south onto Rte. 534 to South River Road West, which runs Doty.
Open: Tues., Thurs., and Sat., noon–8 PM; Wed. & Fri., noon–midnight; closed Sun. & Mon, year-round.
Price Range of Wines: $4.99 to $12.79.

Chalet Debonne is the most visible winery in the Lake Erie region. Its wines are featured in local restaurants, and the winery itself hosts a popular series of events.

Anton Debevc planted his first vineyard here in 1916. His son, Tony, tended the vineyard for many years, and was eventually joined by *his* son, Tony. The grapes at that time were used for grape juice. When the price of grapes dropped in the late 1960s, Tony Sr. and Tony Jr. began to make wine. In 1971, they opened the winery.

Chalet Debonne's winemaker is named — you guessed it — Tony. Tony Carlucci. All the Tonys, along with Rose and Beth (Tony Sr's. and Jr's. wives), produce 25,000 cases of wine annually. They have 60 acres planted in grapes, which is supplemented by additional fruit purchased from other growers.

The winery's appealing wines include a full-bodied Proprietor's Reserve Chardonnay and a soft and pretty Pinot Noir. Classic Red, a medium-bodied, very fruity wine, produced from various

Special Features: Snack shop, indoor and outdoor tables, fireplace.
Special Events: Steak Fries; Hot Air Balloon Race; '50s and '60s Day (with classic cars); Kite Day; Family Day; Summer Concert Series.

French American hybrids, was recommended to me with a steak dinner in a local restaurant one rainy night. The combination was agreeable enough, although my preference would have been for a drier wine. The winery makes several classic labrusca wines — Delaware, Catawba, Niagara — as well as a Riesling, and a dessert Vidal.

The Chalet Debonne winery looks as if it was transported here straight from the Alps, which may be a reflection of the family's Slovenian roots. There's a snack shop where visitors may purchase light fare to be enjoyed with the wine. There's also a pleasant indoor area with tables near a fireplace for relaxing, as well as tables scattered throughout the attractive grounds, including under the grape arbor in front of the winery.

GRAND RIVER WINE COMPANY

Rating: 🍷
216-298-9838.
5750 South Madison Road, Madison, OH.
Directions: From Cleveland, take Rte. 90 east to the Madison-Thompson exit, go 3 miles south to the winery.
Owner: Willet Worthy.
Open: Mon., Wed., & Thurs., 1 PM–8 PM; Fri. & Sat., 1 PM–6 PM.
Price Range of Wines: $6–$7.
Special Features: Picnic area, fireplace.
Special Events: Theatrical productions.

The Grand River Wine Company offers much more than wine. This is the place to come for a good argument about Proust or even Richard Nixon. Owner Willet Worthy willingly debates any number of subjects, but theater, even more than wine, is this former investment banker's real passion — and it is the real reason to visit this winery. The Grand River Wine Company hosts the Mapleleaf Community Theater for 16 weekends between April and November. The plays are performed outdoors on the winery's deck.

Grand River bottles about 5,000 cases of wine annually, made from grapes grown on its own 17 acres, as well as those purchased from other local growers. The best offerings are easy-drinking Beaujolais-style wines. The winery's top seller is its Blanc de Renard ("White Fox"), a sweet Niagara; its best-selling dry wine is Vignoles.

For picnickers, there are tables on the patio or, in cooler weather, indoors by a fireplace. Cheese and crackers are available for visitors who haven't packed their own picnic.

HARPERSFIELD VINEYARD

Rating: 🍷🍷🍷
216-466-4739.
6387 State Route 307, Geneva, OH.

"I believe in doing things small and doing them right," says Wes Gerlosky. He is indeed doing things small: he produces merely 1,200 cases of wine annually, but all the wine is made from grapes grown in his own 10-acre vineyard. He is certainly doing things right, as he is turning out

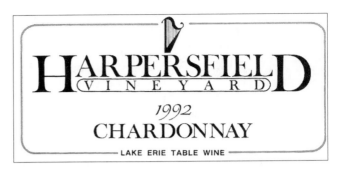

Directions: Call for directions.
Owner: Wes Gerlosky.
Open: By appointment only.
Price Range of Wines: $10 for Pinot Gris to $14 for Chardonnay.

some of the most exciting wines in the Northeast. He is also doing things in a very low-key manner, as there are no tours at Harpersfield, no tasting room, and not even a sign outside to indicate the winery exists.

Wes stumbled into his winemaking career by accident in the early 1970s, when he took over the management of the apple farm his father had purchased as a retirement project. Inspired by the French wines Wes and his wife Margaret had begun drinking, they decided to try their hand at winemaking.

At first, they used the Concord grapes that were growing on the property. "The wine was terrible," he says bluntly. He began talking to people who made wines he liked, particularly Arnie Esterer at Markko Vineyard and Doug Moorehead at Presque Isle. Encouraged by them, he began ripping out apple trees and planting vinifera vines, while refining his winemaking techniques.

In 1985, he built a cellar and decided to start selling his wines. His first vintage was released in 1986. He makes only four wines, all of them white: Chardonnay, Riesling, Gewürztraminer, and Pinot Gris. "These early ripening whites are the strength of our region," he says. Tasting his wines, one cannot help but believe that he is right.

To what does Wes Gerlosky attribute his successes? "Even though I had only seat-of-the-pants training, I made it a point to buy and taste good wines. It can be expensive, but it's really important to be familiar with good wines so you know what you're aiming for. Then, what you need, is the best possible fruit. It's not easy to persuade growers to leave their fruit on the vine until it's thoroughly ripe, but that is critical."

What are Wes's long range goals? "We want to emphasize the influence of the region on our wine," he answers. "Also, we are aiming for consistency. We want to make a living not a fortune, by growing grapes and making wine. I think, eventually, we'll be able to make something as good as anywhere in the world."

Harpersfield winery is on its way to reaching these goals. The Chardonnay has the opulence and character of all good Chardonnays. The Riesling has the aromatic amalgam of floral scents and oiliness that one looks for in a great Riesling. The Pinot Gris and Gewürztraminer resemble the deep-flavored lush wines of Alsace. (Wes suggests drinking the Gewürztraminer with rabbit or chicken stew seasoned with paprika.)

Red wines haven't been ruled out either, particularly Pinot Noir. "Until now, the clones haven't been good enough, yielding undistinguished raisiny wines. But now good clones from Burgundy are available. It will be a challenge to grow the grapes and to make the wine, but when Pinot Noir is good, it's really good. You never forget a great Burgundy." Wes warns, "We don't have picnic facilities. We don't hire an accordionist to entertain, and we don't have events. We just make wine." Most of the wine, incidentally, is sold by mail order.

Defining a Region: Doug Moorehead, Arnulf Esterer & Wes Gerlosky

No vintner can gain recognition for his wines if the region in which he or she works doesn't have a reputation for producing good wine. Simply making outstanding wine is seldom enough, unless it is backed by the prestige of the area from which it comes. I can think of only one important producer in the world who is turning out premium wines in a vacuum: Serge Hochar, who produces the acclaimed Chateau Musar wines in Lebanon. Generally, unless a region has a solid reputation, an individual winemaker stands little chance of attracting attention outside his own vineyard.

It takes strong leadership to develop an identity for a region, and leadership in winemaking, as in the world at large, comes naturally to only a few individuals. In the relatively small Lake Erie area, there are three men with the necessary talent, vision and drive to bring world recognition to the region.

Douglas Moorehead is the pioneer who, after tasting Germany's best wines when he was in the army in the 1950s, resolved to make premium wines back home. He got vinifera vines from Konstantin Frank and hybrids from Philip Wagner. Convinced that the region was suitable for producing fine wines, he encouraged local growers to switch from native American vines to these varieties. He fought for the passage of a Pennsylvania state law that would permit farmers to sell their own wine directly to consumers. When the bill was finally passed in 1969, he opened Pennsylvania's first winery, Presque Isle.

Doug, who is a soft-spoken man with short, graying hair and a pleasant, intelligent face, has worked hard to persuade his colleagues to band together to improve the overall quality of Lake Eerie wines. "We've organized a quality control group," he says, "and we're starting to sort out the varieties we should be working with." It would be best for the region's identity, says Doug, to limit the number of grape varieties grown to a few outstanding examples, rather than obscuring the picture with a bewildering number of indifferent wines made from numerous grapes.

Like Doug, Arnie Esterer also learned about raising vinifera vines directly from Dr. Frank. He founded Markko (named after the Finnish policeman who sold him

→

the property) in 1969, and it was the first of Ohio's modern wineries. Like Doug, he believes the Lake Erie region must build its image on the best possible wine that it can produce. "As far as I'm concerned, the Pinot Gris race is on," he says. "Everybody, everywhere makes Chardonnay, and reds are hard for us to produce consistently. But we do well with Pinot Gris, which Dr. Frank said was the greatest early-ripening grape of all. It's just a question now of who's going to make it the best."

While Arnie is encouraged by the fact that the leading producers are putting their confidence in vinifera, rather than hybrid grapes, he acknowledges that there is still a long way to go. "We have to figure out how to survive the coldest winters, like the one in 1994. That one wiped us out," he said. Despite the problems, Arnie is confident the region has the potential to make a name for itself. "It hasn't happened as fast as I'd hoped, but with the second generation coming along, it *will*."

Wes Gerlosky embodies that second generation. A solidly-built man with a thick mustache, Wes fills a room with his presence. He is perhaps less a diplomat than the two older men and less willing to compromise when quality is the issue. He dismisses the efficacy of the Quality Control Group, for example, claiming that it is more about marketing than about quality.

"Do you know why eastern wine is such a hard sell?," he asks impatiently. "Because so many people have been making schlock in the East. The only thing that got California going was that they stopped making jug wine with screw tops. They started using better grapes and making good wine."

Because of such outspoken ideas, Wes says that he and Arnie Esterer are considered radicals by many of their colleagues. "But, in fact, we're the traditional ones," Wes protests. "We're the ones making the kind of wine everyone else in the world drinks. Some guys up here make wines that aren't accepted anywhere on the planet! You've *got* to have a vision beyond the end of your nose, because the world is awash in good wine. We have to change, and then I think we can do as well as Burgundy . . ." Burgundy? He nods. "I think we can be the Beaune of this region. If we do this right, we can make a mark." Anyone who doubts the veracity of Wes's sentiments need only taste his wine to understand what he's talking about.

Marguerite Thomas

Wes Gerlosky.

Like the talented Italian winemakers known as the "Super Tuscans," who were daring and ambitious enough to make wine outside the sanctioned government regulatory structure, the Lake Erie vintners are refusing to settle for business-as-usual in winemaking. They are doing their best to elevate their region's wine into the global realm.

KLINGSHIRN WINERY

Rating: 🌿
216-933-6666.
33050 Webber Road, Avon Lake, OH.
Directions: From I-90 take the Rte. 83 exit, go north on Rte. 83 to Webber Rd., then go left to the winery.
Owners: Allan, Barbara and Lee Klingshirn.
Open: Mon.–Sat., 10 AM– 6 PM.
Price Range of Wines: $3.69 for a dry Concord to $12.99 for a sparkling wine made with Riesling grapes.
Special Features: Picnic area; swings.

During Prohibition, Albert Klingshirn developed a thriving grape juice business in this small community on the outskirts of Cleveland. Repeal left Klingshirn with a surplus of grapes. He decided to turn them into wine. In 1935, he opened a winery, which his son, Allan, eventually took over. Allan introduced hybrids into the family business and today, Allan and Barbara Klingshirn's own son, Lee, is gradually adding vinifera vines.

The vineyard is currently divided into nine acres of Concord, $2^1/2$ of Vidal, and $1^1/2$ of Delaware, plus smaller acreage devoted to Riesling, Seyval, Chardonnay, Pinot Gris, and Cabernet Sauvignon. With the addition of purchased grapes, winemaker Lee Klingshirn produces 5,000 cases a year. At present, Lee believes Riesling is the best vinifera grape for the region, but he acknowledges there will always be a strong local demand for traditional American labrusca wines. Klingshirn wines, which are simple, clean, and light, rather than rich and complex, include a dry Concord, a snappy Chardonnay, and a sparkling wine made from Riesling grapes. There are picnic tables and swings for the kids, as well as fresh grape juice in season.

MARKKO VINEYARD

Rating: 🌿🌿🌿🌿
216-593-3197.
2 South Ridge Road, Conneaut, OH.
Directions: From I-90 take exit 235, go north on Rte. 193 to Main St; turn left, bear right at South Ridge and continue on to the winery.
Owners: Arnulf Esterer and Tim Hubbard.
Open: Mon.–Sat., 11 AM– 6 PM; closed Sun.; appointment recommended.
Price Range of Wines: $7.50 for Covered Bridge, a generic name for several everyday sipping wines, to $22, for Excelsior, a sparkling wine.

Stone pillars flank the entrance to the curving driveway that leads to this small winery tucked away in the hills. Markko's pups, a group of friendly, gray-bearded dogs with wagging tails, extend their enthusiastic greeting. Arnulf Esterer, who owns Markko with a partner, Tim Hubbard, appears in the doorway of the winery to greet me. His own gray beard matches the dogs'. Inside, there's a cozy tasting room where visitors are treated to some astonishingly good wines, all from vinifera grapes grown on Markko's own 14-acre vineyard.

Arnie, who had two previous careers, one in the Navy and the other as an industrial engineer, has been producing wine here since 1968. In fact, Markko was Ohio's first post-Prohibition winery. "Konstantin Frank got me started," he says, explaining that he was one of the many vintners to be convinced by Dr. Frank that vinifera grapes could be grown in the East. Arnie believes that this region is unusually hospitable to grapes. "We have good soils and a longer growing season than the Finger Lakes," he explains. "The Lake Erie region could produce 10% of the nation's wine. We could do 30 to 50 million gallons — we already do more juice than that."

After we sampled his current Chardonnay, Arnie opened a bottle of 1988 Chardonnay. It was still youthful and fresh, with the distinctive aroma and flavor of roasted almonds and toasted bread picked up from the oak barrels in which the wine was fermented. A 1976 Chardonnay followed, and I was amazed at how vibrant this lovely 20-year-old wine was, with no trace of oxidation or deterioration. "It's the acidity that protects the wine," Arnie explains. "This was a hard wine when it was young, but it's softened and taken on another life with age. This is what we can do with white wine in this region."

"It's harder to make consistently good red wines," Arnie explained, as he poured a Pinot Noir and Cabernet Sauvignon. Both wines were excellent. A 1993 Riesling came as close to a Moselle as any American Riesling I've tasted.

As good as these wines are, however, it is the Pinot Gris that Arnie is really excited about. "This is the grape that can define our region," he says. He described the wide stylistic variations of the grape, a white mutation of Pinot Noir. The wine can range from bone-dry to full, opulent Alsatian Tokay (pinot gris is, confusingly, called *Tokay* in Alsace). "We don't know how we should style ours yet," admits Arnie, "but that's the fun of it." If his fragrant and intensely flavorful Pinot Gris becomes the model for the region, the wine world will surely take note.

Markko produces 2,000 cases of wine a year. All of Markko's wines are excellent, dry libations to enjoy with meals. "We don't cater to the sweet-wine crowd here," warns Arnie. There's a nice picnic area on the winery grounds, or drive three miles north to the excellent beach at Conneaut Park on Lake Erie.

ISLAND WINERIES

In 1870, there were more than 7,000 acres of vineyards in the Lake Erie region, on the mainland and on islands between Toledo and Cleveland. On the Bass Islands alone there were dozens of thriving wineries, including one on Middle Bass Island that was purported to be the largest winery in the nation. By the turn of the century, several wineries in the Sandusky area were winning competitions as far away as Paris.

Vines thrive on the islands because the weather is moderated by the surrounding water, with warmer temperatures and a longer growing season than on the mainland. In addition, they enjoy approximately 25% less rainfall than the rest of the region because storms break up before reaching the islands. Even after the lake freezes in winter, the Lake Erie islands are generally the warmest places in Ohio.

During Prohibition, some island wineries continued producing wine legally for medicinal or sacramental purposes, while others made bootleg wine, which led to occasional confrontations with government officials. Local folklore is full of stories of irate vintners wielding shotguns to chase the officials away.

As in the rest of the East, most of the wineries never fully recovered after Repeal. The few that survived concentrated on sweet Catawba, Delaware, and other native American wines, which still have a local following and attract a substantial number of tourists. The interest in refined, European-style wines that swept the East in the early 1990s is just beginning to be felt here. The region is a charming place to visit, and occasionally one happens upon a very good wine.

Put-In-Bay, Middle Bass, and Kelley Islands can be reached by ferry. There is also a regular jet ferry service. Call 1-800-245-1JET for schedules and prices.

FIRELANDS WINERY
Rating: 👤👤👤
419-625-5474;
  800-548-WINE.
917 Bardshar Road,
  Sandusky, OH.
Directions: From Rte. 2, exit
  at Rte. 6 and follow signs
  to winery.
Owners: Paramount
  Distillers.
Open: June to Sept.,
  Mon.–Sat., 9 AM–6 PM;
  Sun. 1 PM–5 PM; Oct. to
  May, Mon. -Sat., 9 AM–
  5 PM
Price Range of Wines: $4.40
  for a medium dry Vidal
  to $10.95 for the sparkling
  Brut and Rosé.

Although Firelands Winery is not on an island, it is located on Sandusky Bay, the gateway to the island wineries. This strip of land is called the Firelands, after the region along the Connecticut coast that was raided and burned by British troops during the Revolutionary War. Citizens whose property was destroyed were granted parcels of land in the Connecticut Western Reserve, now part of northern Ohio.

The original winery here was established in 1880 by Edward Mantey, a German settler who cultivated grapes and made wine for other German immigrant families. The Mantey Winery was eventually rechristened Firelands. It is owned by Paramount Distillers, a small Ohio corporation that produces wine under five different labels: Mon

Ami, Lonz, Meiers, Mantey, and Firelands. The total production is 50,000 cases annually.

The Mantey wines are all sweet labrusca. "They are our bread and butter," says Ed Boaz, Fireland's president. The wines under the Fireland's label are a testament to the skills of Claudio Salvador, an Italian winemaker from the Veneto region, who has been at this winery for over a dozen years. They include an outstanding Chardonnay and Cabernet Sauvignon, as well as a Pinot Noir.

HEINEMAN WINERY
Rating: 🍷
419-285-2811.
Put-in-Bay, OH.
Directions: Take the jet ferry from Port Clinton, OH to Put-in-Bay and follow signs on the island to the winery.
Owner: Ed Heineman.
Open: April to mid-Nov., Mon.–Sat., 10 AM–10 PM, Sun. noon–7 PM; mid-Nov. to April, Mon.–Sat., 8 AM–5 PM.
Price Range of Wines: $5.18 for Catawba to $9.95 for Chardonnay.
Special Features: German beer garden, snack bar, indoor and outdoor picnic tables.
Special Events: Tours of a cavern filled with green crystal stalactites that was discovered when the winery was being built.

Commodore Oliver Hazard Perry sailed from this island to battle the British fleet in 1813. After the victory, he returned to send his famous dispatch: "We have met the enemy and they are ours. . . ." A peace monument commemorating this event rises over the small harbor at Put-in-Bay Island.

In summer, the island is a lively place, but in the tranquillity of off-season, one senses what the island was like in 1888 when Gustave Heineman arrived. An immigrant from Baden, a wine-producing area along the Rhine River in Germany, he established the first winery on the island. By 1900, there were 17. About 40 acres of vines are still maintained by a handful of growers, but Heineman, which survived Prohibition by making grape juice, is the only remaining winery.

Ed Heineman, great-grandson of the founder, is the present winemaker. He produces about 10,000 cases of wine a year, using grapes from the family's 15-acre vineyard, as well as from other Put-in-Bay and North Bass Island vineyards. Heineman makes 20 different wines, mostly from native labrusca varieties, which is the only grape grown on the island. Recently, Ed began making a Chardonnay from mainland grapes. This and Riesling are the only vinifera wines produced.

In the German beer-garden setting at Heineman, one can sample traditional sweet American wines, as well as variations of native species made into dry wines. Catawba, for example, and Claret, a mixture of Concord and Ives grapes, are well-made, mildly grapey wines. Although they may not convert partisans of Cabernet Sauvignon, they nevertheless offer an agreeable option for anyone who wants to sample an interesting variety of wines. One of Heineman's specialties is a sweet wine made from Ives grape. It is so popular, says Ed, that he has begun stockpiling Ives. "A lot of my colleagues are switching to vinifera grapes," he adds, "but they aren't having an easy time of it. I recognize that tastes are changing, but if this past summer is any indication of how much people like our wines, we will just keep on growing."

OTHER LAKE ERIE WINERIES

LONZ WINERY (419-285-5411, Middle Bass Island, OH), a gothic stone building embellished with turrets and battlements, sits on the southern tip of Middle Bass Island. It began life as the Gold Eagle Winery during the Civil War, and by 1875 it had become the largest wine producer in the nation. The original winery, twice destroyed by fire, was rebuilt in 1942 by George Lonz, whose father had been producing wines on the island since 1884. George sold his Isle de Fleurs Champagne to revelers who sailed regularly to the island after Repeal. Today, most Lonz wines are produced at the Firelands Winery in Sandusky, but some sparkling wine is still made on the island. The winery is an active place, with wine tastings and tours of the century-old cellars, a snack bar, gift shops, playground, and a picnic area. There are a host of special events — from garage sales and grape stomping festivals, to entertainment by barbershop quartets and dancing on the patio in summer.

STEUK WINE COMPANY (419-625-0803, 1001 Fremont Ave, Sandusky, OH), a winery founded in 1855, is now a tasting room and country market. A number of wines may be sampled, although little of the original winery remains. One novelty that makes this a worthwhile stop on a winetaster's tour is a wine made from Black Opal, a grape native only to the Sandusky region. This wine, is a deep maroon color, and comes in either semi-sweet or dry versions. Its assertive American grape flavor has been tamed somewhat by time spent in an oak barrel. In the main part of the market, local fruits, vegetables, homemade candies, fresh cider, and much more, is sold. It's a good place to pick up picnic provisions.

RESTAURANTS AND LODGING

RESTAURANTS

Ohio

OLD FIREHOUSE WINERY
216-466-9300.
5499 Lake Road, Geneva-on-the-Lake, OH.
Open: Lunch and dinner May through Sept.; less frequently off-season. Call for days and hours.
Price: Inexpensive–Moderate.

This unique restaurant in the resort town of Geneva-on-the-Lake is also a winery, although fewer than 1,000 cases of wine are produced annually. Housed in the village's first fire station, there's a large outdoor patio and a gazebo overlooking the lake.

FERRANTE WINERY & RESTAURANT
216-466-8466.
5585 Route 307, Geneva, OH.
Price: Inexpensive–Moderate.

This popular restaurant and winery was partially destroyed by fire in 1995. It is scheduled to reopen by 1996.

MON AMI RESTAURANT & WINERY
419-797-4445; 800-777-4266.
3845 East Wine Cellar Rd, Port Clinton, OH.
Price: Moderate.

Constructed as a co-op winery by European immigrants in 1872, Mon Ami was built from gigantic limestone blocks hauled out of the ground when the cellar was excavated. From the outside, the building looks like a typical French country inn.

The winery is now part of Firelands, where most of the wine is made, although a good deal of it is aged and stored in Mon Ami's historic cellars. The large restaurant menu is eclectic to say the least, ranging from sauerkraut balls through salmon dijon to chicken parmigiana. Varieties of Lake Erie fish are also on the menu, including yellow perch, walleye, and northern Ohio farm-raised trout. A full range of Mon Ami white, blush, red, sparkling, and dessert wines is served here.

LODGING

Ohio

BUCCIA VINEYARDS/ BED & BREAKFAST
216-593-5976.
518 Gore Road, Conneaut, OH.
Price: Moderate.

This small winery, set amidst vineyards and orchards, produces wines from its own hybrid grapes as well as from vinifera grapes purchased locally. A Vignoles wine, made in both dry and sweet varieties, is a specialty. Guests can stroll through the spacious grounds, sample cheese and wine, relax in a private hot tub, and enjoy a sound night's sleep in this peaceful rural setting. No wonder Buccia tends to be booked well ahead.

SWEET VALLEY INN
419-746-2750.
715 Division St, Kelleys
Island, OH.
Price: Moderate.

The Ohio wine industry began on Kelleys Island in the 19th century. The area known as Sweet Valley was so-named because of the vineyards that flourished here. The inn, built in 1892 by the manager of the Sweet Valley Winery, is a large, yellow Queen Anne Victorian with authentic Victorian furnishings and four guestrooms. It sits in a picturesque setting next to the ruins of the winery. Guests can enjoy horse and carriage rides in summer, or sleigh rides in the winter.

New York

THE WHITE INN
716-672-2103.
52 East Main St,
Fredonia, NY.
Price: Hotel:
Moderate–Expensive;
Restaurant: Moderate.

Dr. Squire White, the first medical doctor to settle and practice in Chautauqua County, erected a frame house on this site at the beginning of the 19th century. According to tradition, the pair of stately maple trees flanking the front walk was planted by Dr. White and his young son, Devillo, in 1825. When the original house was destroyed by fire, Devillo built an Empire brick structure, a portion of which was incorporated into later additions. The White house became a hotel in the early 20th century after Isabel White, the last remaining member of the family, sold the house and moved next door. The hotel was recently renovated and now has 23 rooms furnished in antiques or good-quality reproductions. In the capable hands of innkeepers Robert Contiguglia and his wife, Kathleen Dennison, the White Inn is once again a distinguished, comfortable hotel.

The restaurant offers local wines along with traditional fare with an occasional contemporary spin. Examples include fettucine with sundried tomatoes and roasted garlic, saddle of lamb stuffed with almonds, spinach, shallots and garlic, and duck breast with Port.

PART TWO

Atlantic Uplands

I. Northern New Jersey and the Delaware River Region

New Jersey Side of the Delaware River
Pennsylvania Side of the Delaware River

II. Southern Pennsylvania and Maryland

Southern Pennsylvania
Maryland

III. Northern and Central Virginia

IV. Western Connecticut

V. The Hudson River Valley

West Side of the Hudson River
East Side of the Hudson River

VI. The Finger Lakes

Seneca Lake
Keuka Lake
Cayuga Lake
Canandaigua Lake

PART TWO

Atlantic Uplands

Dr. Michael Fisher, owner,
Amwell Valley Vineyard,
Ringoes, New Jersey.

Marguerite Thomas

The Atlantic Uplands lies between the coastal zones that border the Atlantic Ocean and the eastern mountain ranges. This vast plateau runs north to south, and is also sometimes called the Piedmont, or "Up Country." Higher above sea level than the Benchlands, the Uplands are characterized by gently rolling hills easing up toward the Allegheny, Blue Ridge, and Appalachian Mountains. These eastern viticultural Uplands include northern New Jersey, the Delaware River Valley, Pennsylvania (except the central and western mountainous sections), Maryland, northern and central Virginia, western Connecticut, and the Hudson River Valley and Finger Lakes regions of New York.

Because of a long growing season and mineral-laden soils, the best Uplands wines exhibit a beautifully balanced ratio between sweetness, acidity, and alcohol. They are characterized by delicate fruit flavors and, when the grapes come from the region's very best vineyards, have rich and intense flavor components.

The soils that are washed down the mountains are well-drained and rich in calcium and the other minerals that grapes thrive on. With an increasing number of viticulturists gaining greater knowledge of the eastern wine regions, larger capital investments being made, more vineyards being planted, and more wineries opening, this extremely promising area will undoubtedly continue to develop as one of the country's most important viticultural regions.

NORTHERN NEW JERSEY AND THE DELAWARE RIVER REGION

L ike most eastern wine regions, this area is influenced by a great body of water, the Delaware River. The countryside is idyllic, dotted with gracious old stone farmhouses, elegant horse farms, rolling hills, and country retreats. Quaint villages that range from tourist meccas to remote and genuinely charming country hamlets fill the region.

New Jersey's Hunterdon and Warren counties lie on the east side of the river. Their landscape comes as a pleasant surprise to those who think the state is a holding tank for industry and pollution: this is a vista characterized by contentedly grazing horses in spacious green pastures enclosed by white fences, and curving driveways that lead to handsome country estates.

Directly across the river, the Pennsylvania wineries are set in a background that is picturesque enough to attract sightseers from all over the world. Scenic River Road (Route 32), a narrow road that meanders along the Delaware River through Bucks County, is one of the prettiest drives in the East. It was at the southern end of this road on Christmas Day in 1776 that George Washington and the Continental Army crossed the icy Delaware River to deal a crushing blow to the British.

In addition to wineries, there are numerous recreational activities in the area. Historic mansions, such as Pennsbury Manor, William Penn's 17th-century country estate on the banks of the Delaware, and Andalusia, one of the finest examples of Greek Revival domestic architecture in the nation. Both are open to the public. Art galleries, antique stores, and shopping outlets beckon as well.

The wineries are more widely dispersed in this area than in others, so more time may be needed for travel. With a wealth of good restaurants and inns, this region offers plenty of opportunities for lunch and overnight breaks.

NEW JERSEY SIDE OF THE DELAWARE RIVER

AMWELL VALLEY VINEYARD
Rating: 🍂
908-788-5852.
80 Old York Road, Ringoes, NJ.
Directions: From the circle in Flemington, take Rte. 202 south. Take the

A mwell Valley Vineyard is noteworthy in many respects. Founded in 1978 by Dr. Michael Fisher, a London-born scientist at Merck Sharp and Dohme Research Laboratories, this is the oldest winery in this part of New Jersey. One of Dr. Fisher's important contributions to the industry was his successful campaign to improve New Jersey's archaic winery laws. His efforts resulted in

Reavilue exit onto Rte. 514 east. The winery is 1.1 miles further. Old York Road is Rte. 514.
Owner: Dr. Michael Fisher.
Open: Sat. and Sun., 1 PM– 5 PM, and by appointment.
Price Range of Wines: $7 for Pheasant Ridge Blush to $12 for a sparkling Blanc de Blanc.
Special Features: Picnic area.

the passage of the Farm Winery Act in 1981. This act helps regulate the quality of wine produced in New Jersey and encourages the preservation of farm land. It has also opened the door to entrepreneurial winemaking. Until the passage of the act, only seven winemaking licenses had been issued in New Jersey since Prohibition. Dr. Fisher became interested in vineyards after reading an article in *Scientific American* about the various grape growing regions in the world. He contacted one of the contributing authors, Philip Wagner of Boordy Vineyards in Maryland, who guided the Fishers in their first planting of hybrid grapes. After the initial harvest, they began experimenting with other grapes, and today they raise both vinifera and hybrid grapes on 11 acres of their 30-acre farm. They produce about 2,500 cases of wine, ranging from Maréchal Foch, a hybrid, to Gewürztraminer, a vinifera.

"Grapes aren't as hard to grow as I had thought, as long as you select the right kind," said Dr. Fisher. The quality of the grapes you plant is the most important factor in winemaking, he asserts, and climate is the key component. "Riesling, for example, is reasonably easy to grow here. We have better fungicides and pesticides now than we used to, which makes it all possible. Also, the weather is warmer these days."

A large new tasting room should be open at Amwell Valley Vineyards by the summer of 1996. The wines are mostly on the lean side and make nice picnic wines. Picnic benches on the deck overlook the vineyards and a sweep of Amwell Valley's unspoiled land that stretches to the Sourland Mountains in the distance.

KING'S ROAD WINERY
Rating: 🍇
908-479-6611.
Route 579, Asbury, NJ.
Directions: From I-78 take exit 11. Follow signs to Pattenburg on Rte. 614, continue another three miles, then turn right onto Rte. 579 and go .2 mile to the winery, which will be on the left.
Owner: Robert Abplanalp.
Open: Wed.–Sun., noon– 5 PM.
Price Range of Wines: $4 for Chablis to $30 for Chardonnay.

King's Road Winery, which opened in 1981 on the site of a former pig and cow farm, is a leader on several fronts. It is the first winery in New Jersey to have its wines served on an airline (Kiwi Airlines) and it is one of the first to sell its Chardonnay in California (to the Richard Nixon Library).

King's Road is owned by Robert Abplanalp who, trivia buffs will recall, was President Nixon's pal as well as the inventor of the aerosol spray valve. Dutch-born winemaker and general manager Nicolaas Opdam is proud of his winery and of the state it's located in. "New Jersey is more than just Newark," he insists. "People who come out here are always surprised at how nice it is." He's partic-

Nicholaas Opdam, general manager, King's Road Winery, Asbury, New Jersey.

Marguerite Thomas

Special Features: Snack shop, picnic area
Special Events: Evenings with the Winemaker.

ularly proud of the special, small stainless steel fermentation tanks he designed and had custom-made in California.

King's Road has 25 acres of vineyards. The first planting took place in 1980 with native labrusca grapes. The intention was to sell grapes to vintners, but when they proved to be poor sellers, the labrusca was replaced with vinifera vines.

Today, King's Road is the largest producer of Chardonnay and Pinot Noir wines in the state, and the winery's total output is 4,000 cases annually. Nicolaas is also experimenting with different styles of Riesling, one bone-dry and the other sweeter. The latter has a rich, floral perfume. As both of these wines are a little off the mark, the solution might be to blend them together.

King's Road Winery is on a small rural road that in colonial days was a major thoroughfare connecting the northern and southern sections of the state. It was known as "The King's Highway." The tasting room is located in the converted hayloft of a 200-year-old barn. There's a shop where cheese and other light snacks are sold, and there are a few cafe tables inside where visitors can enjoy a glass of wine.

POOR RICHARD'S WINERY
Rating: 🍷
908-996-6480.
220 Ridge Road, Frenchtown, NJ.
Directions: From I-78 take the Clinton/Pittstown Exit. Go south on Rte. 513 to Frenchtown; turn

This winery is as unique as its wines and winemaker. Richard Dilts and his partner, Judy Rampel, have devoted themselves to making honest, unpretentious country wines, a task they proved can be done without the luxury of endlessly deep pockets. "Unlike other wineries, we didn't go to the bank, get a million dollar loan, and then go out of business," Richard explained. "We may not

Richard Dilts, co-owner of Poor Richard's Winery, Frenchtown, New Jersey.

Marguerite Thomas

left on Rte. 12 to Ridge Rd. From Flemington, travel west on Rte. 12 to Rte. 519, and then go north to Ridge Rd.
Owners: Richard Dilts and Judy Rampel.
Open: Thurs.–Sun., 11 AM– 6 PM, or by appointment.
Price Range of Wines: The Vidal is $6 and the Reserve Red is $8.
Special Events: Spring and summer open house; annual chili competition.

be as dazzling as some places because we pay as we go along."

Indeed, the operation is simple. Although plans call for expanding the winery and vineyards, for the moment both the tasting bar and wine making facilities are located in a simple whitewashed underground cellar. The equipment includes plastic "barrels" and a vintage hand-operated corker.

Richard started as a home winemaker but when the Farm Winery Act was passed in the early 1980s, he decided to go into the wine business full time. He planted his own vineyard in the early 1980s. Like many vintners in the French countryside, Richard is part man of the earth, part philosopher. He vigorously defends his decision to raise hybrid rather than vinifera grapes. "They are an expression of American tastes. They are better suited to our soils and climate than vinifera grapes, and the wines go with American food," he declares.

Like Richard himself, the wines tend to be straightforward and full of character. The 1992 Reserve Vineyard Red, for example, is a surprisingly well-balanced and assertive hybrid blend that belies the unsophisticated winery equipment. The rugged, hilly vineyards form a scenic backdrop for picnics.

UNIONVILLE VINEYARDS
Rating: 🍷🍷
908-788-0400.
9 Rocktown Road, Ringoes, NJ.

Unionville Vineyards is one of the youngest of New Jersey's wineries, but the land it occupies has been a productive peach orchard since at least the mid-19th century. "New Jersey was one of the great peach producers in the 1800s," explains

Pat Galloway, co-owner, Unionville Vineyards, Ringoes, New Jersey, in the vineyard's handsome tasting room.

Marguerite Thomas

Directions: From Rte. 202/31 about 10 minutes south of Flemington Circle, turn east onto Wertsville Rd. At the 2nd crossroads turn right onto Rocktown Road. The winery is the first drive on the left.

Owners: Pat Galloway and Kris Nielson.

Open: Thurs.–Sun., 11 AM–4 PM.

Price Range of Wines: $5.99 for Hunters White to $10.99 for Hunters Red Reserve.

Special Events: Summer Fest in August with picnics and live music; October Pumpkin Fest in the fall with live bands, hayrides and activities for the kids.

Unionville owner Pat Galloway. "Then the peach blight hit, and that's when the industry moved to Georgia." In its next incarnation the property became a dairy farm.

Established as a vineyard and winery in 1988 by Pat and her husband, Kris Nielson, the first wines were released in 1992. Since they also jointly own an engineering firm, they rely heavily on their winemaker, John Altmaier, who was trained in Ohio, the Finger Lakes, and Germany. Together, the three have come an impressively long way with the winery.

Eleven acres of hybrid and vinifera grapes have been planted on their 90-acre property. To date, only the hybrids have been harvested and vinified into four wines, including Hunter's White Reserve, an oak-aged Vidal; Hunter's Red Reserve, a fine, oaky Chambourcin. Excellent Chardonnay and Seyval Blanc are made with grapes harvested from a vineyard nearby.

Unionville is already one of the best wineries in New Jersey. If the current wines are an indication of the quality, we can count on this becoming a true leader in New Jersey.

The eye-catching labels depict hunting scenes with foxes and horses, reflecting one of the popular pastimes in this region. The tasting room and winery facilities are located in a former dairy barn. It was handsomely rebuilt by a local Mennonite contractor for the winery, using stones from the original foundation.

OTHER WINERIES ON THE NEW JERSEY SIDE OF DELAWARE RIVER

CREAM RIDGE WINERY (609-259-9797, fax 609-259-1852, 145 Rte. 539, Cream Ridge, NJ). Located halfway between New Jersey's northern Uplands and the Benchlands to the south, Cream Ridge specializes in fruit wines. They also make a credible Red Table Wine from Chardonel grapes and a white wine from Chardonnay. For anyone curious about fruit wines, this is a good place to try them. The Raspberry Wine, a blend of 75% black raspberry and 25% red raspberry, is oak-aged and made into an inky, rich, and slightly tannic dry wine that is truly astonishing. It needs hearty food to accompany it — perhaps stewed venison, duck, or a pork roast with prunes.

FOUR SISTERS WINERY (908-475-3671, Route 519, Belvidere, NJ). This winery is part of a large fruit and vegetable farm owned by Laurie and Robert Matarazzo. The winery, which opened in 1984, is named after the family's four daughters. It produces numerous wines; the most notable being Chardonel. The winery hosts a variety of events and activities, ranging from grape stomping parties to Native American powwows.

LaFOLLETTE VINEYARD AND WINERY (908-359-8833, 64 Harlingen Road, Belle Mead, NJ). Winery owner Mimi LaFollette Summerskill, who is also a writer, and her late husband, John Summerskill, who was President of Cornell University, originally raised Black Angus cattle on their 30-acre farm. This proved to be a daunting challenge, as the cattle often wandered into the gardens of irate neighbors. So, in 1979, they switched to grapes. They decided to concentrate on a single varietal "instead of trying to be all things to all people," says Mimi. They settled on the Seyval grape and planted 10 acres. LaFollette now produces about 1,500 cases of straightforward Seyval and a small amount of oak-aged Seyval. The wine is served in several Princeton restaurants and at some functions at the Faculty House at Princeton University. LaFollette's small tasting room is housed in a former sheep barn. There are picnic facilities outside.

TAMUZZA VINEYARDS (908-459-5878, Cemetery Rd., Hope, NJ). Although the village of Hope is an historic 1769 Moravian village, the far-reaching marketing strategies of Tamuzza winery definitely reflect the 20th century. It claims to be the largest supplier of personalized wine labels and wedding wine favors in New Jersey. The Cabernet Sauvignon is a decent wine.

PENNSYLVANIA SIDE OF THE DELAWARE RIVER

**BUCKINGHAM VALLEY
VINEYARDS**
Rating: 🍷
215-794-7188.
1521 Route 413,
Buckingham, PA.
Directions: From Rte. 202
between New Hope and
Doylestown, take Rte.
413 south for two miles
to the winery.
Owners: The Forest family.
Open: Tues.–Fri., noon–
6 PM; Sat. 10 AM–6 PM;
Sun. noon–4 PM.
Price Range of Wines: $5.25
to $7.25.

Buckingham Valley Vineyards is profitable enough to support an entire extended family: Jerry and Kathy Forest and their grown children, Jonathan, Kevin, and Christopher, who all work at the winery. The Forests started growing grapes in 1966 so they could make wine for their own consumption. One thing led to another, and they now have 20 acres planted in grapes and produce 12,500 cases of wine annually.

Except for a small amount of Riesling, all of the wine is made from hybrid grapes, and it is all top quality. The dry reds, which are aged in American oak, tend to be fleshy wines, and the whites are full-bodied, clean, and flavorful. The wines usually show a good balance between fruitiness and the pronounced acidity that characterizes eastern wines. The sweeter wines have interesting personalities that go beyond mere sweetness.

The winery itself doesn't have a lot of razzle-dazzle charm, as it is basically an addition to a suburban house. A self-guided tour is offered, as well as a help-yourself wine pouring. There are picnic tables outside.

Stormy Skrip of Clover Hill Vineyards & Winery, Breinigsville, Pennsylvania.

Marguerite Thomas

**CLOVER HILL
VINEYARDS &
WINERY**
Rating: 🍷🍷

Set in the bucolic countryside south of Allentown, Clover Hill got its name when John and Pat Skrip (he was formerly a civil engineer and she was a teacher), decided to buy a farm. As they

610-395-246;
   fax 610-366-1246.
9850 Newtown Road,
   Breinigsville, PA.
Directions: From New York
   take I-78/US 22 beyond
   Allentown to Rte. 100
   south. Turn right at the
   2nd traffic light onto
   Schantz Rd.; go to
   Newtown Rd. and turn
   left to the winery.
Owners: John and Pat
   Skrip.
Open: Mon.–Sat., 11 AM–
   5 PM; Sun. noon–5 PM.
Price Range of Wines: $6.50
   for native varietals to
   $10.95 for Chambourcin.
Special Features: Picnic
   area.
Special Events: Seasonal
   open houses.

climbed to the top of their highest hill to admire the view, Pat spotted a four-leaf clover at her feet; within seconds, John had found one too. They immediately named the place after these lucky omens, and a cloverleaf became the logo for their wine labels. The original clovers are framed and hanging in the Skrip's home.

The couple planted their first vineyard in 1975 then, while they waited for the vines to mature, John took courses in viticulture. They opened the winery in 1985. Now, a decade later, Clover Hill produces close to 16,000 cases of wine annually. The Skrips recently purchased another vineyard. The Skrip's son, John III, who earned a degree in enology at California's Fresno State College, is the winemaker. His wife, Stormy, is in charge of public relations.

Clover Hill's winery is immaculate, reflecting the Skrip's passion for cleanliness. The wines are also clean and bright, with the purity of fruit shining through. Oak Vidal, for example, mingles citrusy flavors with a rich taste imparted by aging in French and American oak barrels. The Riesling is moderately sweet but less cloying than many eastern Rieslings. The Chambourcin is a dry, generously-flavored red. Niagara, Catawba, and Alden are native varietals with strong, grapey aromas that are not to everyone's taste or smell, but they are popular in this area. "Most people nearby have grown up with the smell," says Stormy Skrip, "and they love it. It's the taste of the area."

The grove of woods behind the winery provides a scenic picnic setting.

**FRANKLIN HILL
   VINEYARDS**
Rating: 🍷
610-588-8708.
Franklin Hill Road,
   Bangor, PA.
Directions: From Rte. 22
   take Rte. 611 north to
   Pulcini's Restaurant.
   Make a left onto Front St.
   At the top of the hill, go
   right onto Franklin Hill
   Rd. The winery is 1.7
   miles further on the
   right.
Owner: Elaine Pivinski.

Franklin Hill Vineyards is hidden away in the hilly farmland that rises above the Delaware River in Pennsylvania. Elaine Pivinski was a Flower Child in the 1960s: "Yes, I was at the original Woodstock," she smiles. She's now the hardworking owner of Franklin Hill Vineyards.

It all began when Elaine and her former husband decided to buy a farm instead of living on a commune. Having no idea what to do with this former barley field, they wrote to Pennsylvania State University for advice. The university suggested planting the new hybrid grapes people were trying to raise. This appealed to the pair, who planted their vineyard in 1976. A winemaker friend taught

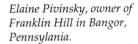

Elaine Pivinsky, owner of Franklin Hill in Bangor, Pennsylania.

Marguerite Thomas

Open: Mon.–Sat., 11 AM–
   4 PM; call for Sun. hours.
Price Range of Wines: $5.99
   a bottle.
Special Features: Picnic
   area.

them the trade, and they released their first vintage in 1982. To their astonishment, it sold out in 15 months. But by 1985, the marriage had broken up and Elaine was left with the winery and three children to tend. "I vowed when I found myself running this business alone, that I would employ only working mothers," she says.

Bonnie Pysher, fit the job description perfectly. She learned how to make wine, run the tractor, spray the vineyards, and fix anything that broke. "She's perfect," sighs Elaine contentedly. Most of the other employees at Franklin Hill are local farmer's wives. "They put their kids on the school bus and then work in the vineyards for a few hours," says Elaine, Eventually, she opened one — then two — retail shops where the wines are sold. This is where she spends most of her time now, assisted by her 75-year-old father. Elaine's blue eyes light up when she speaks of him. "He's the world's best salesman. If you come in to buy a bottle of wine, you'll probably leave with a case."

Franklin Hill wines include Seyval Blanc and Chardonel, a Seyval-Chardonnay cross, Both are crisp, dry whites. The rest of the production is mostly hybrid-based semi-sweet and sweet wines. "The Pennsylvania Dutch around here don't like red wine and they don't like dry wine," Elaine explains. Her own personal favorite is Cayuga White, a very pleasant wine with a fragrance reminiscent of Sauvignon Blanc. Elaine likes it with cheese and crackers, and it's also good with Mexican food and other spicy dishes.

Franklin Hill's tasting room is located among the barrels and fermentation tanks in the winery. Bring your own cheese and crackers for a picnic with a bottle of Cayuga — and, who knows, maybe you'll leave with a case. The retail stores are open every day: The Wine Shop in Stroudsburg, 717-424-2466; The Grape Spot in Easton, 610-559-7887.

PEACE VALLEY WINERY

Rating: 🦆
215-249-9058.
300 Old Limekiln Road, Chalfont, PA.
Directions: From Doylestown, go northwest on Rte. 313 to New Galen Rd. Turn left and go two miles, then turn right onto Limekiln Rd. and go one mile to the winery.
Open: Wed., Thurs., Fri., and Sun., noon–6 PM; Sat. 10 AM–6 PM, except during Dec. when the winery is open every day 10 AM–6 PM.
Owner: Susan Gross.
Price Range of Wines: $5.99 to $11.95.
Special Events: Nouveau Release is held the weekend before Thanksgiving; Spring Fling comes around Income Tax Day.

Peace Valley Winery is situated in an aptly named place — a tranquil, wooded valley that seems light years away from the traffic and industrial blight of contemporary civilization. The first stage in the creation of the winery began in 1968 when Susan Gross planted grapes in a small vineyard on her property. She found a market among home winemakers, so she kept planting more vines. Today she has 24 acres of vines and she's still adding.

In 1984, she opened her own winery. While she produces some so-so Chardonnay and Gewürztraminer, and she's experimenting with Cabernet Sauvignon, she specializes in wines made from blends — mostly native American and French-American hybrids. "The trend is to switch to varietal wines (wines made from a single grape variety)," grumbles Peace Valley's winemaker, Robert Kilmus. "So we're bucking the trend by blending different grapes. But we feel that's the best way to emphasize fruity flavors."

Peace Valley Winery is a good place to sample native American grape wines, such as Niagara and Fredonia, that aren't produced much locally any more. Visitors can also pick their own grapes and apples here. There are no picnic facilities, but Peace Valley Park, on a lake just at the end of the road, is a fine place to picnic.

SAND CASTLE WINERY

Rating: 🦆
800-722-9463.
755 River Road, Erwinna, PA.
Directions: The winery is located on River Road (Rte. 32), which parallels the Delaware River. It is 12 miles north of New Hope and two miles north of the Frenchtown Bridge.
Owner: Joe Maxian.
Open: Mon.–Sat., 10 AM–6 PM; Sun. 11 AM–6 PM.
Price Range of Wines: $11 for Johannesburg Riesling to $19 for Pinot Noir.

This winery has the most stunning location in this region, sitting high on a hilltop overlooking the Delaware River. The tasting room has an undistinguished appearance, but there's talk of building a castle just like the one in Bratislava, Czechoslovakia, where owner Joe Maxian, grew up. If and when this happens, it will be a dramatic landmark in this scenic section of the Delaware River Valley.

The underground caves where wines are stored in barrels and stainless steel tanks are as spectacular as the setting. Seven thousand square feet of space was blasted out of the shale mountain to create the facility. The winery produces 16,000 cases of wine annually from vinifera grapes that are grown on the estate's 40-acre vineyards. The first vines

Special Features: Picnic area.

Special Events: Seasonal festivals include an art festival, a Chardonnay Blossom Festival, and a Cellar Sampler Festival.

were planted in 1983 and the winery opened in 1988.

The wines are all traditional European varietals such as Chardonnay, Cabernet Sauvignon, and Riesling. While most of the wines I tasted had good color and intensity, they were marred by a persistent skunky odor, indicating a serious winemaking problem. A consulting winemaker from Czechoslovakia occasionally provides advice to Joe. With the help of a skilled winemaker, there is the potential here to make excellent wine. Picnic facilities are available at tables set up under a tent.

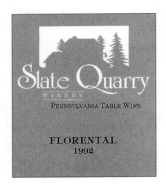

PENNSYLVANIA TABLE WINE

FLORENTAL
1992

SLATE QUARRY WINERY

Rating: 🍷
610-759-0286.
460 Gower Road, Nazareth, PA.

Directions: From Rte. 22 take Rte. 191 north to Nazareth; veer left at the blinking light at the crossroads of Rte. 946; cross over Rte. 248 and travel $^3/_4$ mile further to a group of houses. Turn right onto Knauss Rd. and go $^1/_2$ mile to winery sign; turn right onto Gower Rd; the winery is $^1/_4$ mile more.

Owners: Sid and Ellie Butler.

Open: Feb. through Dec., Fri., Sat. and Sun., 1 PM–

S late Quarry is known as much for the grapes it grows to sell to other vintners as for its own excellent wines. Sid Butler, a science professor from Lehigh University, originally grew a few grapes and produced just enough wine for his family to enjoy. But now that he's retired, he makes about 900 cases of wine a year and oversees his 13 acres of vineyards. He raises mostly hybrids, but he has several acres in vinifera as well.

The Lehigh Valley farm dates back to the colonial days and is located near a slate quarry. The vineyard, with its slate-laced soil, is clearly Sid's passion, and he experiments with a variety of grapes, including several Chardonnay clones — Florental, a little-known Gamay hybrid, and Chardonel, a Chardonnay-Seyval cross that he sells to other wineries in the region. The Butlers believe the mineral-rich soil gives a distinctive character to their wines, and, indeed, one can taste a hint of mineral in the wine's flavor.

6 PM, or by appointment; closed Jan.

Price Range of Wines: $5.75 for Chambourcin to $11 for a sparkling wine made from Vidal grapes.

Special Features: Picnic area.

Special Events: Every autumn Slate Quarry hosts a vigneron-for-the-day event where attendees participate in crushing grapes, followed by lunch and a wine tasting. People usually return the following year to buy a bottle of the wine they helped make.

All of the wines the Butlers make are sold at the winery. Most Slate Quarry wines are "off-dry", or slightly sweet wines. Sid explains that people often claim they don't like sweet wine but, "while they talk dry, they usually end up buying sweet." The best selling wine is "Ellie's Rosé" medium-sweet pink wine with a Muscat grape aroma. He makes an above-average Chardonnay, a good Cabernet Franc, and a dry and rich oak-aged Chambourcin, the red hybrid that many Pennsylvania vintners claim as their signature wine.

OTHER PENNSYLVANIA AND DELAWARE RIVER WINERIES

As in many other wine regions in the East, the Delaware River Valley has many commercial wineries that are so small they are just one step up from home winemaking — "professional hobbyists" is an apt description according to Rushland Ridge's owners. Most of these are open only on weekends as the owners usually have full-time jobs. Visitors who stop in unannounced at other times will most likely be greeted by a "closed" sign on the door.

BLUE MOUNTAIN VINEYARDS (215-298-3068 or 298-7627, Grape Vine Drive, New Tripoli, PA). This young winery promises to be very, very good once it really gets going. Vidal, Chambourcin, Cabernet Sauvignon, and Vignoles are all being raised in the estate's nine-acre vineyard.

HUNTERS VALLEY WINERY (717-444-7211, U.S. Rtes. 11 and 15, Liverpool, PA). With a two-acre vineyard, Hunters Valley makes wine from American grapes such as Niagara and Concord.

RUSHLAND RIDGE VINEYARD & WINERY (215-598-0251, 2665 Rushland Rd, Rushland, PA). This small family-run winery raises 13 varieties of French-American hybrid grapes on three acres. They make about 675 cases of wine annually, including Seyval, Vidal, Cayuga, Niagara, Chellois, and Baco Noir.

VYNECREST WINERY (610-398-1720, 172 Arrowhead Lane, Breinigsville, PA). About 400 cases of wine are produced from a 2 1/2-acre vineyard.

Vynecrest, like many smaller wineries, is open at irregular hours.

Marguerite Thomas

RESTAURANTS AND LODGING

RESTAURANTS

New Jersey

Marguerite Thomas

The Frenchtown Inn, Frenchtown, New Jersey, where local wines are offered and winemaker's dinners are held.

THE FRENCHTOWN INN
908-996-3300.
7 Bridge Street,
   Frenchtown, NJ.
Price: Inexpensive–
   Expensive.

The Frenchtown Inn is in a tranquil small town setting. It's owned by Robert and Holly Long, who trained in some of the best kitchens in France, New York, and Chicago. This restaurant takes its food very seriously, raising its own lettuces and herbs organically and baking its own bread every morning. Irresistible appetizers include the restaurant's house-smoked salmon and homemade pâtés. A Tuscan-style white bean soup garnished with wilted spinach and grilled sausage is delicious. Entrees feature such delights as venison with wild mushrooms and dried cherry coulis, or polenta-stuffed quail. The more casual Grill Room has simpler but equally alluring offerings. The fairly-priced, well-chosen wine list is another plus at this attractive restaurant, where winemaker's dinners are also regularly featured.

THE FERRY HOUSE
609-397-9222.
21 Ferry Street,
  Lambertville, NJ.
Price: Moderate–Expensive.

This small restaurant attracts locals, a few tourists, and a lot of New Jerseyites from Princeton. It's a BYOB place, so plan to pick up some wine at one of the local wineries, or stop at the well-stocked wine shop just across the street. The restaurant is located in a former house, which makes one think of going to a friend's home for dinner. The former living room is now an intimate dining room with forest green walls adorned with paintings. The homey feeling disappears, however, once the food arrives — none of *my* friends, anyway, can cook like this. Everything I ordered was pleasing, from a starter of Asian-marinated quail set on grilled red onion and apple chutney, to the pan-seared salmon served with roasted tomato, white bean, and olive ragout with basil coulis.

Pennsylvania

JOE'S RESTAURANT
215-373-6794.
7th and Laurel Streets,
  Reading, PA.
Price: Expensive.

Joe's is an unusual restaurant. The decor and cuisine are as hard to pigeonhole as the chef/owner himself, and as the clientele who frequent the place. The other diners the night I was there included a few regulars, plus a family who had heard about Joe's back home in Oregon, and a group of students and faculty members from the "Jeune Chef" Program at the Pennsylvania College of Technology, who were having a fine time "studying" Joe's.

The dining room looks as if it was lifted straight from Grandfather's house, which may be exactly what happened, as the restaurant was started by the father of the current owner, Jack Czarnacki.

The menu and the cuisine are as quirky as the decor. The primary theme is mushrooms: lobster lasagna comes with morels, mashed potatoes are made with cèpe gravy, enchiladas feature morels, and venison is prepared with black chanterelles. I enjoyed a plateful of lightly sautéed morels to start, followed by fillets of Talapia fish garnished with black trumpet mushrooms, with Chaddsford Stargazer Chardonnay as an excellent accompaniment.

LODGING

New Jersey

The Woolverton Inn,
Stockton, New Jersey, built in
1792, has been an inn since
1980.

Marguerite Thomas

**THE WOOLVERTON
INN**
609-397-0802 or
   609-397-0168.
6 Woolverton Road,
   Stockton, NJ
Price: Expensive.

Nestled on a hill above the village of Stockton and the Delaware River, the Woolverton Inn was built as a manor house in 1792. For many years, the stately stone house was the country retreat of St. John Terrell, a New York actor, but since 1980 it's been an inn. Woolverton has a formal garden, spacious lawns, and sweeping fields. The house is filled with gracious antique furnishings. The Woolverton Inn is a dream of a country house, and the next best thing to owning it, is to spend the night, thankful that someone else is paying the heating bill and cooking the elaborate breakfast. Breakfast might include an apple-cranberry crisp, followed by ricotta- and walnut-stuffed French toast with strawberry syrup, locally made turkey sausage, and an assortment of homemade muffins. A perfect appetite-whetter for a day of tasting at the local wineries!

SOUTHERN PENNSYLVANIA AND MARYLAND

Southern Pennsylvania's wine region is located along some of the most scenic routes in the nation. Fortunate travelers will amble through the Brandywine Valley, where they can visit Longwood Gardens with more than 11,000 species of plants, and Winterthur Museum, the former du Pont mansion that now contains an unrivaled collection of American decorative arts and antiques.

Visitors will also savor the peaceful countryside around Chadds Ford, immortalized in paintings by three generations of Wyeths. Many of their paintings are on display at the Brandywine River Museum.

The wineries in Pennsylvania are reached by driving through the unspoiled farmland of Lancaster Country, across mile after mile of rolling, fertile fields and pristine farmhouses maintained by Mennonite and Amish farmers, who still use teams of horses to plow the land. The absence of billboards, strip malls, and fast food outlets fills one with nostalgia for simpler times. The same complex soils and moderate climate (with approximately 195 growing days) that make this a good place to grow wheat also provide a hospitable environment for grapes. Pennsylvania produces about 100,000 tons of grapes annually. The wine industry generates thousands of jobs and contributes over a billion dollars to the state's economy.

In Maryland, the undulating countryside is filled with farms and pastures, although throughout the area, horse farms and hay fields, groves of trees, and dairy barns, are rapidly disappearing to make way for housing. The poignant contrast between these two landscapes intensifies one's appreciation for the remaining rural regions, where vineyards help preserve agricultural land and where traditional country houses, surrounded by the kind of simple gardens that reflect the most basic human need to keep in touch with the earth, remain as dignified survivors of a time past.

Another type of garden altogether is the Ladew Topiary Gardens, in Jacksonville, MD, not far from Boordy Vineyards. One of the finest gardens in the world, it has 22 acres of sculptured hedges, as well as animal and geometric figures.

SOUTHERN PENNSYLVANIA

ALLEGRO VINEYARDS
Rating: 🍷🍷🍷🍷🍷
717-927-9148.
Brogue, PA.
Directions: From I-83 take exit 6 onto Rte. 74, traveling about seven miles beyond town of Red Lion to Brogue. Turn right at the Post Office onto Muddy Creek Road. Travel 2 miles and look for the winery sign on the left.
Owners: Tim and John Crouch.

Allegro is the sort of place that inspires musical metaphors. No wonder, as Allegro's owners, brothers Tim and John Crouch, are former classical musicians. To my taste, Allegro wines are among the best in the East (they positively sing!), and well worth the drive to this rather remote spot.

The brothers planted their vineyard in 1973 and the winery building followed in 1980. Today they produce 3,500 cases annually that truly live up to the brothers' original goal "of making excellent European-style table wines that are reasonably priced."

The mid-Atlantic-style Seyval, made dry with a

John Crouch, co-owner of Allegro Vineyards, with a silver medal from the Summit International Competition.

Courtesy Allegro Vineyards

Open: Daily, noon–5 PM.
Price Range of Wines: $6.45 for premium white to $21.50 for Cadenza.
Special Features: Picnic area.
Special Events: Chef series, musical events, an annual festival.

touch of oak aging, has the crisp elegance of Bach's keyboard fugues. The balance and finesse of the Reserve Chardonnay is positively Mozartian, while the stylish Riesling, made like a German *spätlese*, conjures up Schubert's Trout Quintet. The Premium Red, a Chambourcin-Leon Millot blend, is deep, dry and joyful — a Louis Armstrong kinda' wine which, according to the winemaker, is terrific with tomato-based pasta sauces. The Cabernet Sauvignon, blended with a little Merlot and Cabernet Franc to soften the tannins, is a rich, classic Bordeaux-style wine, while the Cadenza is a very fine limited-production Cabernet Sauvignon — try these with *Carmen*.

Many Pennsylvania and Maryland wine shops sell Allegro wines, and it's on several restaurant wine lists. But half the fun of going to a winery is to buy some wine. Take the bottle out on the deck for a picnic, and while you're surveying the countryside you might even find yourself humming a few bars of Beethoven's Pastorale Symphony.

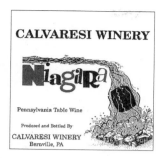

CALVARESI WINERY

Rating: 🍷
610-488-7966.
107 Shartlesville Road, Bernville, PA.
Directions: From Reading, go 10 miles north on Rte. 183; then go right at the elementary school in Bernville to the winery, which will be 1/2 mile on the right.
Owners: Tom and Debbie Calvaresi.
Open: Thurs. and Fri., 1 PM–6 PM; Sat. and Sun., noon–5 PM.
Price Range of Wines: $5.50 for Aurora and Niagara to $8.00 for Chardonnay and Riesling.

This small, unassuming winery northwest of Reading is owned by Tom and Debbie Calvaresi. Like many other small scale vintners, Tom started out as a home winemaker, whose hobby became his profession. Tom began making wine in his basement in Reading. Eventually, the Calvaresis moved to the country, where they built a new home and a simple winery with a tasting room in one corner.

The Calvaresis have only a token five-acre vineyard because Tom believes that most people aren't both good vineyard managers and good winemakers, and he wanted to concentrate his energies on winemaking rather than vine growing. Calvaresi produces a variety of wines from all-Pennsylvania grapes purchased from vineyards around the state. I found them somewhat characterless, although they have a strong local following..

The selection includes Chardonnay, Riesling, Seyval, and Baco Noir, a semi-dry, fruity red that, according to the Calvaresis, local people like with pasta. Aurora and Niagara, two grapey wines, are "just like the grapes grown in Grandma's backyard," says Tom. Calvaresi has no officially designated picnic facilities, but there are lots of grassy fields nearby.

CHADDSFORD WINERY

Rating: 🍷🍷🍷🍷
610-388-6221;
   fax 610-388-7814.
Route One, Chadds Ford, PA.
Directions: From Philadelphia, take I-95

Chaddsford Winery proves that the old real estate dictum of "location, location, location" applies to wineries as well. Situated on Highway One in the beautiful Brandywine Valley, Chaddsford receives thousands of drop-in visitors each year, who cruise the gift shop, take advantage of the wineries self-guided tour, taste the wines,

Marguerite Thomas

Chaddsford Wine is among the finest in the East

south to Rte. 322 west;
turn left onto Rte. 1 and
travel for 6 miles to the
winery.
Owners: Eric and Lee
Miller.
Open: Apr. through Dec.,
Mon.–Sat., 10 AM–5:30 PM;
Sun. Noon–5 PM; closed
Jan. through Mar. on
Mondays.
Price Range of Wines: $6.99
for Chaddsford White to
$26 for Philip Roth
Vineyard Chardonnay.
Special Features: Picnic
area.
Special Events: Fall Wine
Classes; November
introduction to Nouveau;
December Candlelight
Christmas in
Chaddsford.

and buy. Of course, to succeed, wineries, unlike real-estate, also need long range goals, marketing skills, and a talented winemaker.

Chaddsford has been blessed with all of the above. Owners Eric and Lee Miller opened the winery in 1982, in what Eric describes as their "big old Yankee barn." Eric's palate was trained in Burgundy, where he lived when he was growing up, and his winemaking skills were honed in upstate New York, where he was the winemaker at Benmarl, his father's winery.

When they decided to start their own winery, Eric and Lee might have gone straight to California, but Eric preferred the more restrained, complex wines of Burgundy to the low-acid, high-alcohol wines that California was then making. "But California has come around magnificently since then," Eric is quick to acknowledge. After searching for a place where they could make the Burgundy-style wines Eric loves, the Millers finally settled on Chaddsford.

"The soils in the Brandywine Valley are similar to those in Burgundy," says Eric, "and the two regions have almost the same number of growing days — there are 195 here compared to 190 in Burgundy. The rolling hills, with lots of southern exposure, also remind him of Burgundy's terrain.

Eric has no illusions about replicating Burgundy here — "I'm not going to be making Montrachet," he smiles — but the wines he turns out are distinctive, characterized by a bracing thread of acidity, accompanied by a strength and depth of character that make them among the best in the East. Chaddsford's best known wines are the Stargazers Vineyard and the Philip Roth Vineyard Chardonnays. These two wines are expensive, but they can compete in quality with equally high-priced wines from the West Coast and Long Island. Red wines are harder to work with than whites in the East, in part because vinifera red grapes seldom get fully ripe here, but Eric's Pinot Noir is showing great promise, while his Chambourcin (made from a dependable hybrid) and Proprietors Reserve Chambourcin grip the palate with intense, lingering flavors. The winery's annual production is now about 32,000 cases.

Profile: Eric Miller

Eric Miller is among the few contemporary East Coast winemakers whose name is well-known to his colleagues. His wines are recognized by national wine writers and are served in important restaurants in Philadelphia, Washington, D.C., New York, and even California.

An ambitious marketing program has contributed to the steady growth of the winery. Production has expanded in a dozen years from 3,000 to 32,000 cases. How did he propel his winery to such heights? "The most important thing to me as a winemaker, is also being a wine drinker," he says, only half jokingly. "The problem with many eastern winemakers is that they may be foodies, but they aren't drinkers." Pursuing the subject further, Eric elaborates on another aspect of successful winemaking. "I'm trying to become a better businessman, and one thing I've learned, is that you have to have a goal. In winemaking, it's the same thing. You have to have a vision of what you're going to make."

Knowing from the outset that he would never be able to create exact replicas of Burgundian white wines, Eric identified specific characteristics about them that he liked, and that he felt were achievable here. Then, by carefully selecting his grapes and using the right vinification techniques, he has kept his goal in mind. "I like lean, not fat wines," he says. "I like the fruit to be secondary, with nice vanilla showing through, and sometimes, toast. And honey, especially honey. I like a good, firm texture, which is something this region gives us, and I also like a wine that's minerally."

Eric's aim was to establish a regional image for his wines rather than to play David to California's Goliath. "I want my

Courtesy Chaddsford Winery

→

product to have a regional signature," he explains. "I can't out-market the big boys — the Mondavis and those people — but I can make something that is really good and unique to this area. You have to claim your own uniqueness and quality," he adds. "It's all you've got."

Another reason for his success, Eric admits, is that many people are simply curious about anything new. "It's in our human nature to poke around, to try new things." An individual might resist tasting a new wine, explains Eric, because he likes French wine, or he's grown up drinking native American wine. "But then he'll get curious. 'How would it go with the local cuisine?' he might ask. Then he'll say, 'Hmmmm, that crisp, dry, earthy Chardonnay from Stargazers Vineyard sure does taste a lot better with this Chesapeake crabcake than that sticky old Concord. I'll have to try it again sometime.'"

Like his wines, Eric's personality is colorful and intense, yet balanced by a playful streak that keeps peeking through. His conversation darts from idea to idea the way a hummingbird works a row of flowers.

"There are two distinctly different characteristics of white wine," he might announce suddenly, having run out of nectar from the previous conversational topic. "First, there are the big, rich wines for keeping," he'll continue, "then there is the second category of lean, fresh, flowery wines that are meant to be drunk young. People don't distinguish between the two, but they're as different as vegetables and beef." He explains that people don't go into a store and ask for a nice, *old* apple. Instead, they want it to be fresh and crisp. Eric believes that we don't think about wines in those terms enough. "Of course, he admits, "price is a factor — those light, lean wines are admittedly less expensive . . ." There he goes, whirring off toward another subject. I think I'll pour myself a glass of Chaddsford Chambourcin, finish up the last of the delicious *cassoulet* Eric has made to go with it, and do my best to follow wherever this new discussion leads.

YORK COUNTY
Dry Riesling

NAYLOR VINEYARDS & WINE CELLAR
Rating: 🌲🌲
717-993-2431 or
  800-292-3370.
Ebaugh Road,
  Stewartstown, PA.

Nestled among the rolling hills and lush green valleys of southern York County, the warehouselike winery sits on a hill overlooking the 27-acre vineyard where eastern labrusca, French American hybrid, and European vinifera grapes grow. This plateau, rising 1,000 feet above sea

Directions: From I-83 take exit 1 in Shrewsbury to Rte. 851 east and go four miles to Stewartstown. Take Rte. 24 north for 2 more miles to winery.

Owner: Richard E. Naylor.

Open: Mon.–Sat., 11 AM– 6 PM; Sun., noon–5 PM.

Price Range of Wines: $8.95 for Riesling to $18.95 for Cabernet Sauvignon Reserve.

Special Features: Picnic area, gift shop.

Special Events: June Grape Blossom Festival, October Harvest Festival (including a grape stomping contest).

level, was known as "The Barrens" during the Revolutionary days because it was devoid of trees. Early Indian tribes burned off all the trees so that grass could grow to provide a habitat for game. For a brief period in 1777–1778, York, the nearest city, served as the site of the Sixth Continental Congress.

The area was settled by Scotch, Irish, and German immigrant farmers in the late 1700s and has been primarily used as farmland ever since. In 1975, Richard E. Naylor began planting vines on his property. The winery, which was founded in 1978, currently produces 6,000 cases of wine annually, including more than 20 varieties of table wine.

Dick Naylor's winemaking goals are very clear. "Wines to remind one of fresh fruit. Big on flavors, low in alcohol (11%). Wine that will complement food. A wine for everyone. A wine that is local in nature but, to the connoisseur, reminiscent of European wines." Connoisseurs as far away as Manhattan are discovering the charms of Naylor wines: Peter Morrell, one of New York's most reputable wine merchants, is among the many proponents of Naylor Chambourcin.

A visit to Naylor Wine Cellars provides more than a sampling of wines. It's also an opportunity to stock up on wine accessories, gift baskets, and home winemaking supplies, as well as to receive a colorful and entertaining education. Dick Naylor's wine labels literally talk to consumers. For example, the Riesling label reads as follows: "Hi, I'm Dry Riesling . . .The scent of spring blossoms across a sunlit meadow quickens your senses in anticipation of an ultimate sensation. Then there's a gentle brush of flavor like a lover's lips, as you sample the essence of my lively, green, gold nectar. I'm crisp, fruity, yet very smooth . . . I prefer salads or lite soups, sandwiches and quiches . . . my favorite dish is broiled seafood . . . As you can see I'm very flexible and so much fun to be with socially." It's hard to resist picking up a bottle to take to the picnic pavilion, where your senses might quicken. . . .

NISSLEY VINEYARDS AND WINERY ESTATE

Rating: 🍷

717-426-3514.

140 Vintage Drive, Bainbridge, PA.

Directions: From Lancaster take Rte. 30 west to

Nissley is a family-run winery that makes solid, local wines from hybrid and native American grapes. Set on a 300-acre estate that's enhanced by a row of stone arches, the winery has been a favorite tourist destination for almost two decades. Wines range from Niagara to "Red Wine," a blend of red hybrid grapes with some white added to

Columbia and exit onto Rte. 441. Follow 441 north for 8 miles; turn right on Wickersham Rd. and continue 1.5 miles, following signs at the intersection to the winery.
Owners: The Nissley family.
Open: Mon.–Sat., 10 AM– 5 PM; Sun. 1 PM–4 PM.
Price Range of Wines: $5.50 for Niagara to $10.50 for "Red Wine."
Special Features: Picnic area.
Special Events: "Music in the Vineyards"; summer lawn concerts; an October foot race.

keep the potion light and simple. Visitors are urged to bring a picnic lunch to enjoy on the tree-shaded picnic patios.

SEVEN VALLEYS VINEYARD AND WINERY

Rating: 🍷
717-236-6281.
Gantz Road, Glen Rock, PA.
Directions: From I-83 take Exit 1 in Shrewsbury, and go west on Forest Avenue (Rte. 851) to the stop light at Main St. Turn right and go .2 mile to Clearview Drive. Turn left and go 1.3 miles to Gantz Road. Turn right and follow signs to the winery.
Owners: Fred and Lynn Hunter.
Open: Weekends 10 AM– 5 PM and by appointment.
Price Range of Wines: $6.75 for Limerick, a blend of Vidal, Seyval, Cayuga, and Steuben, to $12 for Cabernet Sauvignon.

After driving along country roads, one comes to an idyllic, isolated small valley where one of Pennsylvania's newest wineries is situated. Fred and Lynn Hunter had looked at 106 other farms before agreeing that this old homestead was the right place for their winery. They chose this site because they believed its elevation, its well-drained soil, and its extended growing days were right for growing grapes.

For several years the Hunters commuted to Philadelphia, where they were psychologists. In the interim, they planted vines on their property and sold grapes to Pennsylvania wineries. Finally, on Labor Day in 1994, they opened their own winery in an old stone-walled cellar furnished with old-fashioned horse stalls. They now grow nine varieties of grapes on their 25-acre vineyard.

Seven Valley's wine production is still limited and still very young, but it is clearly off to an excellent start. The Riesling and Gewürztraminer are pleasant, slightly sweet wines, that are still dry enough to accompany a wide range of foods. Country Red, a blend of Chambourcin, Cabernet Sauvignon, and Chancellor is an assertive wine.

"I'm not an expert at any of this," says Lynn candidly. "Just like everyone else, I taste the wine and if I like it, then it's good."

If ever there was a landscape made for picnics, Seven Valleys is it.

SMITHBRIDGE CELLARS

Rating: 👥
610-558-4703.
159 Beaver Valley Road, Chadds Ford, PA.
Directions: From the intersection of Rtes 1 and 202, go south on Rte. 202 for 2.2 miles. Then go right on Beaver Valley Rd. for 1/2 mile to the winery.
Owner: Trip Stocki.
Open: Tues.–Sun., noon–6 PM; closed Jan. and Feb.
Price Range of Wines: $6.50 for Valley White; $14 for Cabernet Sauvignon or Chardonnay.
Special Features: Picnic area.

This winery is a one-man show, and that man is Trip Stocki. Although he gets occasional help from his parents and girl friend, Trip regularly puts in 80 hour weeks, with 6 to 12 hours a day in the vineyard alone. Trip has a self-described "checkered past" that includes stints in the nuclear power business and in the armed services during the Vietnam conflict.

It was while he was in the service that Trip was introduced to fine wine. Eventually, he acquired some land and planted a few acres of table grapes. In 1983, he ripped those out to plant wine grapes. "That was the last time I made money," says Trip wryly, although he admits things are finally beginning to turn around.

"I've always wanted to grow great grapes," he explains. "I want to make a great wine, and that starts with good grapes. I don't know anyone in Pennsylvania who's making wine up to their potential yet." By the accounts of his colleagues, however, Trip may be the first who does. "Mine's good now," he says modestly. He now produces about 800 cases of wine annually from his five-acre plot.

Visitors to the rustic winery will find that it's housed in an old dairy barn. The Valley White, a blend of Chardonnay and Sauvignon Blanc, and the fine barrel-fermented Cabernet or Chardonnay are all excellent sampling choices. There are picnic facilities.

TWIN BROOK WINERY

Rating: 👥
717-442-4915.
5697 Strasburg Road, Gap, PA.

The 70-acre parcel of land that Twin Brook Winery sits on has a rich history. It's said that it was once the site of an Indian village, and in 1748 William Penn's brother granted the land to the Sadsbury Quakers. The stone and frame barn

Directions: From Rte. 202 take Rte. 30 west through Exton to Rte. 30 Bypass; continue west on Rte. 30 for 2.1 miles to Swan Rd.; turn left and follow signs 3 miles to winery.

Owners: Richard Caplan and Cheryl Caplan.

Open: Apr. through Dec., Mon.–Sat., 11 AM–5 PM; Sun. noon–5 PM; Jan. through Mar., Tues.–Sun., noon–6 PM.

Price Range of Wines: $6.50 for Clock Tower White to $16.95 for Cabernet Franc.

Special Features: Picnic area.

Special Events: Art exhibits throughout the year; outdoor concerts in summer.

where the winery is located, was originally constructed in the 1800s, although it was partially destroyed by fire in 1933. A notation found on a board indicates it was re-built "in 9 days by 56 men and Charlie Celos." Today, the winery building is distinguished by its original hand-hewn beams — one of which is over 65 feet long — and by the stained-glass windows that were salvaged from a demolished church. The Lancaster Historic Preservation Society recognizes Twin Brook as a significant historic site.

Twin Brook Winery, which was named for a pair of brooks that run through the property, was founded in 1988 by two lawyers, Richard Caplan and Cheryl Caplan. The winery's grapes all come from the estate's own 20-acre vineyard. It produces about 5,000 cases of wine annually, with 50% coming from vinifera grapes and the rest from hybrids.

Particularly notable among the genenerally excellent wines are Cabernet Franc and a Cabernet Franc/Cabernet Sauvignon blend. Both are aged in American oak, although Twin Brook has been experimenting with Hungarian oak for some of its Chardonnays. Vignoles is another appealing wine with pleasing acidity behind the sweetness. Several local restaurants pour Twin Brook's wine. Picnic tables on the gazebo, next to the vineyards, or among the trees along one of the brooks, provide a scenic environment for picnicking.

MARYLAND

BOORDY VINEYARDS
Rating: 🌲🌲
410-592-5015.
12820 Long Green Pike, Hydes, MD.
Directions: From the Baltimore Beltway take exit 29 (Cromwell Bridge Rd.) east to Glen Arm Rd.; go left and travel 3 miles to Long Green Pike, turn left, and go 2 miles to winery.

Philip Wagner, the founder of Boordy Vineyards, is the most important figure in the contemporary chapter of winemaking in the eastern United States. He was the London correspondent for the Baltimore Evening Sun in the 1930s when he was introduced to the hardy French hybrid grapes, which he felt produced a more appealing wine than native American grapes. A home-winemaker himself, Wagner was intrigued enough by these vines to bring some back and plant a vineyard at his home in Maryland. He was soon con-

The 19th-century stone and wood barn at Boordy Vineyards, Hydes, Maryland.

Marguerite Thomas

Owner: Rob Deford.
Open: Mon.–Sat., 10 AM–
   5 PM; Sun. 1 PM–5 PM.
Price Range of Wines: $5.75
   for Maryland White to
   $11 for Cabernet
   Sauvignon.
Special Features: Picnic
   area.
Special Events: Spring
   Champagne Release
   Celebration, Mother's
   Day Clambake, Father's
   Day Pig Roast.

vinced that French hybrids were the solution to the problems American vintners faced in trying to grow European vinifera grapes in an era before technology made such an endeavor possible.

Wagner and his wife, Jocelyn, tirelessly promoted the establishment of an American wine industry in the East. They provided fledgling vintners with everything from vines to advice. In 1943, the Wagners founded Boordy Vineyards (they always insisted the name has no meaning). Today, Boordy is the oldest and largest winery in Maryland. Though now in his nineties, Philip Wagner is still the guru of eastern wine makers.

In 1980, Rob Deford, a friend of the Wagners and one of Boordy's grape suppliers, bought the winery and moved it to his 250-acre beef and grain farm a few miles away from the original site. Located in the scenic Long Green Valley, an area listed in the National Register of Historic Places, the winery is housed in a charming 19th-century stone and wood barn. In addition to the grapes grown on the estate's 16-acre vineyard, additional fruit is purchased from the Eastern Shore of Maryland, the central Piedmont region, and the Catoctin Mountains.

The annual output of Boordy Vineyards is now 8,500 cases. This includes Maryland White, a pleasant, dry blend of Seyval, Vidal, and Chardonnay and a nicely balanced, medium-bodied Cabernet Sauvignon. Picnic tables on a terrace overlook the winery and farm buildings.

CATOCTIN VINEYARDS
Rating: 🍇
301-774-2310;
 fax 301-681-6855.
805 Greenbridge Road,
 Brookeville, MD.
Directions: From Frederick,
 take I-70 west to Rte. 29;
 take Rte. 29 south to
 Columbia; then take Rte.
 108 northwest to Ashton;
 then take Rte. 650 (N.
 Hampshire Ave.) 4 miles
 to the winery, which will
 be on the right.
Owners: Bob Lyon; Jerry,
 Ann, and Molly Milne;
 and Shahin Bagheri.
Open: Sat. and Sun.,
 noon–5 PM; Mon.–Fri. by
 appointment.
Price Range of Wines: $4.95
 for two pink wines, Eye
 of the Oriole and Eye of
 the Beholder, to $11.95
 for Chardonnay Oak and
 Cabernet Sauvignon
 Reserve.
Special Features: Picnic
 area.

"Winemaking with vinifera grapes is still in the experimental stage on the East Coast," insists Bob Lyon, Catoctin's winemaker and one of its four owners. With a background in California winemaking, including a degree from U.C. Davis, and work at Chateau Montelena and Byrd Vineyards, Bob knows as much as anybody about the comparative challenges of winemaking in the East, but he is also aware of the advantages. "This is the perfect climate for Cabernet Sauvignon. It's hot, but not too hot," he explains, nodding towards the 32-acre vineyard at the base of the Catoctin Mountain. Bob's aim is to make classic-style Cabernet Sauvignon, with little fining, and aging the wine in French oak for two years. The wines have good color and a pleasing intensity, but their charm is often diminished by a musty aroma that hints at dirty barrels.

The vineyard was planted in 1975 and the winery opened in 1983. It now produces some 3,500 cases annually, with half in vinifera and the rest in hybrid. Catoctin Vineyards provides a nice, rural setting for a picnic.

**FIORE WINERY AND LA
 FELICETTA
 VINEYARD**
Rating: 🍇
410-836-7605 or 836-1860.
3026 Whiteford Road,
 Pylesville, MD.
Directions: From I-95 take
 exit 77B to Rte. 24 north.

Fiore and La Felicetta remind one of small, family-run wineries in Italy. Mama sits in the shade of the terrace on a hot summer morning, while Mike Fiori is down the hill on a tractor, spraying the vineyards. Bees buzz in the roses, the trees are filled with birds whistling Verdi, and one expects the smell of espresso to waft from the house. But

Picnic area at Fiore Winery and La Felicitta Vineyard, Pylesville, Maryland.

Marguerite Thomas

Travel 22 miles to Rte. 136. Go east one mile to the winery.
Owners: Mike and Rose Fiore.
Open: Sat. and Sun., noon–6 PM, or by appointment
Price Range of Wines: $5.50 for Blush to $20 for Caronte, a blend of Cabernet Sauvignon, Merlot, and Sangiovese.
Special Features: Picnic area.
Special Events: August wine festival, jazz and art festival.

Rose Fiori isn't in the kitchen brewing coffee. She's working in the vineyard. She zips up now on a golf cart, wearing blue eye shadow and a film of vineyard dust.

As we taste wines, Rose tells me the vineyard was named in honor of the La Felicetta Vineyard in the Calabria region of Italy, where the Fiori family has been making wine since the 16th century. Mike grew up in Italy, working in a vineyard planted by a Fiori whose ancestor came to America 200 ago to help Thomas Jefferson grow grapes.

The Fioris planted their first grapes in 1982 and opened the winery in 1986. They now produce 3,000 cases of wine annually, but they hope to expand to 5,000 in a few years. They believe the attractive Seyval and Vidal Blanc wines owe their distinctively dry and fruity flavor to the influence of the nearby Susquehanna River and the Chesapeake Bay. The soil composition here, where marble and slate quarries abound, also adds a distinctive, minerally flavor, faintly reminiscent of rain-dampened pebbles.

Fiori Chambourcin has the rich aroma of cedar and licorice. The Fioris are convinced that Chambourcin does better in the Mid-Atlantic regions than elsewhere in the East. "It's too cold in upstate New York and too hot in Virginia," says Rose. The Fiori Cabernet Sauvignon is nicely balanced, with a good fruity finish. One of the most popular wines at Fiori is Scarlette, a sangrialike sweetish blend that, when poured over ice cubes, makes a refreshing summer beverage. Visitors can picnic on a nicely landscaped stone patio overlooking the vineyard.

Woodhall
Seyval

Maryland
White Wine
1993

Dry table wine produced and bottled by
Woodhall Vineyards and Wine Cellars, Inc., Sparks, Maryland
Contains Sulfites   Alcohol by volume 11.0%

**WOODHALL
VINEYARDS & WINE
CELLARS**
Rating: 👤👤
410-357-8644.
17912 York Road, Parkton,
MD.
Directions: From I-695, take
I-83 north to exit 27. Turn
right on Mt. Carmel Rd.
to York Rd.; turn left to
winery, which will be on
the left.
Owners: Chris and Patricia
Lang, Al Copp.
Open: Sat. and Sun.,
noon–4 PM, or by
appointment.
Price Range of Wines: $7
for Vidal to $25 for
Copernicus, a well made
Cabernet Sauvignon.
Special Features: Picnic
area.

Woodhall Vineyards makes only dry table wines. As Chris Lang, a former airline pilot explains, referring to partner Al Copp, "Al hates sweet wine, so we don't make any. People say that selling sweet wine is how you make money. I guess we'll never have any money," he adds with a rueful smile.

Woodhall gets most of its grapes from a 20-acre vineyard on Maryland's Eastern Shore; the rest come from smaller vineyards nearby. Its Seyval, which is aged in American oak, and made from grapes grown in Virginia, Maryland, and in the Finger Lakes region, is Woodhall's best seller. Cabernet Sauvignon, a nicely structured wine, with good but not overbearing tannins, is their second most popular. Woodhall produces a very nice Meritage, a Bordeaux-style blended red wine from 65% Cabernet Sauvignon, 25% Merlot, and 10% Cabernet Franc. The winery has picnic facilities.

OTHER SOUTHERN PENNSYLVANIA AND MARYLAND WINERIES

ADAMS COUNTY WINERY (717-334-4631, 251 Peach Tree Rd, Orrtanna, PA). Located minutes from Gettysburg, this winery is a good example of a small, local winery that produces a variety of table wines from vinifera and hybrid grapes.

FOX MEADOW FARM (610-827-9731, 1439 Clover Mill Rd, Chester Springs, PA). This tiny winery, producing merely a few hundred cases, is owned by a retired chemist and his wife.

FRENCH CREEK RIDGE VINEYARDS (610-286-7754, Grove Road, Elverson, PA). This new winery is very small but it shows excellent potential for growth and for making superior wines.

RESTAURANTS AND LODGING

RESTAURANTS

Philadelphia is noted for its many fine restaurants and inns, but there are also a few unexpected eateries outside the city that serve simple but good food. The two listed here make particularly satisfying lunch stops.

BARNACLE BILLS
410-452-9109.
Rte. 165, Pylesville, MD
(located .6 mile north of
Rte. 24).
Price: Inexpensive.

Most of us wouldn't know what to do with 1,200 bushels of crab a year, but Bill and Anita Sokal do. They make crab cakes, crab sandwiches, and an excellent vegetable crab soup. They also steam 8,000 gallons of shrimp annually. Their small, informal roadside restaurant seats merely 83 people but the wholesome, unpretentious food keeps fans coming back. A crab sandwich would be a good thing to take to Fiori Winery to enjoy on the stone terrace with a glass of Vidal Blanc.

**BRANDYWINE RIVER
  MUSEUM**
608-388-2700.
Route One, Chadds Ford,
  PA.
Price: Inexpensive.

The museum restaurant, in a glass tower overlooking the Brandywine Museum, provides a spectacular setting in which to have an informal lunch or other refreshment. The menu is simple, and includes soups, salads, sandwiches, and hot dishes. Chaddsford wine is served by the glass.

LODGING

HICKORY BRIDGE INN
717-642-5261.
96 Hickory Bridge Road,
  Orrtanna, PA.
Price: Moderate.

This quiet, unassuming country inn, in a former farmhouse in the Pennsylvania Dutch countryside, offers seven guestrooms decorated with comfortable and cozy furnishings. It also has a dining room that's open Friday, Saturday, and Sunday nights. There's no wine list, so this is the perfect place to bring a bottle from a local winery. The menu features wholesome traditional Pennsylvania Dutch dishes such as fried chicken. For dessert, the innkeepers might offer blueberry cobbler, or walnut pie, or coconut custard pie.

The Brandywine River Museum has an outstanding restaurant in a spectacular setting.

Courtesy The Brandywine River Museum

ANTRIM 1844
410-756-6812 or
  800-858-1844.
30 Trevanian Road,
  Taneytown, MD.
Price: Expensive.

Elegance and style are evident from the moment one enters this stately mansion built in 1844. The brick plantation house on 23 acres witnessed events unfold before the Battle of Gettysburg and this is the era to which it's now been restored. Magnificent antiques decorate the bedrooms, common rooms, and the dining room. The acclaimed restaurant serves a formal prix fixe dinner every night and the wine list is exceptional.

NORTHERN AND CENTRAL VIRGINIA

It's a quick transition from bustling, cosmopolitan Washington, D.C. to the graceful farmland of northern Virginia. This is steeplechase and fox hunting country, where America's gentry retreats. The beautiful horse farms, peaceful country roads, rolling vineyards, and alluring villages are compelling reasons to visit the area, but for history buffs the numerous Civil War sites are the lure.

Manassas National Battlefield Park, where the battles of the First and Second

Ruins of the plantation house once belonging to James Barbour, on the grounds of the Barboursville Vineyards, Barboursville, Virginia.

Marguerite Thomas

Manassas (better known as Bull Run) were fought, is a few miles from the peaceful vineyards. It's in these hills that Stonewall Jackson got his name, when Bernard Bee, the Confederate general, rallied his men by calling out, "There is Jackson standing like a stone wall. Let us determine to die here, and we will conquer."

The town of Culpeper, where George Washington received his surveyor's license, was also the place from which Minute Men marched to battle carrying flags inscribed "Don't Tread On Me" and "Liberty or Death." Almost 100 years after the Revolutionary War, the town was the headquarters for the Union Army.

American history lives in this bucolic region snuggled between the coast and the Blue Ridge Mountains, which Virginians call the Piedmont. The countryside near Charlottesville is graced by many historic estates, including Monticello, Jefferson's former estate. James Madison's home, Montpelier, is nearby. This is also Virginia's heartland and the center of her wine industry.

Virginia could be the most promising eastern wine-producing state. Lying between the cold weather extreme of the northeast and the intense heat and humidity of the south (where Pierce's Disease, a deadly vine ailment, thrives), this region may prove to have the most grape-friendly climate. Forty-six Virginia wineries are now in operation, a remarkable number considering that the first successful vinifera grape wines were made here less than 20 years ago. Remarkably supportive state legislation that encourages growers and wineries is one of the principal factors contributing to this success. Virginia has one of the most liberal farm winery laws in the nation. Unlike many other states in the East, wine can even be sold in Virginia's food stores. Another bonus is the affluent and educated population in the Washington, D.C., area, which supports the local wine industry.

Luca Paschina, manager, Barboursville Vineyards, Barboursville, Virginia.

Marguerite Thomas

BARBOURSVILLE VINEYARDS

Rating: 🍷🍷🍷🍷
540-832-3824.
17655 Winery Road (Route 777), Barboursville, VA.
Directions: At the junction of Rtes. 20 & 33, take Rte. 20 south for 200 yds.; turn left on Rte. 678 and travel for .5 miles, turn right onto Rte. 777 (Winery Rd.), turn right at the 1st driveway and follow the signs.
Owners: The Zonin family.
Open: Mon.–Sat., 10 AM– 5 PM; Sun. 11 AM–5 PM.
Price Range of Wines: $6.99 for Rosato, $18.99 for the 1991 Cabernet Sauvignon Reserve, and $35 for the 1988 Cabernet Sauvignon Reserve.
Special Features: Picnic area.
Special Events: Spring Festival, Old Fashion Pig Roast, Shakespeare in the Ruins, Autumn Explosion & Barrel Tasting, and Hollyday Celebration.

Barboursville is a Virginia winery with an Italian accent. It is owned by Italians, the Zonin family, who are also proprietors of eight wineries in Italy. It is guided by an Italian winemaker, Luca Paschina, a graduate in viticulture and enology from the Institute Umberto Primo in Alba who came to Barboursville in 1990.

Barboursville was one of the pioneering Virginia wineries, founded in 1976 by Gianni Zonin. In addition to establishing an outstanding winery, Zonin's great contribution to the Virginia wine industry was to bring a gifted young agronomist named Gabriele Rausse from Italy to manage the Barboursville property. Despite the skepticism of everyone, Gabriele was the first to show that vinifera grapes could be raised successfully in Virginia. His successor, Luca Paschina, continues the tradition of creating exciting wines.

The winery is part of a lovely, large estate that also includes the picturesque ruins of a plantation house that once belonged to James Barbour, who was Governor of Virginia from 1812–14, a U.S. Senator, and a Secretary of State. The house was designed by Barbour's close friend, Thomas Jefferson.

Extensive renovations on the winery's Tuscan country-style tasting room were completed in 1995. It includes a large brick fireplace, an Italian terracotta floor, and a long tasting bar.

Such Italian classics as Pinot Grigio and Barbera are made here. In addition to the Italian varietals, the winery also makes French varietal wines such as Cabernet Franc, Pinot Noir, and Cabernet Sauvignon. All are characterized by deep color, complex and inviting flavors, and a long aftertaste that lingers satisfyingly in the mouth. Rosato, a slightly sweet but very flavorful Rosé, is also notable. The Traminer Aromatico (the Italian name for Gewürztraminer), is a fresh white wine with citrusy overtones. Malvaxia Reserve, a dessert wine produced from late-harvest, honey-flavored Malvasia grapes, explodes in the mouth like a comet of golden fruit.

After visiting Barboursville, one can only exclaim, "*Andiamo*, y'all!" Translation: "Go see this great place."

In addition to its other attractions, Barboursville is a fine place for a picnic.

Profile: Gabriele Rausse

I was born taking care of flowers and plants," says Gabriele Rausse. His family owned two farms 50 miles northwest of Venice that included greenhouses where fruits and flowers were propagated. When Gabriele arrived in Virginia to start up Barboursville Winery, the overwhelming opinion in the U.S. was that vinifera grapes could never be grown successfully in the East. But Gabriele is not the sort to go along with prevailing opinion if his own judgement points him in another direction.

Logic told him that if grapes could be successfully grown in his part of Italy, they ought to survive here too. "The data I gathered showed that while there are extreme differences in the two regions, there are also many similarities," he explains. "The average rainfall is the same; the temperatures are similar. Yet, everyone kept saying, disease, disease.' We have high humidity where I come from too, so we spray. That's not new to me."

Convinced there was a possibility of growing vinifera grapes here, Gabriele persisted. As happens to many pioneers, his peers were skeptical and sometimes disdainful. For the first three years, he worked alone. "Nobody else was brave enough to try vinifera," he recalls. "Part of the problem was a negative attitude. If you are convinced you won't be successful, I assure you, you won't be. People give up the minute the first problem comes up."

One of the prevailing reasons for failure in the East, Gabriele decided, was that vintners were relying too much on California techniques. "California doesn't spray against any fungus except powdery mildew. They don't use anything against Black Rot or the other related problems we have in the East. Furthermore, people were following an American grape program here, which is a different species, with different characteristics. The skin of the Chardonnay grape, for example, is probably the thinnest of any grape in the world, while the Concord is probably the thickest. Obviously, it's much easier for fungal disease to enter the Chardonnay. So the problem was that they were applying the wrong rules. They never looked at the grapes the right way." With Barboursville's 1979 releases, opinion changed abruptly. "Until that point we had been propagating only for ourselves," says Gabriele. "By 1980 we had sold 100,000 vines to other people. They bought everything we had. It was a very exciting time."

→

Every vintner and wannabe-vintner in Virginia suddenly sought advice from Gabriele Rausse. Today, there is hardly a vineyard owner or winemaker in the state who doesn't credit Gabriele for generously sharing his time and wisdom with that first generation of vintners. For many of them, consultation developed into a closer bond. Tom Corpora, of Afton Vineyards, tells a typical story: "Gabriele Rausse acted as consultant for the purchase of our property. We consulted him about restoring the old vineyards, and he helped us with the winemaking. And then, after being our paid consultant, he became our close friend."

For Gabriele Rausse, success was almost as hard to cope with as neglect had been, and in 1981 he left Barboursville. "My life had become impossible," he says candidly. "It was completely turned over by this earthquake. My wife and I needed our own life back." Gabriele did not drop out of the wine world completely. He continued counselling others who sought his advice — "I have always liked to help people," he explains in his rolling Italian accent. "That is my nature."

He was the winemaker at Simeon (now Jefferson Winery) for a few years. But now Rausse's vision is focused on a larger horticultural scene. He has just been named Assistant Director of Monticello's gardens and grounds. Does he like this work which has, in some ways, returned him to his origins? You bet. "Monticello is the most wonderful place imaginable. I used to go there once a year to visit, and now I'm paid to go there every day!" he enthuses. "What could be better than having a beautiful garden with lots of people to take care of it?"

Gabriele finds the sense of purpose at Monticello particularly satisfying. "Everyone from the head gardener to the newest worker, is immersed in what Jefferson did or didn't do. The person who mows the edge of the flower bed, for instance, knows that he does it because Jefferson would have done it that way."

Don't think for a minute that Gabriele has really retired from winemaking. At the moment, he is producing a small amount of wine from grapes raised in Jefferson's own vineyard. This wine, which is served at private Monticello functions, is not available to the public. And sometime soon Gabriele will be back in the wine business full time. If his dreams materialize, he may even start his own winery some day. "I don't miss the commotion or politics of a winery," he says. "But I love to grow things, and crush grapes, and make wine."

DOMINION WINE CELLARS

Rating: 🍷🍷
540-825-8772.
1 Winery Avenue,
  Culpeper, VA.
Directions: From Rte. 29
  Bypass, take Culpeper
  exit onto Rte. 3; turn right
  on McDevitt Dr. and
  continue to Winery Ave.
Owners: Williamsburg
  Winery.

In 1985, a group of successful Virginia grape growers — among the first to grow vinifera grapes in Virginia — created Dominion Wine Cellars. Their contributions to the burgeoning wine industry are remembered in a collection of plaques on display in Dominion's tasting room. Several years ago, however, in an effort to improve its financial and marketing positions, they sold their co-op interests to Williamsburg Winery, who now manages Dominion. Several of the original growers do continue to supply grapes to Dominion.

Although much of the winery operation is

Open: Tue.–Sat., 10 AM–
5 PM; Sun. 11 AM–5 PM.
Price Range of Wines: $6.50
for Blancs de Blancs to
$11 for the Cabernet
Sauvignon.
Special Features: Picnic
area.

shared with Williamsburg, including the wine-maker, Steve Warner, Dominion wines are still processed individually and it has its own wine labels. Among Dominion's offerings are Blanc de Noir, a white wine made from red grapes (in this case Cabernet Sauvignon) and Cabernet Rosé, a wine that is fermented on the grape skins just long enough to extract a hint of pinkish color. Both of these are well structured and very pleasant. The winery makes a commendable Cabernet Sauvignon as well.

The winery is located in an industrial park. Its picnic tables are located on a deck and in a courtyard, taking advantage of views over the scenic countryside.

Cheryl and Al Kellert, owners and winemakers, in the gazebo at Gray Ghost Vineyards, Amissville, Virginia.

Marguerite Thomas

**GRAY GHOST
VINEYARDS**
Rating: 🍇🍇
540-937-4869.
14706 Lee Highway,
Amissville, VA.
Directions: From
Warrenton, take Hwy.
211 west for 11 miles to
the winery, which will be
on the left.
Owners: Al and Cheryl
Kellert.
Open: Sat., Sun. and some
holidays, 11 AM—5 PM;
other days by
appointment.

This winery is named for John Mosby, the Confederate colonel who headed the only unit that never surrendered during the Civil War and who, by disappearing like a ghost, persistently avoided capture. Colonel Mosby was also a wine drinker. Al and Cheryl Kellert, the owners and winemakers at Gray Ghost Vineyards, share both an interest in the Civil War events that unfolded near their property and a passion for wine.

Al began making wine when he was a college student. Later, he and Cheryl planted vines in their suburban garden near Washington, D.C. In 1986, they bought this farm, which had earlier been an apple orchard and a horse farm, and they moved

Price Range of Wines: $7.50
  for Vidal Blanc to $12 for
  Chardonnay.
Special Features: Picnic
  area.

their vines here. They now have nine acres of vine-yards, planted mostly with vinifera grapes, supplemented by small amounts of Vidal and Seyval.

Al still works for the Postal Service in Washington, while Cheryl, who trained at several Virginia wineries, runs Gray Ghost. The 1,400 cases of wine produced annually include an excellent Chardonnay that is fermented in new French oak barrels and an unfiltered Cabernet Franc that has a deep, inky color and a full-bodied flavor.

When tasting from the barrels in the cellar, I noticed that the reds have a pronounced, pleasantly smoky aroma. "We've noticed that too," Al remarked. "We suspect it might be something in the soil." Hmmm, I wonder if John Mosby smoked. . . . There are picnic tables, and I can relate from personal experience that a bottle of Vidal and a hunk of cheese taste mighty good in the shade of the gazebo at Gray Ghost.

HORTON VINEYARDS
Rating: 🍴🍴🍴
804-971-8947.
Route 33, Gordonsville, VA.
Directions: From Rte. 29
  take Rte. 33 east for 8
  miles to the winery
  entrance which will be on
  the left. From
  Gordonsville, take Rte. 33
  west for 4 miles to the
  winery entrance which
  will be on the right. The
  winery is $1/2$ mile from
  the town of Barboursville.
Owners: Dennis and Susan
  Horton; Joan Bieda.
Open: May through Dec.,
  Mon.–Sun., 11 AM–5 PM;
  Mar. & Apr. Sat. & Sun.
  11 AM–5 PM; closed Jan. &
  Feb.
Price Range of Wines: $6.99
  for Vidal Blanc to $20 for
  Viognier.
Special Events: Annual Pig
  Roast in June.

Like many winery proprietors in the East, Dennis Horton started in 1983 by planting a small vineyard at his home. As his interest and knowledge grew, he began to realize that the humid conditions in the East favored grapes with thick skins and loose clusters. In his search for the ideal grape, he gravitated to the Rhone Valley in southern France, where he was impressed by the refined wines produced despite hot summer weather that rivaled Virginia's.

Viognier, a thick-skinned, loose-clustered, heat-loving grape used for Condrieu and Chateau Grillet wines, particularly struck his fancy. When Dennis and his business partner Joan Bieda began planning their vineyard, they concentrated on Viognier and other Rhone varieties, such as Marsanne, Mourvedre, Sirah, Grenache, and Malbec. The vineyard was planted in 1988 under the supervision of Dennis's wife, Sharon.

But the Rhone was not Dennis Horton's only fixation. He also had a crush (so to speak) on Norton, a true Virginia grape propagated in 1835 in Richmond, Virginia, by D. N. Norton, who wanted to develop a grape suitable for Virginia's climate. The Norton was so successful that it became the backbone of the Monticello Wine Company in Charlottesville, and as early as the late 1800s, the Monticello Company made Virginia the capital of the Eastern Wine Belt. It retained its position until the state's entire wine industry collapsed under the pressure of Prohibition.

Dennis, who had found a few Norton survivors in his home state of Missouri, became interested in reviving this historic grape. Perhaps Horton's Norton (do you think the name is one reason Dennis loves this grape?) will help Virginia regain its earlier leadership. The wine has an astonishingly dark, inky color and a pronounced aroma reminiscent of cherries and plums. Horton Viognier also has an intense aroma — putting nose to glass is like burying your face in a hedge of honeysuckle. It has the dryness and depth one associates with fine Viognier, and a satisfying long finish. Robert Parker wrote about the 1993 vintage, "While it will not replace a great Condrieu from the likes of Marcel Guigal or Andre Parret, it represents a major breakthrough in what can be achieved in specific micro-climates in the mid-Atlantic region . . . Bravo!" Horton's total production, including that of its affiliate winery Montdomaine, is 20,000 cases.

JEFFERSON VINEYARDS

Rating: 🍷
804-977-3042 or
800-272-3042;
fax 804-977-5459.
Highway 53,
Charlottesville, VA.
Directions: On Hwy. 53
between Monticello and
Ashlawn-Highland just
southeast of
Charlottesville.
Owner: Stanley
Woodward, Jr.
Open: Mar. through Nov.,
daily, 11 AM–5 PM except
major holidays; by
appointment Dec.
through Feb.
Price Range of Wines: $9.50
for Monticello Red to $16
for Merlot/Cabernet
Franc Reserve.
Special Features: Picnic
area.

In 1774, Filippo Mazzei, an Italian viticulturist and a friend of Thomas Jefferson, planted vinifera wine grapes on this site. Mazzei's efforts to grow grapes and make wine were ultimately unsuccessful, but today 16 acres of vines that were planted in the same spot in 1981 have fared well, and the winery now produces 4,000 cases of wine annually.

Jefferson Vineyards went through several transitions in 1995. The name was changed from Simeon to Jefferson, and a new winemaker, Michael Shaps, from Mallea Vineyards in Massachusetts came on board.

The wines, 95% of which are made from grapes grown in the estate's own 16-acre vineyard, show promise, although my own palate would prefer more intense flavors than these somewhat insipid wines offer. Perhaps all that's needed is a winemaker who will stick around long enough to give this deserving cellar some undivided attention. Let's hope Michael Shaps pulls it off.

Jefferson wines include a Reserve Chardonnay that is aged in French oak for six months, and two Sauvignon Blancs, one that is aged in stainless steel and the other in oak. Reflecting Italian winemaker Gabriele Rausse's previous tenure here, Jefferson produces both Pinot Grigio and Sangiovese. A pretty picnic site overlooks the same countryside that Thomas Jefferson loved so much.

The view from Loudoun Valley Vineyards, near Leesburg in northern Virginia, is spectacular.

Marguerite Thomas

LOUDOUN VALLEY VINEYARDS

Rating: 🍷
540-882-3375.
Route 9, Waterford, VA.
Directions: From Leesburg, take Rte. 7 west for 2 miles to Rte. 9 west. Go 5 miles to the winery on the right.
Owners: Dolores and Hubert Tucker.
Open: Apr. through Dec., Wed.–Sun., 11 AM–5 PM; Jan. through Mar., Sat. and Sun. 11 AM–5 PM.
Price Range of Wines: $8 for table whites to $14 for Cabernet and Chardonnay Reserves.
Special Features: Picnic area, cafe, view.
Special Events: Wine seminars, winemaker's dinners, Octoberfest, summer Bull Roast, Tex-Mex Fiesta.

Loudoun Valley Vineyards sits on a plateau overlooking vineyards and farms, with the Blue Ridge Mountains to the west and the Catoctin Mountains to the east. The view is spectacular enough to have inspired neighboring artist Rowan LeCompte to create several paintings, one of which is reproduced on Loudoun's labels. LeCompte also designed stained glass windows and mosaic murals for the National Cathedral in Washington. Once visitors pull themselves away from the mesmerizing view, they proceed along a gravel path through a small herb garden, fragrant with lavender and spicy smells, into the handsome, contemporary winery.

Hubert Tucker, an aeronautical engineer with the Federal Aviation Administration, and his wife Dolores, are the winery owners, and Hubert is the winemaker as well. He grows a variety of grapes in his 25-acre vineyard that includes a preponderance of vinifera. At present he produces 4,000 cases a year. He also operates a nursery from which he sells grafted vinifera root stock to wineries. Could it be that gazing out over that tranquil view charges Hubert up with enough energy to wear all these different hats?

Loudoun's Chardonnay is crisp and flinty, reflecting the vineyard's rock and clay soil. The Riesling, which is aged in American oak, has an intriguing peppermint aroma. Gewürztraminer, Gamay Beaujolais, and even Zinfandel are also made here. Loudoun was the first winery in the East to plant California's popular Zinfandel, and although California doesn't have much to worry about yet, perhaps some day it may prove a winner here too.

The winery has a small kitchen behind the tasting room, where light fare such as a cheese and bread plates, pâtés, and baked Brie are prepared. These can be enjoyed from a wraparound deck as you drink some wine and drink in the view as well.

Owner and winemaker Archie Smith of Meredyth Vineyards, Middleburg, Virginia.

Marguerite Thomas

MEREDYTH VINEYARDS

Rating: 🍷🍷
540-687-6277.
Route 628, Middleburg, VA.
Directions: From Washington, D.C., take I-66 to exit 31; go north on Rte. 245 to Rte. 55; then go right for 1 block, turn left on Rte. 626 and travel 3.75 miles; turn right on Rte. 679 and go 1 mile to Rte. 628, the winery will be on the left. From Middleburg, turn south at the traffic light, go 2.5 miles to Rte. 628, then turn right and go 2.5 miles to winery.
Owner: Archie Smith.
Open: Daily, 10 AM–5 PM except major holidays.
Price Range of Wines: $6.99 for a blush, $7.49 for the

One approaches Meredyth Vineyards along lazy country roads that skirt the Bull Run Mountains. A long driveway leads up through fields and vineyards, past the ruins of an old farmhouse, to the winemaking facility and tasting room. Meredyth's vineyards were planted on the family farm in 1972 and the first harvest was in 1975, making it the second oldest winery in Virginia. (The oldest is Farfelu, which, after suffering from personal and winemaking problems, is currently in the throes of change.)

Winery owner Archie Smith was teaching philosophy at Oxford when his father summoned him back to help with the Meredyth winery in the mid-1970s. After commuting to England for awhile, Archie finally moved back to Virginia to become a full-time winemaker.

The 216-acre farm includes vineyards of both vinifera and hybrid grapes. Archie defends the hybrids energetically, arguing that they are well-suited to the Virginia climate. "Our vines represent

Harvest Red, $10.99 for the Cabernet.
Special Features: Picnic area.

both our old and the new world heritage," he maintains, exhibiting glimpses of the philosopher lurking beneath the winemaker's jaunty surface. "A wine like De Chaunac is hard to sell off the supermarket shelf, but it's interesting from a winemaker's point of view. If grown right, it's chock full of fruit flavors, but it doesn't have much tannin. Personally, I like a wine like this. I don't like wine that sticks to your teeth." The downside of De Chaunac is that it oxidizes easily. "It can taste like rubber boots," Archie acknowledges. Others apparently share his enthusiasm, since the wine consistently sells out.

Another of Meredyth's popular old world/new world wines is Harvest Red, a blend of Cabernet Franc and Maréchal Foch grapes. It's fresh and light, with a faint rose petal aroma. "We call it our white wine in drag," smiles Archie. For those of us who like "wine that sticks to your teeth," Meredyth's Cabernet Sauvignon is softly tannic, with good flavors. From 10,000 to 12,000 cases of wine are produced at Meredyth annually. Picnic tables look out toward the Bull Run Mountains.

MONTDOMAINE CELLARS

Rating: 🍷🍷🍷
804-971-8947.
Route 720, Charlottesville, VA.
Directions: From I-64 take exit 121. Follow Rte. 20 south about 10.5 miles. Turn right at Rte. 720 and go approx. 2 miles to the winery.
Owners: Joan Bieda and Dennis Horton.
Open: Mar. through Nov., Wed.–Sun., noon–5 PM; Dec. through Feb. by appointment.
Price Range of Wines: $5.99 for Vidal Blanc to $15 for Heritage and Ivy Creek Chardonnay.
Special Features: Picnic area.

Montdomaine was established in 1984 by a group of growers who had been raising grapes since 1977. In 1991 the winery operation was assumed by Joan Bieda and her business partner, Dennis Horton, who also own Horton Vineyards. Shep Rouse, one of Virginia's leading winemakers, was Montdomaine's winemaker for four years, but left in 1995 to start his own winery. He continues to be a consultant at Montdomaine.

Although Montdomaine is affiliated with Horton Vineyards, the wines are very different. Horton specializes in Viognier, Marsanne, and other wines typical of the Rhone Valley. Montdomaine, on the other hand, produces excellent Chardonnays, Cabernets, and Heritage, a well-balanced and pleasing blend of Merlot, Cabernet Franc, and Cabernet Sauvignon. At present, 8,000 cases of wine are produced annually. There is an inviting picnic site under the tall tulip trees overlooking the vineyard.

OASIS VINEYARDS

Rating: 🍷🍷🍷🍷
540-635-7627.
Highway 635, Hume, VA.
Directions: Going west on I-66, take exit 27 at

Oasis Vineyards has the oldest plantings of Chardonnay and Cabernet Sauvignon grapes in Virginia. It was also the first in the state to plant only vinifera grapes and the first to make a sparkling wine.

Marguerite Thomas

Tareq Salahi, winemaker, Oasis Vineyards, Hume, Virginia.

Marshall, follow Rte. 647 south for 4 miles to Rte. 635, turn right and go for 10 miles to the winery.
Owners: Dingham and Corinne Salahi.
Open: Daily 10 AM–5 PM.
Price Range of Wines: $9 for Riesling to $25 for Meritage, of which no more than a hundred cases are produced annually.
Special Features: Cafe, picnic area.
Special Events: Spring Open House, with hors d'oeuvres and live music; Polo Wine and Twilight Dine.

Since its initial vintage in 1980, when 186 cases of wine were produced, Oasis has expanded to 20,000 cases in 1994, and it's still growing. The winery owns 80 acres of vineyards at the winery site, plus 20 additional acres. It is owned by Jerusalem-born Dingham Salahi and his Belgian wife Corinne. Their son, Tareq, recently joined the business as wine-maker. He graduated in enology from the University of California at Davis and then worked at Napa's Domaine Carneros, which is known for its sparkling wines. Whether Oasis Vineyards makes its excellent sparkling wine because of Tareq's experience at Carneros, or whether he went to Carneros because of an interest in sparklers, is irrelevant. What counts is that the winery's sparkling Oasis Brut Cuvée D'Or is simply outstanding. Actually, it's hard to find fault with any of the Oasis wines, from the buttery Barrel Select Chardonnay to the intense, soft Cabernet Sauvignon.

Oasis has a small cafe which offers cheese, pâtés and other informal foods. This is a lovely spot for a picnic, with splendid views of the surrounding mountains.

PIEDMONT VINEYARDS & WINERY
Rating: 🍷🍷🍷
540-687-5528.
Route 626, Middleburg, VA.

Piedmont Winery was started in 1975 by 73-year-old Elizabeth Furness, who converted her former dairy farm to a winery when she realized grapes were more profitable than milk. She planted Semillon grapes because she was a fan of French

Directions: From Washington, D.C. take I-66 to Rte. 50 west, following it to Rte. 626 south. From Middleburg, it's 3 miles south on Rte. 626.
Owner: Elizabeth Worrall.
Open: Daily, 10 AM–5 PM, except major holidays.
Price Range of Wines: $6 for Little River, a Seyval/Chardonnay blend, to $15 for Semillon wines.
Special Features: Picnic area.

Semillon wines, thereby putting Piedmont on the wine map as the first winery in the East to raise this varietal. She also planted Chardonnay grapes. The winery is now owned by her daughter, Elizabeth Worrall.

White wines are Piedmont's forte. The Semillon/Sauvignon Blanc wine is excellent, an aromatic libation with pleasing fruit flavors. Merrill/Hubbard, a blend of Chardonnay, Semillon, and Sauvignon Blanc is also very good, with aromas of melon and honey touched by oak. The winery is also experimenting with Pinot Gris, and it is about to release a Chardonnay made with native yeasts.

Recently, Cabernet was added to the all-vinifera vineyards (the winery does buy hybrid grapes from local vineyards for blending). It is about to release its first Cabernet Sauvignon, which will be excellent if it is up to the standard of the whites. The winery now bottles 6,000 cases of wine each year.

Piedmont winery has distinctive labels designed by local artists, whose paintings are exhibited at the winery. You'll know you've reached Piedmont when you spot the family's striking green-shuttered, ocher Greek Revival house. The winery is behind the house, near the picnic tables that are set against a pastoral backdrop.

Marguerite Thomas

Chris Johnson, Prince Michel and Rapidan River Vineyards, Leon, Virginia.

PRINCE MICHEL and RAPIDAN RIVER VINEYARDS
Rating: ♟♟♟
540-547-3707;
fax 540-547-3088.

Chris Johnson is the all-American winemaker. Born and educated in California, where he obtained a degree in enology from Fresno State University, he worked in the Niagara Falls area of Canada and at Taylor Great Western in upstate

Route 29, Leon (near Culpeper), VA.
Directions: 10 miles south of Culpeper on Rte. 29.
Owner: Jean Leducq.
Open: Daily, 10 AM–5 PM.
Price Range of Wines: Rapidan River: $9.95 for Riesling to $11.66 for Gewürztraminer. Prince Michel: $12.95 for Chardonnay to $18.95 for Cabernet/Merlot Reserve.
Special Features: Wine museum, gift shop, restaurant.

New York before coming to Prince Michel. He has experienced every possible kind of weather in America's vineyards, from frigid to scorching.

This varied background enables Chris to put Virginia's conditions in perspective. "We are in a marginal area for vinifera," he states unequivocally, "so we have to do extreme things to get the fruit as ripe as possible. Vigorous canopy management, good air circulation to keep the vines dry, and an effective spraying program are very important to get good, clean fruit."

Prince Michel, established in 1983, and its affiliate, Rapidan River Vineyards, are owned by French businessman Jean Leducq. The combined acreage, which includes 100 acres at Prince Michel and 50 acres at Rapidan, makes this one of the largest vineyard holdings in Virginia. Furthermore, Prince Michel's 30,000 case annual production is one of the largest in the state. It is among the few Virginia vineyards to machine-harvest its grapes.

Grapes from an affiliated 20-acre vineyard in California's Napa Valley are blended with some Virginia grapes and bottled at the winery under the label of "LeDucq." To distinguish these wines from those made from grapes grown only in Virginia, the label will identify it as "American" instead of a wine from Virginia.

Jacques Boissenot, a noted wine consultant from Bordeaux, is often called upon to share his expertise at Prince Michel. Among Boissenot's other clients are some of France's most illustrious chateaux, including Pichon-Longueville, Léoville-Barton and Lafite-Rothschild. Global winemakers such as Boissenot, who is also affiliated with Lafite's operations in Chile, and Bruno Prats, the owner of France's prestigious Cos d'Estournel winery who also consults at Millbrook Winery in New York's Hudson River Valley region, are exerting a positive influence on the quality of American wines.

Rapidan River wines (primarily Riesling and Gewürztraminer) are styled like the white wines of Germany and Alsace, very fruity and semi-dry, which is to say, somewhat sweet. The red wines of Prince Michel are modeled after Bordeaux wines, while the whites are full flavored and full bodied with a deep, fruity aroma reminiscent of California. The Merlot has good color and strength, with an aroma of berries and herbs, while Cabernet-Merlot Reserve, made with 45% Cabernet Sauvignon grapes, 33% Merlot, and 22% Cabernet Franc, offers a more complex bouquet of berries and cherries, plus a hint of cedar.

Prince Michel has a small but interesting wine museum and a superior gift shop. Visitors are encouraged to take an informative self-guided tour of the winery, where detailed, illustrated explanations of each aspect of winemaking are clearly illustrated. There are no picnic facilities, but the winery does have a good restaurant.

View of the fields at Swedenburg Estate Vineyard, Middleburg, Virginia.

Marguerite Thomas

SWEDENBURG ESTATE VINEYARD
Rating: 🍷🍷
540-687-5219.
Route 50, Middleburg, VA.
Directions: From Middleburg, take Rte. 50 for 1 mile east to the winery.
Owners: Wayne and Juanita Swedenburg.
Open: Daily, 10 AM–4 PM.
Price Range of Wines: $7 for Riesling, $9 for Chardonnay, and $14 for Cabernet Sauvignon.
Special Features: Picnic area.

Swedenburg Estate Vineyard is part of a working farm that was established 225 years ago by a royal grant instructing the lessee "to build a dwelling house twenty feet long and sixteen feet wide." That original house is now part of the Swedenburg family residence.

Wayne Swedenburg, whose parents were Swedish, was in the Foreign Service when he and his wife, Juanita, bought the farm in 1976, 10 years before Wayne retired. First they raised a few head of cattle and some hay. Then, in 1980, feeling grapes would be more profitable, they planted a few vines. Eight years later, they opened the winery.

Swedenburg now has about 15 acres of grapes. All are vinifera except for a small amount of Seyval. It produces about 2,000 cases of wine each year.

Swedenburg makes German-style wines. All of the winery equipment is German, and many German practices are followed in the vineyard, including trellising. Swedenburg Riesling, for example, which has more appeal than the average American Riesling, has a lower alcohol content (about 9.5%), similar to its German counterparts. While it may be too sweet to accompany most fish dishes, it makes a pleasant sipping wine. The oak-aged Chardonnay is harmonious and the Cabernet Sauvignon, a grape that does well in the region's limestone soil, is very drinkable. A Scandanavian-style picnic — smoked salmon, say, with a glass of Riesling — would be enjoyable here.

TARARA VINEYARD & WINERY

Rating: 👥👥
703-771-7100 or
703-478-8161.
13648 Tarara Lane,
Leesburg, VA.
Directions: From Leesburg,
take Rte. 15 north about
8 miles to Lucketts. Turn
right onto Rte. 662 and
go 3 miles to the winery
sign. The driveway is on
the left.
Owners: Margaret and
Whitie Hubert.
Open: Thurs.–Mon.,
11 AM–5 PM; Tues. and
Wed. by appointment;
Jan. and Feb. open
weekends only.
Price Range of Wines: $6.99
for Terra Rouge to $18
for the Pinot Noir.
Special Features: Picnic
area, hiking trails,
softball diamond,
volleyball court,
horseshoe pit.

Margaret and Whitie Hubert named their 475-acre farm after the Tarara River, which flooded the area in 1985, the year they bought it. Tarara is also "Ararat" spelled backwards, which was the name of the mountain where Noah landed after the great flood. This idyllic spot overlooking the Potomac River is further enhanced by ornamental trees, ponds, fields of asparagus, blackberry bushes, a 10-acre orchard, and a 50-acre vineyard. It's hard to believe it's only 60 minutes from the turmoil of Washington, D.C.

This is a hospitable environment for a vineyard, as the constant breeze from the river moderates the temperatures. To provide a cool, stable climate in which his wines could age gracefully in their French barrels, Whitie (a retired contractor and developer) blasted a 6,000-square-foot cave out of the land. In the tasting room above the caves, samples are poured from bottles with colorful labels designed by the Huberts' daughter Martha, a San Francisco artist.

Terra Rouge is a non-vintage blend of Cabernet, Chambourcin, and Vidal Blanc that the Huberts describe as a light, Beaujolais-style wine. It has broad appeal and is good with burgers and barbecues. Serious wines are made here as well, including Cabernets, a Bordeaux-style blend of Cabernet Franc, Cabernet Sauvignon, and Merlot; Pinot Noir, and Chardonnay.

Tarara is an exceptionally lovely spot for an al fresco lunch, and it also offers hiking trails, a volleyball court, a softball field, and a horseshoe pit.

TOTIER CREEK VINEYARD & WINERY

Rating: 👥
804-979-7105 or
800-683-6174.
Route 720, Charlottesville,
VA.
Directions: From I-64 take
exit 121, then take Rte. 20
south for 10 miles to Rte.
720. Turn right and go 1
mile to the winery which
will be on the right.
Owners: Mary and Jamie
Lewis.

Totier Creek is named for the French-Canadian Indians who farmed this land in the 19th century. In the early 1980s Wally Dahl, one of nearby Montdomaine Cellar's original partners, planted a vineyard here. Mary and Jamie Lewis bought the vineyard in 1990.

Soon, Jamie, who also owns parking lots in Georgetown, was so hooked on grapes that in 1992 he opened a winery. Gabriele Rausse, the original winemaker at Barboursville Vineyards, helped guide Jamie through the early stages of his winemaking career.

Totier Creek Vineyard produces about a dozen

Open: Mar. through Dec.,
Wed.–Sun., 11 AM–5 PM;
Jan. & Feb., Sat. & Sun.
only, 11 AM–5 PM; closed
Christmas through New
Years.
Price Range of Wines: $8 for
Cardinal Blush, a blend
of Riesling, Merlot,and
Pinot Noir to $15 for
Cabernet Sauvignon.
Special Features: Picnic
area.

**WILLOWCROFT FARM
VINEYARDS**
Rating: 🍷🍷
703-777-8161.
Mt. Gilead Road (Route
797), Leesburg, VA.
Directions: From Leesburg,
go south on Rte. 15. At
Rte. 704, turn right and
then immediately left
onto Rte. 797 (a dirt
road). The winery will be
in 3.1 miles.
Owners: Lew and Cindy
Parker.
Open: Sat. and Sun.,
noon–5 PM.
Price Range of Wines: $8
for Seyval to $14 for
Cabernet Sauvignon.

wines from vinifera grapes, including several barrel-fermented Chardonnays and Cabernets, a Riesling, and a Merlot. Cardinal Blush is a blend of Riesling, Merlot, and Pinot Noir with a residual sugar content of 2.2. Most of the wine is aged in French oak, but Jamie is also experimenting with Virginia oak. The wines are light and pleasant, although a little too lightweight for my taste. A deck, overlooking the 19-acre vineyard and the wooded Green Mountains, is an attractive place for a picnic.

The approach to Willowcroft is along a dirt and gravel road that dips and sweeps across the side of Mt. Gilead and presents astonishing views of hayfields, green countryside, and distant mountains. When Lew and Cindy Parker were raising their daughters, this was a small farm with a few chickens, goats, and horses. The farmhouse was originally an 1800s log cabin, although it has seen many renovations in the interim.

Lew, an executive consultant to the chemistry and biotechnology industries, planted his first 10-acre plot of grapes early in the 1980s. They were mostly vinifera, supplemented by some Seyval. In 1984, he opened the winery in the old Civil War-era barn. Winemaker and vineyard manager, David Collins, who trained at Virginia Polytechnic Institute and in California, was hired in 1987.

The model for Willowcroft is Burgundy. Barrel maturation, malolactic fermentation, and other traditional Burgundian winemaking techniques are followed here. "We are looking for wine that is rich and full," explains David. "We've come a long way in the last few years. Five years ago our cold-fermented Chardonnay was more acidic. Now we're rounding out the flavors better. We've learned how to work with eastern acidity."

Actually, improved winery techniques have played a minor role in achieving the winery's success, according to David. "You make the wine in the vineyard. It's the vineyard practices that create quality," he insists, listing the importance of canopy shoot position, pulling leaves to expose fruit to the sun, and above all, harvesting at the right moment. "We strive for picture-perfect ripe fruit, 22-23 degrees Brix (a scale for measuring the amount of sugar in grapes)," he explains. Then David smiles and pours some Chardonnay for visitors. "I'm really pleased with where we are," he says. And he should be. The wines, including Riesling, Seyval, Cabernet Franc, and Cabernet Sauvignon, are well made, well structured, well rounded, and flavorful. The current annual production is 2,500 cases.

RESTAURANTS AND LODGING

Please also refer to restaurants and lodging under the Virginia Highlands section of Part Three, *The Mountains* for other nearby places.

RESTAURANTS AND LODGING

THE ASHBY INN
540-592-3900.
Paris, VA.
Price: Expensive.

Reminiscent of an English country inn and pub, this cozy inn is located in a tiny rural village in Virginia Hunt Country. There are six bedrooms upstairs filled with lovely antiques and country furniture. Downstairs, the dining room and pub are welcoming and convivial. This is a very serious restaurant: all herbs and many vegetables are grown in the gardens, fresh fish is trucked to the restaurant straight from the Eastern Shore, and wines from the nearby vineyards are featured.

THE INN AT LITTLE WASHINGTON
540-675-3800;
   fax 540-675-3100.
Middle and Main Streets, Washington, VA.
Price: Very Expensive.

The inside cover of the wine list at the Inn at Little Washington contains this inscription, "Water separates the people of the world; wine unites them." It's a credo the owners live by. Their award-winning wine list is almost as long as the script for *Gone with the Wind*, and it has an entire page devoted to Virginia wines. The cellar contains more than 9,000 bottles.

The menu at this outstanding restaurant changes "with the seasons, the weather, and the wind." A diner might start with a napoleon of potato crisps and Maine lobster, or homemade boudin blanc (white sausage) with sauerkraut braised in Virginia Riesling on apple coulis. The main course selections include barbecued grilled boneless rack of lamb in a pecan crust with shoestring sweet potatoes, and a "portobello mushroom pretending to be a filet mignon with a roasted shallot and tomato fondue."

If you're a pauper pretending to be a prince, don't even think of dining here, as it's very expensive. But if you do have a princely bank account, or have saved for just such a treat, the Inn at Little Washington is perfect. A member of the prestigious Relais & Chateaux association of fine hotels and restaurants, the inn also features 12 guestrooms. All are furnished with English antiques, canopy beds, fine fabrics (even the windows are better dressed than most of the people I know), and marble bathrooms with brass fittings and fresh flowers.

Washington, Virginia, is a small village of 158 inhabitants that was surveyed by George Washington in 1749.

Clifton, The Country Inn, Charlottesville, Virginia.

Courtesy Clifton, The Country Inn

CLIFTON, THE COUNTRY INN
804-971-1800.
1296 Clifton Inn Drive,
Charlottesville, VA.
Price: Expensive.

At Clifton, guests can experience gracious Southern hospitality in a historic house. Although Thomas Jefferson's daughter once lived here, it's hard to believe she ate as well as todays guests do, for Chef Craig Hartman creates exceptionally fine cuisine. Dinner might start with shrimp bisque garnished with croutons and scallions, followed by a refreshing salad of mixed baby greens, accompanied by Iron Rod chèvre, a creamy and flavorful goat cheese from a local farm. Pan seared yellowfin tuna with leek marmalade and tomato relish is a perfect gastronomic partner for a bottle of Horton Viognier. For dessert, the white and dark chocolate terrine with berry confiture and ginger snap cookies is a delicious ending. The dining room is on a pleasant glassed-in terrace. Comfortable bedrooms are furnished with attractive antiques.

RESTAURANTS

THE FIREHOUSE CAFE & MARKET
540-672-9001.
137 W Main St, Orange, VA.
Price: Inexpensive.

This informal deli/market/wine shop is a good place to stop for a bowl of soup and a sandwich, or to pick up supplies for a picnic. The menu includes many interesting, homemade selections, such as curried asparagus soup and spicy African peanut soup, which, by the way, is excellent with a glass of Horton Vidal.

FOUR AND TWENTY BLACKBIRDS
540-675-1800.
Rtes. 522 and 647,
Flint Hill, VA.
Price: Moderate.

This acclaimed restaurant, considered one of the best in the foothills of the Shenandoahs, offers eclectic cuisine in a charming setting crisscrossed by stone walls. The menu changes every three weeks to reflect the regional local bounty. All ingredients are house-made including the breads, pastas, and ice creams. Halibut baked in parchment with Italian white beans, roasted red peppers, portobello mushrooms, and sundried tomato rouille is one of the most popular dishes. Yes, local wines are featured.

TASTINGS
804-293-3663.
Corner of 5th and East Market St,
Charlottesville, VA.
Price: Moderate.

Tastings is a unique wine shop and restaurant, where lunch or dinner can be enjoyed along with a half-glass, a full-glass, or a bottle of wine. I sometimes browse through selections in a wine shop and get hungry just imagining certain foods that might go with a particular wine. This is a fine place to let imagination run wild. The shop sells over 30 Virginia wines, and the restaurant wine list includes 10 from the home state. The contemporary American food includes salads and soups (the wild mushroom soup was outstanding), as well as appetizing and well-prepared entrees. The shop carries more than 1,000 bottles of wine, and the owners are unusually knowledgeable about eastern wines.

WESTERN CONNECTICUT

Connecticut is a tough state in which to grow grapes and produce wine. This is partly due to lack of local support both from the public and the government. Connecticut, in fact, has some of the most unfriendly rules in the nation regulating the sale and distribution of wine.

The western section of the state also has to cope with more challenging weather than any of the surrounding regions because it doesn't have the advantage of a large body of water to moderate the climate. Wineries have come and gone since the passage of the state's Farm Winery Act in 1978, but the four current wineries in western Connecticut have survived for almost twenty years.

It's difficult to maintain healthy vinifera vines here, so the wineries have built their image on wines made from hybrid grapes. In recent years, however, some vintners have begun to flirt with vinifera by purchasing grapes from Long Island or the Finger Lakes regions, or they have discovered ways to raise Chardonnay, Cabernet Franc, and other vinifera varietals themselves.

They have also turned to more refined winemaking techniques, such as the judicious use of oak aging. The wines produced in the past few years have generally shown a great improvement over the lackadaisical quality of earlier efforts. People who are partisans of hybrid wines will find much to interest them in this region, but even the confirmed consumer of European wines will be in for some pleasant surprises. Furthermore, the rural scenery, the splendid old houses, and the charming villages in this part of Connecticut are well worth the trip.

The Connecticut vintners hold several events annually, including a Connecticut Wine and Food Festival. Call any Connecticut winery for information.

HAIGHT VINEYARDS
Rating: 🍷
860-567-4045 or
  800-325-5567 (CT only).
29 Chestnut Hill Road,
  Litchfield, CT.
Directions: From Rte. 8 take
  Exit 42 and then go west
  on Rte. 118 for 3 miles to
  the top of the hill. Just
  beyond the intersection
  with Rte. 254, turn left.
  The winery is on the left.
Owner: Sherman P. Haight.
Open: Mon.–Sat., 10:30
  AM–5 PM, Sun. noon–5 PM.
Price Range of Wines: $6.98
  for Covertside White to
  $9.98 for Merlot.
Special Events: Spring:
  Barrel Tasting with food
  and music; Summer:
  Taste of the Litchfield
  Hills, with food from
  local restaurants and
  inns, music, hayrides;
  Fall: Crafts Fair.

Textile manufacturer Sherman P. Haight was one of a handful of men who successfully fought for the passage of Connecticut's 1978 Farm Winery Law. In anticipation, he planted a vineyard in 1975, so the winery that bears his name was ready to open in 1978. Today, Haight produces 6,000 cases annually and has a 30-acre vineyard. It is planted in approximately 20% of vinifera vines.

Among the Haight wines, Covertside White, a predominantly Seyval blend, outsells all others 3:1. The wine is named for the coverts — thickets where foxes live — that are found near one of the vineyards. It has great appeal to the sweeter wine trade. Recolte, a blend of Seyval with about 15% Chardonnay, is a dry white with pleasant fruit flavors. The winery, which does not have its own picnic facilities, recommends the picnic tables in nearby Litchfield.

HOPKINS VINEYARD
Rating: 🍷
860-868-7954;
  fax 860-868-1768.
Hopkins Road, New
  Preston, CT.
Directions: Take Rte. 202
  to New Preston. Then
  take Rte. 45 north for 2.5
  miles; take the first left
  after passing North Shore

Hopkins Vineyard may have the most scenic location of any vineyard in the East, set on the slope of a hill overlooking Lake Waramaug, a large, tranquil lake surrounded by hills and woods and a scattering of picture-perfect country houses. The original farm has been in the Hopkins family for over 200 years. The winery was founded by William Hopkins, a home winemaker, in the mid-1970s, when he switched from dairy farming to vineyards, making it the oldest continuously oper-

Road, and then take the second right onto Hopkins Rd. The winery is on the right.

Owner: William Hopkins.

Open: May through Dec., daily, 10 AM–5 PM; Jan. through Apr., Fri.–Sun., 10 AM–5 PM.

Price Range of Wines: $6.99 for New England Rosé to $16.95 for sparkling wine.

Special Features: Lake nearby for picnics.

Special Events: Annual Spring Barrel Tasting.

ating winery in Connecticut. The winery now produces 6,000 cases of wine a year, all from grapes grown in the 30 acres of vineyards.

This is still a family enterprise, with Bill Hopkins and his son-in-law, Gerald Corrigan, making the wines. Vinifera planting has increased over the years to account for about 20% of the total. "That's where it will probably stay," says Gerry Corrigan. "We sell mostly to tourists here, and tourists are not vinifera buyers." But vinifera buyers won't be unhappy here either: the newest Chardonnays, made from grapes harvested in the winery's own vineyards, have a firm texture and well-developed flavor. Previous Chardonnays, made from Finger Lakes grapes, tended to be lighter and less interesting. Recent plantings of Cabernet Franc and Merlot may produce similarly winning wines. I tasted some newly released wines that had good color and a full, pleasing flavor. The light and airy tasting room is set in a renovated 19th-century barn. The lake is an ideal setting for a picnic.

McLAUGHLIN VINEYARDS, INC.

Rating: 🍇

203-426-1533; fax 203-270-8722.

Albert Hill Road, Sandy Hook, CT.

Directions: From I-84 take exit 10 and go in the direction of Sandy Hook. Take the first left onto Walnut Tree Hill. Go 2 miles to the island and bear left onto Albert's

The most isolated winery in this region, McLaughlin is located at the base of a mountain where eagles and hawks soar. In an odd twist of events, the McLaughlin family owns this winery as well as another in Colorado. Morgen McLaughlin oversees Sandy Hook, while her parents, Bruce and Taffy, operate the Colorado facility. It seems that her father inherited his parent's 160-acre Connecticut farm in the 1970s and he decided to plant a vineyard on it. Later, her mother inherited *her* family's dairy farm in Colorado, and they

Hill Rd., the winery is 100 yards on the right.
Owners: The McLaughlin family.
Open: Daily noon–5 PM.
Price Range of Wines: $6 for White Table Wine to $16 for Merlot.
Special Features: Picnic area, eagle-watching.
Special Events: Jazz Under the Stars, a summer-long series.

elected to replicate the experience there. Morgen, a recent graduate of Boston University, initially resisted joining the family business, but after staying to fill in one summer, she was seduced by the lure of wine and never left.

McLaughlin's is a good place to taste hybrid and vinifera wines side by side. Both are well-made and flavorful here. The White Table Wine, a semi-dry blend, shows off the strengths of hybrids with a full, enticing aroma and a rich flavor that fills the front of the mouth. McLaughlin wines also offer a good example of a well-made hybrid's ability to age. I sampled a ten-year-old Seyval that had gained in richness and complexity, unlike the average Chardonnay, which usually declines after a few years. It had maintained a freshness, with a slight trace of bubble-gum fragrance. The only flaw was a slight tendency, common in older wines made from hybrids, to lose flavor at the back of the palate. It is "short," meaning that it lacks the pleasant aftertaste that characterizes the finest wines. Overall, McLaughlin wines have a distinct personality and are appealing examples of good regional wines.

This is a lovely setting for a picnic and for eagle watching. Serious bird watchers may want to visit during November and March when, according to the McLaughlins, more eagles come to perch and feed at their farm than at any other site on the Housatonic River.

OTHER WINERIES IN WESTERN CONNECTICUT

DiGRAZIA VINEYARDS AND WINERY (203-775-1616 (tel and fax), 131 Tower Road, Brookfield, CT) Known principally as a producer of sweet wines, DiGrazia does also make a dry Seyval, called Winners' Cup, and a Seyval-Vidal blend, called Vintage Festival. Paul DiGrazia, who has been the owner and winemaker at this family winery since 1978, also pursues a full-time medical practice.

All the DiGrazia grapes come from the winery's own 20-acre vineyard. One of Dr. DiGrazia's best-selling wines is Honey Blush, which is made by using honey, rather than sulfites, as a preservative. It is popular among people who are troubled by sulfites. Brookfield is a picturesque small town with an historic district.

RESTAURANTS AND LODGING

RESTAURANTS AND LODGING

THE BOULDERS
860-868-0541;
   fax 860-868-1925.
Rte. 45 (East Shore Road)
   New Preston, CT.
Price: Moderate.

Located on a hillside overlooking Lake Waramaug, this elegant country inn has antique-filled guestrooms in the main house, as well as spectacular modern furnishings in separate guesthouses and in a carriage house. There are whirlpool tubs, fireplaces, and window seats overlooking the lake. The dining room, also with a view of the lake, is noted for its fine cuisine and for its exceptional wine list. Several local wines are available.

Summer at the Hopkins Inn, New Preston, Connecticut.

Marguerite Thomas

THE HOPKINS INN
860-868-7295; fax
   860-868-7464.
22 Hopkins Road, New
   Preston, CT.
Price: Moderate.

Like the Hopkins Winery, which is just across the street, this inn is set on a gentle slope overlooking Lake Waramaug, in the Berkshire foothills. Built as a summer boarding house in 1847, it was converted to an inn in 1945. Incidentally, there is no relationship, other than name and location, between the inn and the winery, although Hopkins Vineyard wines are featured on the inn's list.

The Austrian background of owners Beth and Franz Schober is reflected in the decor of the inn, in the dress of the servers, who wear dirndl skirts and peasant blouses, and on the restaurant menu. It features such items as Backhendl (Austrian fried chicken) with Lingonberries, as well as filet mignon, grilled salmon, and other conventional entrees. The decor of the newly renovated bedrooms feels somewhat Alpine, with floral patterned wallpaper, country antiques, and pristine white-tiled bathrooms. Some have spectacular views of the lake.

RESTAURANTS

DOC'S
860-868-9415.
Rte. 45 and Flirtation Ave.,
  Lake Waramaug, New
  Preston, CT.
Price: Moderate–Expensive.
Open: Dinner only,
         Wed.–Sun.
Special features:
  Reservations required;
  no credit cards accepted;
  BYOB.

Doc's bills itself as an Italian cafe, pizzeria and bakery, but this humble description barely hints at some of the elegant items on the menu. Dinner entrees might include braised rabbit with shiitake mushrooms, red peppers, sage, and tomatoes; or roasted chicken with white beans and garlic. There are numerous pastas and salads, as well as pizzas garnished with all manner of ingredients, from fennel, to eggplant, to pepperoni. Doc's is a tiny, but very popular place, so don't even think of coming without a reservation. No wine or spirits are sold, so it's the perfect opportunity to bring your own wine.

WEST STREET GRILL
860-567-3885.
43 West Street,
  Litchfield, CT.
Price: Moderate–Expensive.

Situated on the village green in Litchfield, one of the most historic and handsome villages in Connecticut, this enormously popular restaurant features an exceptional wine list and an interesting menu. In a crisp and smart setting, grilled pork chops come with a compote of roasted figs and a port wine sauce, and salmon is served with roasted corn, braised leeks, and whipped potatoes. The restaurant, like the town, attracts well-known novelists, film stars, and politicians. Reservations are absolutely necessary.

GOOD NEWS CAFE
203-266-4663.
694 Main Street South
  (Route 6,)
  Woodbury, CT.
Price: Moderate–Expensive.

Popular restauranteur Carole Peck opened the Good News Cafe in 1993 and it's been packed ever since. The menu features innovative contemporary American fare. Basil-wrapped scallops come with caramelized onions and a tomato-pineapple sage chutney is a typical offering. The wine list is thoughtful and reasonably priced, with over 16 selections by the glass, including a few from local wineries. The dessert selection is renowned. The decor in the art-filled dining room is light and airy.

THE HUDSON RIVER VALLEY

The Hudson River Valley has one of the most impressive winemaking histories in America, as it is the oldest commercial grape-producing region in the United States. As early as the mid-1600s, the Hudson River was recognized as a major trading artery for the New World. It was then used by English, German, and Dutch farmers in upstate New York to ship their products to the booming market in New York City.

When the French Huguenots arrived in the valley in the 1670s, they established vineyards along the river where, once they learned that European vinifera grapes couldn't tolerate East Coast diseases and climates, they raised table rather than wine grapes.

In 1877, Andrew Caywood moved from Modena, New York, to Marlboro, in the Hudson Valley, where he developed many successful hybrids, most notably the Dutchess grape. Caywood's contributions marked the beginning of this region's foray into commercial winemaking. Prohibition put a temporary halt to the industry, which was revived by Mark Miller when he replanted Caywood's original vineyards in the 1960s (now called Benmarl Vineyards).

The Hudson River Valley is a lovely spot that attracts nature lovers who come for the hiking trails and water sports, antiques hunters, art aficionados, and history buffs. The homes of several of the famous 19th century Hudson River painters, who lived and worked here are open to the public. Also, historic sites such as the 17th-century stone Huguenot houses in New Paltz and the museum at George Washington's Headquarters in Newburgh are interesting to visit. And, of course, wine lovers can spend a day or a week visiting wineries and sampling the local wines in delightful settings.

WEST SIDE OF THE HUDSON RIVER

ADAIR VINEYARDS
Rating: 🍷
914-255-1377.
75 Allhusen Road, New
Paltz, NY.
Directions: The winery is 6
miles south of New Paltz.
From Rte. 32, turn east on
Allhusen Road.
Owners: Jim and Gloria
Adair.
Open: Mar. through Dec.,
daily, noon–6 PM; Jan. &
Feb. by appointment.
Price Range of Wines: $6
for the Seyval and Picnic
Red to $14.50 for
"Champagne Brut."

Like many eastern vintners, Jim Adair started as a home winemaker while pursuing another career as an executive art director in a Manhattan advertising agency. When he finally succumbed to the siren song of the grape in 1982, Jim and his wife, Gloria, moved to a lovely 200-year old farm and planted their 10-acre vineyard.

In 1983 they opened their winery in the handsome red barn that has a National Historic Landmark plaque at the entrance. From a window in the tasting room, visitors can look out at a splendid oak that resembles the tree on the Adair wine bottle, although the tree on the label is actually a replica of "The Solitary Oak," a 19th-century painting by Asher B. Durand, a leader of the Hudson River School.

Adair produces 1,500 cases of wine that include a crisp, dry Seyval and a medium-bodied Chardonnay. Picnic Red, a light Beaujolais-style red, and Landmark Red, a more deeply-flavored dry wine, are made from Maréchal Foch grapes. The winery makes sweeter wines also including Mountain White, an engaging blend of Seyval, Vidal, and Ravat (or Vignoles, as the grape is now more commonly called), and Mountain Mist, a dessert wine made from late harvest Ravat that has a faint hint of botrytis, the so called "noble rot" that gives French Sauternes its inimitable personality. A bottle of Adair Picnic Red would be just the thing to accompany an al fresco lunch in the shade of that arty oak.

BALDWIN VINEYARDS
Rating: 🍷
914-744-2226.
176 Hardenburgh Road, Pine Bush, NY.
Directions: From the New York State Thruway (I-87) take exit 17 in Newburgh and follow Rte. 52 east to Pine Bush; from the light at the intersection of Rtes. 52 and 302 follow the signs north one mile to the winery.
Owners: Jack and Pat Baldwin.
Open: Apr. through Nov., daily, 10 AM–5:30 PM; Dec. through Mar.,

Jack Baldwin had never even tasted wine until 1974 when he and his wife, Pat, took a trip to France. His epiphany came in the Côtes-du-Rhône region over a bottle of Châteauneuf-du-Pape. From that moment on, Jack was a man obsessed with becoming a winemaker.

Jack began reading everything he could find about the subject, and he bought grapes to vinify at home. Soon the couple founded a chapter of Les Amis du Vin in New Jersey, where they were then living, to pursue their hobby with other like-minded individuals. They also started looking for a piece of property where they could raise vines. Eventually they found a 200-year-old former dairy farm in the Hudson River Valley that included a charming stone house, plus an enormous old barn that might be adapted to winemaking. They moved

Fri.–Mon., 11 AM–5 PM or by appointment.
Price Range of Wines: $5.99 for Seyval to $15 for Cabernet Sauvignon. The Strawberry Wine is $8.99.
Special Events: 4th of July Strawberry Wine release party, November Nouveau Party, Christmas party.

to their dream house in Pine Bush in 1982, and planted a vineyard the same year.

For the first two and a half years Jack commuted 150 miles each day to his job in the marketing research division of Hoffmann-LaRoche, a pharmaceutical firm in New Jersey. Like many others who pursue a utopian goal, the Baldwins were not entirely prepared for the staggering amount of work involved in starting a farm, or for the ups and downs of the grape and wine market, or for the sheer exhaustion that went along with it all.

Happily, there were rewards as well. Sales doubled and tripled each year from the Baldwin's first production in 1983 until the stock market crashed in 1987. Today Jack and Pat impress anyone who visits their tasting room as people who are truly happy with the life they've chosen, especially now that their daughter Wendy, and her husband Alex, have joined the business.

Jack makes a variety of wines including a Chardonnay, Riesling, Gewürztraminer, and Pinot Noir. He is particularly proud of his Strawberry Wine, which is popular in Canada and has recently been favorably received in England. For the most part, all the wines produced here are decent *vins du pays* — good regional country wines. Baldwin currently produces about 3,000 cases annually from its 10 acres of vines.

If you plan to picnic under the trees next to the old barn at Baldwin Vineyards, think about bringing some brownies to enjoy with the strawberry wine — chocolate, say the Baldwins, has found its ultimate gastronomic partner with this wine.

BENMARL WINE COMPANY

Rating: 🍷🍷
914-236-4265.
156 Highland Avenue, Marlboro, NY.
Directions: From I-84 take exit 10 north; then take Rte. 9W north for four miles to Conway Road; turn left and then bear right and travel 1 mile to the winery.
Owner: Mark Miller.
Open: Mon.–Fri., 11 AM–5 PM; Sat. and Sun., noon–5 PM.
Price Range of Wines: $6.99 for Seyval and $15 for Estate Red, a combination of Baco

"This is the oldest vineyard in America," states Mark Miller. As he gazes out over the magnificent panorama of mountains and valleys bisected by the mighty Hudson River, he declares that this is also one of the world's most beautiful sights. He ought to know. He's lived in some classically beautiful places, including a chateau in Burgundy.

The son of Oklahoma farmers, Mark Miller followed his own muse to become an artist, first as a Hollywood costume designer, and later, during the 1950s and 1960s as the world's most widely published magazine illustrator. It was during these years, while living in France, that Mark discovered "that the ultimate destiny of a grape is not necessarily grape juice."

When Mark and his wife, the late Dene Miller, moved to the Hudson River property they had pur-

Noir, Chellois, and Maréchal Foch.

Special Features: Picnic area, hiking trails, art gallery.

Special Events: Concerts, art shows focusing on contemporary Hudson Valley painters, picnics, and medieval events.

chased years earlier, his newly developed passion for wine led him to take an interest in the property's historic vineyards. The vineyard had been cultivated successfully for hundreds of years because of its proximity to the Hudson River, which made transportation easier and had a moderating influence on the local microclimate.

With the help of France's famous wine consultant, Emile Peynaud, Mark replanted the vineyard, concentrating principally on hybrids, which he defends staunchly. "We are a hybrid nation. I don't want to spend my life making Chardonnay when the French already do it so well. We must distinguish ourselves with something different." He promotes New York state wines tirelessly, and he was instrumental in the passage of New York's Farm Winery Act. Mark and his architect-wife built the winery compound that is focused on a courtyard inspired by their homes in French chateaux.

"Konstantin Frank and Philip Wagner are the grandfathers of the eastern wine industry," he says. "I am the father." He is also the father of Eric Miller who, after working as winemaker at Benmarl during the 1970s, struck out on his own to found Chaddsford Winery in Pennsylvania. Mark clearly regrets that Eric left Benmarl, but he is also pleased to have passed the torch along to his son. One can only hope that Benmarl soon finds another energetic and talented winemaker, for both the winery and the wines seem a bit tired now.

Most of Benmarl's wine is distributed to members of its private Societé des Vignerons. Wine drinkers who become members of the Societé receive wine every year as part of their membership, a unique system through which members help support the 36-acre vineyard. The winery produces about 6,000 cases of wine a year, including Seyval and an Estate Red.

In addition to the wines, visitors can also enjoy an art gallery, where Mark Miller's delightfully romantic illustrations are displayed, and they can picnic under the pines. There are paths and trails through the estate's 12 acres of woods.

BRIMSTONE HILL VINEYARD

Rating: 🍷

914-744-2231.

49 Brimstone Hill Road, Pine Bush, NY.

Directions: From the New York State Thruway (I-87) take exit 17 in Newburgh and follow Rte. 52 east to Pine Bush; turn right onto New Prospect Rd and follow signs to the winery.

Valerie and Richard Eldridge are Hudson River Valley pioneers, having planted some 20 varieties of French hybrid grapes when they moved here in 1968. In recent years, they added vinifera grapes, speculating that these will do well in their vineyard's heavy, rocky soil. "It's hard soil to plant and cultivate," says Valerie, "but it tends to retain the heat."

The Eldridge's aim is to produce reasonably priced quality table wines with a French character, much like the wines from France's Upper Loire Valley where Valerie was born. The white wines, including Seyval and Chardonnay, tend to have the delicacy

Owners: Valerie and
Richard Eldridge.
Open: May through Oct.,
Thurs.–Mon., 11:30 AM–
5:30 PM; Nov. through
Apr., Sat. and Sun.,
11:30 AM–5:30 PM, or by
appointment.
Price Range of Wines: $6
for still wines to $12 for
sparkling wines.
Special Features: Picnic
area.
Special Events: July Bastille
Day celebration with
fruit, quiche, and
Valerie's homemade
bread, as well as French
art and music.

typical of wine from cool climates, although they
lack the elegance and finesse of good Loire wines.
The reds, including Baco Noir and Vin Rouge, a
blend of various red hybrid grapes, are light, with
pleasant aromas. Brimstone Hill's first Cabernet
Franc looks promising. The vines, according to the
Eldriges, seem to do exceptionally well here.
Brimstone Hill produces a very crisp sparkling wine
called Domaine Bourmont, Valerie's family name.

Dick and Valerie, who are also full-time acade-
mics at local universities, maintain the seven-acre
vineyard, and produce 650–700 cases of wine annually. This is strictly a family operation, and you'll
find them in the tasting room themselves. Picnic
tables are set up under the trees.

BROTHERHOOD WINERY

Rating: 🍷
914-496-9101.
35 North Street,
Washingtonville, NY.
Directions: From the New
York State Thruway
(I-87) take exit 16; then
travel Rte. 17 west to exit
130; take Rte. 208 north
for 7 miles to Rte. 94 east;
turn right and then take
the first left onto North
Street; follow signs to
winery. From I-84 follow
signs to Stewart Airport
on Rte. 207; go 2 miles
and take a left at the sign
onto Toleman Rd.; go 3
miles to winery entrance
on left.
Owners: A partnership.
Open: Daily (except
Christmas and New
Year's Day), 11 AM–5 PM.
Price Range of Wines: $4.99
for Holiday Wine to
$18.39 for Mariage
Reserve, a blend of 75%
Cabernet Sauvignon and
25% Chardonnay.

Brotherhood Winery is the oldest continuously
operating winery in America, founded by John
Jacques, a former New Jersey shoemaker, in 1920.
Shortly after he moved to the area, he decided to
plant a vineyard after noting his neighbors were
receiving high prices for their grapes. Unfortunately, by the time his own vines were mature,
the price of grapes had dropped, so Jacques
decided to go into the wine business. He began his
winery by digging a deep cellar, which today has
been expanded into extensive subterranean aging
vaults. Above the cellar, he built his winery. Today,
this historic building houses a cafe and art gallery.

When Prohibition was forcing most American
wineries to close in 1919, Brotherhood Winery
switched to making sacramental and medicinal
wines. This production was sanctioned by the government, enabling it to ride out the rocky years.

During its long history, Brotherhood has changed
ownership only three times. The most recent purchase, in 1987, included Cesar Baeza among the
partners. A native of Chile, Cesar has a background
in winemaking in France and California.

Brotherhood owns no vineyards. Instead, it purchases its grapes from Hudson Valley growers, as
well as from other nearby places including Long
Island. Altogether, the winery produces 50,000 cases

Special Features:
  Brotherhood Village, a
  complex of shops, an art
  gallery, cafe, wine
  museum; winery tours.
Special Events: Events at
  Brotherhood are frequent
  and diverse. A few
  include line dancing,
  luaus, a July 4th BBQ,
  lobster fests, car shows,
  art shows, Murder
  Mystery Dinners, and a
  September Grape
  Stomping Festival.

of wine ranging from straightforward Chardonnay and Riesling to several unusual wines such as "Burgundy," a blend of two hybrid grapes, Baco Noir and Chellois. There is even a Ginseng wine, sold primarily in Taiwan, and a sweet treat called Holiday Wine, a blend of Concord and Baco Noir seasoned with cinnamon and cloves. It's nice poured over ice cubes or ice cream in the summer, or heated in the winter to create an instant mulled wine.

Although most of the wines are acceptable mass-market beverages, wine is the tail that wags the Brotherhood dog. The real draw for the 10,000 visitors who come here each year, is the Brotherhood Village, a complex of shops, an art gallery, cafe, wine museum, and more. It's a shopper's paradise.

Oh, yes, there are also wine tastings and winery tours. In fact, Brotherhood claims to have invented the concept of winery tours in the 1950s, before California even thought about them.

Bring your own food for a picnic on the deck or under the covered pavilion, or stock up on simple food items at the General Store. Or let someone else take care of the preparations and grab a snack in the cafe.

RIVERVIEW

Rating: 🍷
914-236-1370,
  fax 914-236-1371.
656 Route 9W, Newburgh,
  NY.
Tasting Room: 1338 Route
  9W, Marlboro, NY.
Directions: From I-84 take
  the first exit on the west
  side of the Beacon-
  Newburgh Bridge onto
  Route 9W. The winery is
  eight miles north.
Owners: Tim Biancalana
  and Diane Lagamma, the
  Charbot family.
Open: Sat. & Sun., 10 AM–
  5 PM, or by appointment.
Price Range of Wines: $6
  for Chardonnay to $20
  for Blanc de Blanc, a
  sparkling wine made
  from Chardonnay
  grapes.

The Charbot family has a long history of Champagne making in France. Now Charbot has crossed the ocean to team up with Tim Biancalana who, with his wife, Diane Lagamma, owns the Biancalana & Lagamma Wine Cellars in the Hudson River Valley. Tim, who earned his winemaking degree from the University of California at Davis, moved East in 1980. Less than a decade ago Riverview began producing sparkling wines from Chardonnay and Pinot Noir grapes purchased from other vineyards in New York State. They now produce about 4,000 cases of sparkling wine as well as a Chardonnay and a Pinot Noir. The sparkling wine shows promise of being a top contender for the region, and the other wines are also excellent. The winery is not open to the public, but there's a tasting room in nearby Marlboro. There are no picnic facilities.

ROYAL KEDEM WINERY
Rating: 🍇
Winery
914-236-4281.
1519 Route 9W, Marlboro, NY.
Directions: From I-84, take the first exit on the west side of the Beacon-Newburgh bridge, go north on Rte. 9W for 1¹/₄ miles beyond Marlboro to the winery.
Open: Fri. and Sun., 10 AM–5 PM.
Tasting Room
914-795-2240.
Dock Road, Milton, NY.
Directions: From the Kedem Winery in Marlboro, take 9W north to the 1st traffic light. Turn right into the village, continuing across Main St. to the stop sign; turn right on Dock Rd. and go to the river.
Open: Daily except Sat., 10 AM–5 PM.
Price Range of Wines: $4.99 for extra dry Chablis, and $5.50 for a dryish sparkling wine.
Owners: The Herzog family.
Special Features: Tasting room in old railway station overlooking the Hudson River.
Special Events: Seasonal wine parties, with music and "finger foods."

Eight generations of Herzogs have been making kosher wines since 1848, when they were the sole purveyor to Emperor Franz Josef I of Austria. The Herzog family survived World War II because they were hidden from the Nazis by their own loyal employees, but in 1948 they fled the Communist takeover of Czechoslovakia, settling on New York's lower East Side. The Herzogs did what they knew how to do best in their new country; they made wine. The word "Kedem" comes from a Hebrew expression that means "going forward," which aptly describes the Herzogs.

Eventually, they expanded to New York's Hudson River Valley, where they now produce a staggering amount of kosher wine — a quarter million cases annually, plus another quarter million cases of kosher grape juice, which makes them the world's largest supplier of kosher wines. In addition to the U. S. market, the wines are widely distributed in Europe, Russia, Taiwan, Hong Kong, and Latin America.

Kedem owns merely 20 acres of vineyards, purchasing most of its grapes from other growers. The grapes are vinified at the Marlboro facility, then the wine is shipped to the Herzog's Brooklyn plant for final "polishing," i.e. filtration and bottling. The family also produces a line of premium kosher wines, called Baron Herzog, in California.

Although many excellent, dry kosher wine is produced in the world, including Baron Herzog, people continue to associate kosher with sweet, grapey wines. But, according to the Kedem winery itself, "kosher" simply means that the wine is made "with no additives, preservatives, or artificial color, and with a rabbi on the premises to supervise the process." "*No* preservatives?" I ask. "What about sulfites?" Well, yes, it seems that it's okay to add a minimal amount of sulfites (one tenth of a gram).

The Kedem winery in Marlboro has a small tasting room. A few miles away, in Milton, there is a large Kedem tasting room in an old railroad station at the edge of the Hudson River. Cafe tables are set up in the former waiting room and a variety of kosher snacks are for sale. An enormous number of wines are available to taste, including selections from the firm's wineries in California, Israel, France, and Italy. The New York wines are mostly sweet and strong flavored, although there is an "extra dry Chablis" and a dryish sparkling wine. Visitors might as well try the sweet wines here. That's what the Hudson River winery is all about. Try the Cream White or Red, which show off the essence of Concord grapes. Incidentally, Kedem grape juice is outstanding.

EAST SIDE OF THE HUDSON RIVER

The Winery   by Peter Corbin
1993
Coeur de Lion
New York State Red Wine
PRODUCED AND BOTTLED BY
CASCADE MOUNTAIN VINEYARDS
FLINT HILL ROAD, AMENIA, NEW YORK
ALCOHOL 11.5% BY VOLUME

CASCADE MOUNTAIN WINERY
Rating: 👤👤
914-373-9021.
Flint Hill Road, Amenia, NY.
Directions: From the Taconic Pkwy. take the Millbrook-Poughkeepsie Exit, take Rte. 44 east through Millbrook to Amenia. Turn north onto Rte. 22 and follow signs to the winery.
Owner: William Wetmore.
Open: Daily, 10AM–6 PM.
Price Range of Wines: $7.99 for Harvest Rosé to $14 for Reserve Red, a blend of 75% Cabernet Sauvignon and 25% Baco Noir or Maréchal Foch.
Special Features: Restaurant.
Special Events: Wine dinners.

Novelist William Wetmore left New York City for the serenity of the Hudson Valley. He found a quiet atmosphere in which to write, but then, in 1972, he planted a vineyard. In 1977 a winery followed, and next he opened a restaurant. So much for his peaceful life.

Bill is now talking about turning the reins over to his son, Michael, a New York actor, who is bringing vigor and a fresh outlook to the winery, "We're going for a premium level," acknowledges Michael. "We're appealing to today's more sophisticated palate. Semi-dry wine used to be the way to go, but now people prefer a drier style. The California style has overlapped into the East." Indeed, in the past couple of years, Cascade Mountain wines have greatly improved. If the trend continues, they'll soon appeal to even the most finicky palates.

Cascade has 12 acres of vineyards, high on a hill overlooking fertile farmland. It grows French-American varietals, a term Michael likes better than "hybrids." "The word 'hybrid' is sometimes used by people who work only with vinifera, in a negative marketing way," he explains. Cascade's own grapes are supplemented by fruit purchased from growers in the Hudson Valley and in the Finger Lakes. 5,000-6,000 cases are produced annually. Wines include a Harvest Rosé and a Reserve Red, a very good blend of 75% Cabernet Sauvignon and 25% Baco Noir or Maréchal Foch.

The attractive wooded setting is a fine place for hikes. It would be a nice place to picnic, except that Cascade's own restaurant is so good that I recommend eating there instead.

Profile: Coach Farm and Hollow Road Cheese

The U.S. will never rival France, a country where virtually every community produces its own distinctive cheese. Nevertheless, we have progressed from a nation where cheese was mostly processed in a factory, ready for store shelves in perfect, odorless, tasteless, sandwich-sized slices, individually wrapped in plastic, to one where increasing numbers of entrepreneurs are making flavorful, fresh regional cheeses.

COACH FARM (518-398-5325; 105 Mill Hill Rd, Pine Plains, NY. Open: 3 PM daily to watch the milking.)

Some people plant a vineyard because they want to help preserve agricultural land. Miles and Lillian Cahn were concerned about saving the rural character of the 300-acre farm they purchased in the Hudson Valley, but instead of planting a vineyard, they started a goat farm. At first, the Cahns continued to run their successful leather company, Coach Leatherworks, while they commuted back and forth from Manhattan. When they sold the leather business to the Sara Lee Corporation, however, they turned to raising goats and producing cheese full-time.

A French cheesemaker was brought in as consultant, teaching the staff at Coach Farm how to pasteurize the fresh goat milk, how to add a culture and enzymes to cause the milk to curdle, and then how to mold the fresh goat curd into rounds and pyramids, logs and loaves, and the tiny, delectable lumps called "buttons." The farm now has 900 goats and produces over 4,000 pounds of goat cheese a week, ranging in style from soft and fresh to dry and aged. It's all delicious and an excellent accompaniment to wine.

HOLLOW ROAD FARMS (518-758-7214; fax 518-758-1899; RR 1, Box 93, Stuyvesant, NY. Not open to the public.)

One of the pioneers in the fledgling American farm cheese revolution is Joan Snyder, whose Hollow Road Farms brings joy to epicures. Hollow Road cheese is made from sheep's milk or, to be specific, from ewe's milk. While sheep dairying has been in existence for centuries in Europe, it is a relatively new form of agriculture in America.

Fresh sheep's milk cheese is similar to cheese made from goat's milk. "Like chevre, but from fuzzier animals," says Joan Snyder. In French, it's called *brebis*. It is soft, spreadable, and with only 45 calories and 3 grams of fat per ounce, com-

→

pares favorably with cream cheese, which has 120 calories. Actually, the amount of fat in a cheese depends on the type of cheese made rather than on the kind of milk used to make it: fresh cheese, whether from goat, sheep, or cow's milk, will always be lower in calories than aged cheese.

The farm consists of about 200 acres, on which pesticides and chemical fertilizers have never been used. None of the animals at the farm are treated with antibiotics on a routine basis, and homeopathic remedies are always the first path of treatment if an animal becomes sick. The philosophy is that naturally-raised, humanely-treated animals yield a higher quality cheese.

Hollow Road produces about 12,000 pounds of pure white, clean-tasting cheese a year. It comes in fresh logs, fresh cheese for spreads or for cooking, aged logs,and aged *tommes*, as well as ricotta and a camembert-type cheese. The cheese is served in many restaurants, including the one at Cascade, and it may be purchased at specialty stores nationwide.

CLINTON VINEYARDS
Rating: 🌲🌲
914-266-5372.
Schultzville Road, Clinton Corners, NY.
Directions: From the Taconic Pky. take the Salt Point Turnpike exit. Turn right and go straight through Clinton Corners. Take a sharp left onto Schultzville Rd. at the 10 mph sign and proceed to the winery.
Owner: Ben Feder.
Open: Daily, 10 AM–5 PM, or by appointment.
Price Range of Wines: $8.50 for Seyval, $15.50 for sparkling wine, $15 for Riesling.
Special Features: Picnic area, walking trails on 80-acre estate.
Special Events: Press release party, summer picnics, a harvest party.

Like several other eastern vintners, Ben Feder, formerly a New York City graphic designer, went into the cattle business before turning to grapes. When he did succumb to the lure of Bacchus, Ben decided to plant only Seyval grapes. Recently, however, he added one acre of Riesling to his 15 acres of Seyval, but since the Riesling appears to be too temperamental for his site, it's doubtful he'll expand the plantings.

Clinton Vineyards produces 1,800 cases of crisp, fruity Seyval Blanc annually, which is vaguely reminiscent of Sancerre and Muscadet from France's Loire Valley. He also makes a small amount — 100 cases — of sparkling wine, with a clean, fruity flavor, as well as a small amount of Riesling (from zero to 40 cases, depending on the vintage).

In addition to picnicking at the winery, visitors can enjoy walking trails on the 80-acre estate.

MILLBROOK VINEYARDS & WINERY
Rating: 🌲🌲🌲🌲
914-677-8383 or 800-662-9453.

One of the best and most innovative wineries in the East, Millbrook was the first vineyard in the Hudson River region to concentrate exclusively on vinifera grapes. The concept for Millbrook Vineyards began in 1976, when John Dyson, then

John Dyson, Millbrook Vineyards and Winery, Millbrook, New York.

Courtesy Millbrook Winery

Wing Road, Millbrook, NY.
Directions: From the
Taconic Parkway, take
the Millbrook exit to Rte.
44. Take Rte. 44 east to
Rte. 82 north, go three
miles to Shunpike Rd.
(Rte. 57); turn right, go
three miles to Wing Rd.,
turn left to the winery.
Owner: John Dyson.
Open: Daily, noon–5 PM.
Price Range of Wines: $7
for Pinot Noir, $16 for
Reserve Chardonnay, $17
for Reserve Cabernet
Sauvignon.
Special Features: Picnic
area.
Special Events: Annual
Harvest Party on
Columbus Day weekend.

New York State Commissioner of Agriculture, met Dr. Konstantin Frank, the Russian-born winemaker who operated Vinifera Wine Cellars in the Finger Lakes. Frank's success with European vinifera vines greatly impressed John Dyson, who reasoned that the same grapes might also do well in the Hudson Valley, where he owned a farm. He planted an experimental acre and found that his Chardonnay, Cabernet Sauvignon, and Pinot Noir did perform remarkably well.

Armed with the success of this experiment, plus the knowledge that vinifera grapes offer considerably higher gross returns than other crops, John bought an old dairy farm in 1979, where he planted 50 acres of vines. (John firmly believes that vineyards can help save family farming in the East.) He converted the dairy barn into a state-of-the-art winery. Next, he invented and patented a new trellising system, and then he hired John Graziano, a talented graduate of Cornell University, as his winemaker.

God may have rested after creating the world, but John Dyson just keeps going. In 1989, he purchased two top-quality vineyards in California's Central Coast region, where he grows grapes for important California wineries such as Glen Ellen, Robert Mondavi, and Joseph Phelps. As neither of these vineyards has winemaking facilities, John began shipping grapes from his California properties to Millbrook to be made into wine, which he markets under the "Mistral" label.

Millbrook's outstanding wines include Sangiovese, Merlot, and Cabernet

Franc, as well as Pinot Noir, Reserve Chardonnay, and Reserve Cabernet Sauvignon. Picnic tables overlook the scenic ponds that John created to provide a modifying influence on the climate.

RESTAURANTS AND LODGING

West Side of the Hudson River

RESTAURANTS AND LODGING

DEPUY CANAL HOUSE
914-687-7700.
Rte. 213, High Falls, NY.
Price: Moderate.

History permeates every creaky floorboard, hand-hewn beam, and paneled fireplace of this former locktender's cottage with its charming little rambling rooms. The quaint stone house was built in 1797 to watch over Lock 16 of the Delaware and Hudson Canal, but it's been the acclaimed restaurant of Chef John Novi since 1969. His cuisine is contemporary American with French and Oriental influences. Ask to eat at the table in the kitchen to watch the pro at work. Several local wines are featured on the wine list. Across the street the Locktender's Cottage has one suite and three rooms.

MOHONK MOUNTAIN HOUSE
914-255-1000.
Lake Mohonk, New Paltz, NY.
Price: Moderate.

Mohonk Mountain House is one-of-a-kind. This Victorian wood and stone castle, overlooking beautiful Lake Mohonk with the majestic Catskill Mountains in the background, sits atop a ridge of the Shawangunk Mountains. There are 283 rooms, 151 working fireplaces, 200 balconies, and Victorian antiques in every room, including the numerous common rooms. Outdoors on the 7,500 acres there are formal gardens blazing with color in summer, more than 100 gazebos situated in picturesque sites, and enough outdoor activities to bring everyone to the dining room with jumbo appetites. There's hearty American food on the menu plus a wine list that includes Hudson River Valley wines.

RESTAURANT

MAGNANINI WINERY RESTAURANT
914-895-2767.
172 Bordens Road, Wallkill, NY.
Price: Moderate.

The Magnanini family were winemakers in the Emilia-Romagna region of northern Italy for many generations. Today the tradition is being continued in the Hudson River Valley of New York. French-American hybrid grapes are cultivated and made into wine that is sold at the winery and served in the Magnanini's restaurant. Local winemakers love this lively place that specializes in northern Italian cuisine served family-style. "It's like going to a big Italian wedding," says one of the vintners. "Eating there is like being part of a big, happy Italian family," enthuses another. All the food at Magnanini's Restaurant, including the pasta, is homemade. And, of course, so is the wine.

East Side of the Hudson River

RESTAURANTS AND LODGING

OLD DROVERS INN
914-832-9311;
   fax 914-832-6356.
Old Rte. 22, Dover Plains,
   NY.
Price: Expensive.

The dining room of this historic 1750 tavern is divided by a mammoth stone fireplace. Low, hand-hewn beams, tapered candles in etched hurricanes, and intimate little corners, make this one of the most romantic dining rooms in the Northeast. Specialties include a hearty cheddar cheese soup and double thick lamb chops with the house tomato chutney. Local wines are on the list. Upstairs, four charming rooms (three with fireplaces) ensure a cozy night's sleep.

BEEKMAN ARMS
914-876-7077.
Rte. 9, Rhinebeck, NY.
Price: Moderate–Expensive.

This hostelry claims to be the oldest continuously operating inn in America, although several others dispute the fact. Nevertheless, the sleeping rooms in the historic old inn have recently been refurbished and the Delamater House, a restored 1844 American Gothic mansion just down the street, offers excellent, antique-filled rooms. Additional accommodations in the complex include those clustered around a conference center, a little group of motel rooms, and accommodations in several additional village buildings. The dining room is managed by Larry Forgione, who also owns Manhattan's An American Place. The food is outstanding, and the extensive and well-chosen wine list includes local wines.

RESTAURANT

**CASCADE MOUNTAIN
   RESTAURANT**
914-373-9021.
Flint Hill Road, Amenia,
   NY.
Open: Apr. through Dec.
   lunch daily noon–3 PM;
   dinner Sat. only;
   restaurant closed Jan.
   through Mar.

In cool weather, it's a cozy place warmed by a wood burning stove. In summer, the restaurant is cool and soothing, both indoors and outside on the shady porch. Any time of year, the simple but well prepared food is welcome and satisfying. Appetizers include homemade pâté, or potato pancakes with smoked salmon, which is just right with an accompanying glass of Cascade Seyval Blanc.

Main course selections might include grilled breast of chicken filled with goat cheese, or chicken salad with maple mustard dressing. The fruit and cheese plate, which includes selections from the local Hollow Road and Coach Cheese Farms, makes a very satisfying light lunch. What kind of wine is best with goat or sheep's cheese? Some people prefer a fruity white, others insist on red. Order a glass of Cascade's Private Reserve White and one of Coeur de Lion, a light-bodied red, and decide for yourself.

THE FINGER LAKES

Most of the wineries in upstate New York are clustered around three of the Finger Lakes. Cayuga is the longest of the lakes. Keuka, the most scenic, is known as "the jewel of the Finger Lakes" because its waters are unusually clear and clean. Seneca is the deepest. Wineries line both shores of Seneca in such profusion that it's easy to visit several of them in a single day.

A pleasant way to break up a day of wine tasting is to stop to eat at one of the vineyard picnic sites overlooking a lake. Several wineries in the Finger Lakes also have restaurants with splendid views and local wines.

The whole region is one of spectacular scenic beauty, where vine-covered hills roll down to the edge of the lakes. Hundreds of examples of the Greek Revival architecture that once dominated the Finger Lakes region remain. Many of them are open to visitors, including Rose Hill Mansion, one of the most beautiful Greek Revival houses in America (Rte. 9A, Fayette, NY).

Originally, the Finger Lakes region was home to the Seneca and Cayuga Indians of the Six Nations, whose lands were devastated by the Clinton-Sullivan military expedition of 1779. The area opened up for settlement after the American Revolution. When Cayuga and Seneca Lakes were linked by the Erie Canal in 1830, the population grew and industry flourished.

History has played its role here as well. It's known as the birthplace of women's rights, as the first Women's Rights Convention was held in Seneca Falls in 1848. Locals claim it's also the birthplace of American aviation because Glenn Curtiss pioneered the first flying airplanes here in 1908. It is also the birthplace of the wine industry in the eastern United States.

The Finger Lakes are blessed with soil that is a good host for grapes and with a climate moderated by the lakes themselves. It has another advantage as well. "One of our great secret weapons is Indian summer," says Willy Frank, describing the exceptional warm period that arrives in late fall to extend the growing season. Because of these advantageous conditions, the Finger Lakes region has produced strong-flavored, sweet wines made from native American labrusca grapes such as Niagara and Catawba for generations. As it was universally believed that Chardonnay, Riesling, and other European vinifera grapes could not survive New York's freezing winter climate, native labrusca was what everyone focused on.

The first vintner to challenge the labrusca tradition was Charles Fournier who, at the end of Prohibition, came from the French Champagne firm of Veuve-Cliquot to work at the Urbana Wine Company, later known as the Gold Seal Wine Company. Fournier began experimenting with the hybrid grapes that had been developed in France to withstand phylloxera and other vine diseases. As a result of his work, other vintners began focusing on hybrids. Fournier's most lasting contribution, however, was the trust he put in Dr. Konstantin Frank, the Russian emigré whom he hired in 1953 to help plant vinifera grapes at Gold Seal.

Konstantin Frank had managed vineyards in the Ukraine, where it was not unusual for winter temperatures to drop to 20 or 30 degrees below zero; if vinifera grapes could survive those temperatures, Frank reasoned, there was no reason for them not to do well here. First at Gold Seal, and later at his own winery at Keuka Lake, Frank proved that vinifera vines could be grown in upstate New York. Frank's influence on the entire eastern wine industry is inestimable. He inspired, encouraged, and educated leading trailblazers Philip Wagner (Maryland's Boordy Vineyards), Louisa and Alex Hargrave (Hargrave Vineyard on Long Island), and John Dyson (Millbrook Winery in the Hudson Valley), among many others.

The next important pioneering European immigrant was German-born Hermann J. Wiemer, who arrived in the Finger Lakes in 1968. He first made wine from hybrid grapes at Bully Hill Vineyards, but switched to vinifera when he acquired his own vineyard and winery in 1979. He established one of the nation's largest grape nurseries. Now, in addition to producing some of the region's most successful wines, Wiemer provides rootstock not just to the Finger Lakes, but to vineyards all over the country, including California.

Many of today's leading vintners are descended from growers who began raising labrusca grapes for the Taylor Wine Company, and who then replanted with hybrids to keep pace with demand. For years, the powerful Taylor Wine Company was the major player in the eastern wine business, and most Finger Lakes viticulturists sold their grapes to this giant. When Taylor was taken over by Coca-Cola, many growers resisted becoming a link in the impersonal and exploitative chain of corporate farming. By contrast, the family-run Taylor Company was widely perceived as being benevolent and fair.

By the early 1980s, tastes in New York State, as elsewhere, had shifted from sweet wines towards drier, European-style wines, with an analogous decline in the labrusca and hybrid grape industry. Some growers, who have not made the switch, have not been able to stay afloat economically. "One of the unspoken reasons why hybrid wines are still around is that the grapes are a cinch to grow," one vintner told me. "Vinifera is definitely harder work, and a lot of growers just don't want to make the extra effort."

Today, a new generation of talented winemakers and well-informed wine drinkers, is working in the Finger Lakes. Growers have decided to take control of their own destiny by founding wineries themselves. As a result, the Finger Lakes is unique among eastern wine regions in that, rather than being dominated by wealthy "outsiders," its upcoming stars are vintners who know the land intimately from working it for generations. They have experienced all the ups and downs of the region's winemaking history, and they are determined to make the kind of serious wines that will garner world recognition.

The strength of the Finger Lakes region rests in the type of wines that are characteristic of cool weather regions, notably Riesling, Pinot Noir, Chardonnay, and Champagne-style sparkling wine. Other currently popular varietals such as Merlot are also doing well here, but they may be a greater challenge than in places such as Long Island, where the growing season is longer and the extremes of temperature not as great.

Profile: Riesling

Of the many vinifera grape varieties thriving in the Finger Lakes region today, Riesling stands out as the brightest star in the firmament. For a variety of reasons, Riesling is a misunderstood and underappreciated wine in this country. Part of this has to do with a misunderstanding that all Riesling is sweet. Indeed, a lot of Riesling *is* sweet, ranging in style from spineless schlock to some of the greatest dessert wines in the world, such as Germany's Trockenbeerenauslese. But the trend worldwide — Riesling is grown in virtually every wine-producing country in the world — is toward a drier wine, a wine that is adaptable to a variety of foods.

The Riesling grape is believed to have originated in Germany, where it was probably cultivated by the Romans. Many connoisseurs consider it to be the noblest of all wines. Today, Germany, Austria, and Alsace produce the ultimate Rieslings, recognized throughout the world as unrivaled in style and taste. But in the last few years a handful of eastern vintners, particularly in the Finger Lakes region, have begun to produce Rieslings that may soon take their place beside the great European Rieslings.

One of the charms of an excellent Riesling is its beguiling aroma which, in youth, is fresh and floral, and becomes more subtle and intriguing with maturity. As it ages, it may even develop a gasolinelike bouquet known as "petrol," one whiff of which is enough to quicken the pulse of any true devotee of Riesling.

Riesling's character depends, more than most other grapes, on *terroir*, or the site on which it is grown. Mediocre Riesling can vary from watery and insipid

→

versions to those that are cloyingly sweet. Fine Riesling, on the other hand, will range from the light and delicate elegance found in Rieslings from Germany's Moselle region, to a full, vivacious elixir, such as that from the Rheingau region. In the mouth, all fine Rieslings, whether dry or sweet, show a notable streak of acidity backed up by a suggestion of honey, flower blossoms, or fruit concentrate.

One of Riesling's many attributes is its ability to age well. Unfortunately, today most top-grade Riesling is consumed in its infancy, before it has the chance to develop the full charm and multi-faceted personality of an adult wine.

Riesling is one of the best wines to drink with food. "A dry Riesling is the most versatile wine you have in the house," declares Vinifera Wine Cellars' Willy Frank. Dry Rieslings are an excellent match for grilled food, for most poultry, for sausage and other pork dishes, and for such classic dishes as *choucroute* (sauerkraut). Slightly less dry Rieslings are excellent accompaniments for spicy Cajun, Mexican, and Thai cuisine. When it carries a hint of sweetness, Riesling is a far more satisfying aperitif than most bone dry wines — "Better than a dry martini," claims Willy Frank — and late-harvested or other dessert-style Rieslings are uniquely satisfying at the end of a meal.

There is nothing mysterious about the promise of eastern Riesling. Despite its small, tightly-clustered berries that are vulnerable to injury and disease, Riesling also has thick bark and a habit of budding late that enables the plant to resist freezes. Riesling grapes depend on cool nights to develop a bracing thread of acidity, and warm days for their characteristic honeyed sweetness. They do particularly well when the growing season is long enough for flavors to develop slowly. If the weather is too warm, as in many parts of California, the grapes ripen before the full balance of fruitiness, acidity, and finesse are complete. "Our Riesling has wonderful acidity," exclaims Willy Frank. "In California they have to add acidity to make a palatable wine." On the other hand, when Riesling is grown in a climate that is too cool, the grapes don't ripen completely and lack sufficient alcohol to produce a harmonious wine.

Also favoring Finger Lakes Riesling are substances called monoterpenes. These various compounds, which are responsible for the perfume of certain aromatic grapes such as Riesling and Gewürztraminer, are particularly prevalent in this region's grapes.

Finger Lakes vintner Scott Osborne says, "We can get the acids we need here to balance the sugars. That's what makes Riesling great. The fact that we can get up to 12% alcohol adds to the overall balance."

"The Finger Lakes is Riesling country," adds Willy Frank. "We produce some of the most delicate and elegant Rieslings in the world." Fox Run's winemaker, Peter Bell, concurs. "We can make Rieslings that can exceed anyone else's."

Most winemakers in the Finger Lakes agree with these sentiments. So, increasingly, do consumers.

SENECA LAKE

ANTHONY ROAD WINE COMPANY

Rating: 🍷🍷
315-536-2182.
1225 Anthony Road, Penn Yan, NY.
Directions: From I-90 take exit 42 to Rte. 14 south, turn west on Anthony Rd. to the winery.
Owners: John and Ann Martini and Derek Wilber.
Open: Apr. through Dec., Mon.–Sat., 10 AM–5 PM, Sun. noon–5 PM; Jan. through Mar., Sat. 10 AM–5 PM, Sun. noon–5 PM.
Price Range of Wines: $5.98 for Poulet Rouge, $6.49 for Vignoles, $7.99 for Vintners Select, $8.99 for Chardonnay.
Special Features: Picnic area.

John and Ann Martini bought their farm on Seneca Lake in 1973. They planted grapes and sold them to other wineries. John, meanwhile, continued working as the Field Research Coordinator at the New York Agricultural Station. In 1989, the Martinis joined forces with winemaker Derek Wilber, a Cornell University graduate in Pomology (the science of fruits), and founded Anthony Road Wine Company.

Derek, who was born in Penn Yan, has been around vines most of his life. His father managed Windy Heights, a 200-acre vineyard that grew grapes that were sold to the Taylor Wine Company. When Coca-Cola bought Taylor, Windy Heights and many other local vineyards were forced out of business. Derek tried to wean himself away from the wine business by studying oceanography in Florida, but he finally succumbed to Bacchus' lure. He returned to his origins, to work as a winemaker for various wineries.

Derek found his niche at Anthony Road, an unpretentious winery that overlooks the 25-acre vineyard. This is a family-run winery. One afternoon when I was visiting, John was pouring wine in the crowded tasting room. Derek was in the back pasting labels on bottles. "Why does he have to do that on a Sunday afternoon?" I asked John. "Because we sold so much wine yesterday we ran out of labeled bottles. That's good, of course," he hastened to add. "After all, selling wine is our goal." Then he looked up and grinned. "Well, that and having fun." He went back to pouring wine. Derek continued pasting labels on bottles of wine. They both looked as if they were, indeed, having fun.

The winery produces 4,500 cases of wine annually. Anthony Road's wines include Vintners Select, a spicy blend of Seyval, Riesling, Vignoles, and Cayuga; a crisp and refreshing Chardonnay; Vignoles, a rich, well-balanced dessert wine that is great with cheese and fruit; and Poulet Rouge ("It flies out the door," explained John, "and besides, it's good with chicken"), a semi-dry red.

Bring along some cold chicken and enjoy it with a bottle of Poulet Rouge at the picnic table on the concrete pad right outside the winery where the grapes are crushed.

ARCADIAN ESTATE VINEYARDS

Rating: 🍴
607-535-2068 or
800-298-1346 (NYS only).
4184 Route 14, Rock
   Stream, NY.
Directions: From NY Rte.
   17 take exit 32 to Rte. 14.
   Travel north for 16 miles
   to Watkins Glen. The
   winery is four miles
   north of Watkins Glen.
Owners: Mike Hastrich and
   Charlie Langendorfer
Open: Apr. through Dec.,
   Mon.–Sat., 10 AM–5 PM,
   Sun. noon–6 PM; Jan.
   through Mar., Fri. & Sat.,
   10 AM–5 PM, Sun. noon–
   6 PM.
Price Range of Wines: $6
   for Dechaunac to $10
   for Pinot Noir or
   Chardonnay.
Special Features: Deck for
   picnics.
Special Events: Equinox
   Celebration, Cinco de
   Mayo Celebration, Folk
   & Blues Music Event,
   Midsummer's Play, Clam
   Bake, Chocolate and
   Wine Pairing, Halloween
   Vineyard Walk, Venison
   and Wine Pairing, St.
   Nicholas Event, and
   much more.

Arcadian, formerly the Giasi Winery, released its first vintage in 1979. It has been owned by Mike Hastrich and winemaker Charlie Langendorfer since 1991. Mike and Charlie are determined to build their reputation on red wines, although it's still too early to predict the outcome. They grow grapes on two plots of land totalling about 110 acres.

The tasting room, located in a refurbished 170-year-old barn, was warm and cozy on the gray, stormy day I visited. It was the perfect setting for the stories Mike told about the resident ghost, a Civil War soldier who, it seems, hangs around the winery pining for his lost love.

The current production of the winery is at 3,000 cases. There's a deck for picnics in nice weather. Buy a bottle of Arcadia's Dechaunac, or the nice Pinot Noir or Chardonnay, for a picnic if the weather's nice. And if a shadowy figure in a gray uniform flits by, you might offer him a glass of wine too.

CASTEL GRISCH ESTATE WINERY

Rating: 🍴
607-535-9614.
3380 County Road 28,
   Watkins Glen, NY.
Directions: From NY Rte.
   17 take exit 32 to Rte. 14
   north. From Watkins
   Glen, follow Rte. 414 (4th
   St.) west to Rte. 28. Turn
   right to the winery.
Owners: Tom and Barbara
   Malina.

Castel Grisch was founded in 1982 by a chemist named Alois Baggenstoss, and his wife Michelle. The Baggenstosses, who had been searching for a spot that reminded them of their native Switzerland, felt they had arrived home when they saw this site looming high above the lake. They planted vines and produced their first vintage in 1984. They also built a chalet-style winery and opened a restaurant on the spot.

In 1992, Tom and Barbara Malina bought Castel Grisch. Tom, who had previously been a regional sales manager with Banfi Vintners, a Long Island-

The main house at Castel Grisch, Watkins Glenn, New York.

Marguerite Thomas

Open: Apr. through Dec., daily, 10 AM–10 PM, Jan. through Mar. call for hours.
Price Range of Wines: $6.99 for Cayuga to 11.99 for Gewürztraminer.
Special Events: Oktoberfest, including hay rides and live music.

based wine importer, is delighted to be living in such spectacular surroundings. The couple enjoy overseeing the restaurant, winery, and the 135-acre estate, of which 20 acres are planted in vines. The Malinas have also converted the manor house, where the Baggenstoss's lived, into a bed and breakfast.

While the Malina's imprint on the wines is only beginning, the future looks good. At present, 4,000 cases of wine are produced annually, including oak-aged Chardonnay and Baco Noir that is aged in Hungarian oak. They also make Cayuga and Gewürztraminer.

CHATEAU LaFAYETTE RENEAU

Rating: 🍷🍷🍷
607-546-2062.
Route 414, Hector, NY.
Directions: From NY Rte. 17 take exit 32 to Rte. 14 north. In Watkins Glen take Rte. 414 north. The winery is 7.4 miles NE of Watkins Glen.
Owners: Dick and Betty Reno.
Open: Mar. through Oct., Mon.–Sat., 10 AM–6 PM, Sun. noon–6 PM; Nov. & Dec., Sat. noon–5 PM, Sun. noon–4 PM; Jan. & Feb. by appointment.

One of the hazards of visiting the Finger Lakes region is that people are sometimes so charmed that they end up buying a vineyard here. That's what happened to Dick and Betty Reno a few years ago. They purchased their lakeside parcel in 1985, and commuted to the site on weekends, while they replanted the old vineyard and rebuilt the winery.

The Reno's hired winemaker David Whiting, whose stylish, well-crafted wines have helped place Chateau LaFayette Reneau near the top of the region's quality producers. David has since gone to Swedish Hill Vineyard, but Chateau LaFayette Reneau continues to win awards and has become particularly well-known for its red wines.

The winery maintains 38 acres of vines, from

Price Range of Wines: $6.49 for Cuvée Blanc to $20 for Pinot Noir.
Special Features: Picnic area.
Special Events: Hayrides through the vineyards, barbecues, and a fall pick-your-own-grapes event.

which the Renos produce about 9,000 cases annually. Among their offerings are a Cuvée Blanc, a blend of Riesling and Seyval, and a Pinot Noir. Picnic tables on the terrace afford a beautiful view of the lake.

Scott Osborne, co-owner, and Peter Bell, winemaker, of Fox Run Vineyards, Pen Yann, New York.

Courtesy Fox Run Vineyards

FOX RUN VINEYARDS
Rating: 👤👤👤
315-536-4616.
670 Route 14, Penn Yan, NY.
Directions: From I-90 take exit 42 to Rte. 14 south. The winery is on Rte. 14 between Geneva and Dresden.
Owners: Scott Osborne and Andy Hale.
Open: Mon.–Sat., 10 AM–6 PM; Sun. 11 AM–6 PM.
Price Range of Wines: $4.99 for Arctic Fox, $7.99 for Riesling, $13.99 for Blanc de Blanc, and $14.99 for Pinot Noir.
Special Features: Picnic area.

My biggest problem is how to expand while keeping the quaint, small-winery feeling of the place," muses Fox Run Vineyard owner, Scott Osborne. He and his partner Andy Hale, bought the winery from Larry and Adele Wildrick in 1993. The "feeling of the place" is indeed appealing. The winery is housed in a converted 1867 barn that's attached to a contemporary tasting room.

Scott's career began as a real estate salesman in northern California. "When interest rates went up to 22%, I looked around for something else. *Anything* else. I got a job in a winery and that was the beginning." Over the course of several decades, Scott never looked back. He has progressed from that first menial job on a bottling line to owning and managing his own winery.

Scott is soft spoken and modest. He is also hard working, smart, and ambitious, and he's recognized as a leader who is working to propel the Finger Lakes into the national spotlight as a premium wine-producing region. He has absolute confidence in his cause.

Shortly after purchasing Fox Run, Scott hired Peter Bell, a talented Canadian winemaker with a degree in enology from Australia. Peter is a firm believer in the influence of climate and soil on Finger Lakes wine. "For example, wine made from Riesling grapes grown on Keuka Lake tastes different than wine made from grapes grown on Seneca Lake. Both are excellent; they're just different," he says. "Both are aromatic and steely, but those from Seneca have more apricot and tropical fruit flavor elements. The wines from Keuka have more apple blossom, lime peel, and slate. I have really gotten into Riesling since I came here," Peter adds, with a small grin of apology for his enthusiasm.

He is scarcely less excited about the potential of Fox Run's Pinot Noir, even though he describes this grape as his "biggest challenge." Nevertheless, Peter is convinced that, in the long run, Pinot Noir will be one of his signature wines. "We're in this for the long haul," he insists. In addition to Riesling and Pinot Noir, the winery makes Arctic Fox, a light, off-dry Chardonnay-based wine with the aroma of a juicy melon; Blanc de Blanc, an excellent, crisp sparkling wine; a flavorful Merlot; and the Pinot Noir, which has a distinct cherry aroma.

A bottle of Fox Run wine would be a terrific addition to a picnic on the winery's deck. The pretty setting includes a sweep of vines down the hill behind the building and a view of the lake stretching out in front.

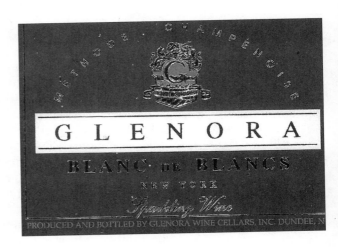

**GLENORA WINE
CELLARS**
Rating: 🍷🍷🍷
607-243-5511 or
800-243-5513;
fax 607-243-5514.

Surrounded by vineyards sweeping down to the lake, Glenora Wine Cellars has one of the best views in the region. The winery was founded in 1976, right after the passage of the New York Farm Winery Act.

5435 Route 14, Dundee, NY.
Directions: From I-90 take
exit 42 to Rte. 14 south.
The winery is west of
Dundee.
Owners: Gene Pierce, John
Potter, and Ed
Dalrymple.
Open: Jul. & Aug., daily,
10 AM–8 PM; Sept.
through Oct., daily, 10
AM–6 PM; Nov. through
Apr., Mon.–Sat., 10 AM–
5 PM, Sun. noon–5 PM;
May & June, daily,
10 AM–6 PM.
Price Range of Wines:
$12.99 for Brut, $14.99 for
Blanc de Blancs, to $19.99
for Brut Rosé.
Special Features: Cafe.
Special Events: Summer
Jazz Concert Series,
Leaves and Lobsters (an
autumn harvest festival),
Down East Lobster Bake
(includes live jazz).

HAZLITT VINEYARDS
Rating: 🍷
607-546-5812.
Route 414, Hector, NY.
Directions: From NY Rte.
17 take exit 32 to Rte. 14
north. In Watkins Glen
take Rte. 414 north. The
winery is north of
Hector.
Owners: The Hazlitt family.
Open: May through Nov.,
Mon.–Sat., 10 AM–5 PM,
Sun. noon–5 PM; Dec.
through Apr., daily,
noon–5 PM.
Price Range of Wines: $6
for Cayuga White and
White Stag to $8.75 for
Riesling and $9.75 for
Chardonnay.
Special Features: Schooner
for charter on Lake
Seneca.

The owners were quick to recognize that the climate and soil of the region were ideal for Chardonnay and Pinot Noir, the classic Champagne grapes. Glenora has carved out a distinctive niche for itself by focusing on sparkling wine made from the same grapes and produced in the same manner as classic French Champagne. Although the winery owns 15 acres of vines, most of its grapes are purchased from local growers, and a small percentage (especially the red wine grapes) come from Long Island.

The winery averages 30,000 cases of wine a year. Among the very fine sparkling wines produced at Glenora are a Brut, made from a blend of Pinot Noir, Pinot Blanc, and Chardonnay; a creamy Blanc de Blancs, made with Chardonnay and Pinot Blanc; and an elegant Brut Rosé. Glenora also makes a semi-dry sparkler that would be a good match for a wedding cake, as well as several non-sparkling wines, including classic Chardonnay and Riesling.

Visitors can enjoy a light snack or meal in Glenora's Wine Garden Cafe.

The Hazlitt family has been growing grapes in this region since 1852, which makes theirs one of the oldest vineyards still held by its original family. Elaine and Jerry Hazlitt opened a winery in 1985 when the grape market declined. "But making wine was nothing new to us," says Elaine. "We'd always made our own wine at home."

They started with 1,500 cases, but the Hazlitt production has grown every year. Today, they produce 12,000 cases, and son Doug Hazlitt is the winemaker.

The Hazlitt family presents a classic example of how tastes in wine are changing. "We like the older-style sweeter wines," says Elaine. "Our sons and daughters, however, prefer the dry, red table wines." The 45-acre Hazlitt Vineyard reflects this shift in taste. They previously grew primarily Cayuga and Catawba grapes but recently they planted Merlot, Cabernet, and Gewürztraminer.

The Hazlitt tasting room is located in a barn that resembles a hunting lodge, with animal and fish trophies decorating the walls. Their wines include Chardonnay and Riesling, as well as Cayuga White and White Stag. The latter is a blend of Aurora, Cayuga, and Vidal. Schooner White, a Chardonnay, Riesling, and Seyval blend, is a reminder that Doug Hazlitt is also the Captain of Chantey, a Seneca Lake schooner that is available for charter. Hazlitt reds include Cabernet, Merlot, and Pinot Noir, as well as Red Cat, a blend of Catawba and Baco Noir. According to the Hazlitts, Red Cat inspires hot tubs in the moonlight. If it's daylight when you're visiting, you might have to settle for something more modest, such as a cruise on Chantey, or even a simple picnic at the winery.

Three members of the Stamp family at Lakewood Vineyards, near Watkins Glenn, New York.

Marguerite Thomas

LAKEWOOD VINEYARDS
Rating: 🍷
607-535-9252.
4024 Route 14, Watkins Glen, NY.
Directions: From I-90 take exit 42 to Rte. 14 south. Winery is between Dundee and Watkins Glen.
Owners: The Stamp family.
Open: May through Dec., Mon–Sat., 10 AM–5:30 PM, Sun. noon–6 PM; Jan. through Apr., Fri. & Sat. 10 AM–5:30 PM, Sun. noon–5 PM, weekdays by appointment.
Price Range of Wines: $4.99 for Delaware, Niagara, and White Catawba,

Lakewood is a family-operated winery, and it's family-friendly as well. On any given day you might find a young mother — perhaps Liz Stamp — standing behind the tasting bar pouring wine with one hand and holding a baby with the other. Visitors bring their kids, who dive happily into the toys piled on the floor while their parents taste wine.

Four generations of the Stamp family have farmed the sloping hillside vineyards at Lakewood. Monty and Beverly Stamp now run the place. Their son, David, manages the vineyards, and Christopher, the oldest son, is the winemaker. Christopher graduated from Cornell with a degree in Food Sciences, and trained at Glenora Wine Cellars and at Cayuga Ridge.

Lakewood produces several American native labrusca wines such as Delaware, Niagara, and

$5.99 for Long Stem Red, $7.99 for Chardonnay.
Special Features: Children's indoor play area, swings outdoors, picnic area.
Special Events: Steak and wine dinners, other food and wine pairings.

White Catawba. They make them because, "a lot of people don't sell this anymore," says Beverly, explaining that many customers request it. The winery's Chardonnay spends only a brief time in American oak barrels before it's transferred back to stainless steel tanks, "so you don't get splinters in your tongue," jokes Beverly. Long Stem Red is a dry blend of the hybrids Baco Noir and Leon Millot.

The whole family will enjoy a picnic here, and the kids can play on the swings if they get bored.

Lamoreaux Landing Winery, Lodi, New York.

Marguerite Thomas

LAMOREAUX LANDING WINE CELLARS
Rating: ▯▯▯▯▯
607-582-6011;
   fax 607-582-6010.
9224 Route 414, Lodi, NY.
Directions: From NY Rte. 17 take exit 32 to Rte. 14 north. In Watkins Glen take Rte. 414 north. The winery is south of Lodi.
Owner: Mark Wagner.
Open: Mon.–Sat., 10 AM–5 PM, Sun. noon–5 PM.
Price Range of Wines: $7 for Estate White, $8 for Dry Riesling, $15 for Chardonnay, $16 for Pinot Noir.
Special Features: Picnic area.

Lamoreaux Landing is possibly the most exciting young winery in the Finger Lakes region. It produces a variety of wines that have been earning high praise from critics and top prizes in competitions. One of the most surprising of the recent awards was bestowed in Los Angeles at the New World International Wine Competition, known as the "Oscars of the Wine World." Lamoreaux Landing's 1993 Chardonnay was judged best Chardonnay in the "New World," beating out contenders from some of the world's leading wine regions, including California, Australia, South America, and South Africa.

"People don't think of Chardonnay growing here, but we're finding that with proper canopy management you can get some really good flavors," says Lamoreaux Landing owner, Mark Wagner. Mark, whose family has been growing grapes in the Finger Lakes region since the 19th century, raises both vinifera and French-American varietals on his 150-acre vineyard. He sells the hybrids to other wineries, but his own wines are made exclusively from vinifera grapes. Mark, incidentally, is only distantly related to Bill Wagner, owner of neighboring Wagner Vineyards.

In 1990, Mark founded his own winery and in 1992, the striking Lamoreaux Landing winery building was built. Designed by architect Bruce Corson, who has offices in Ithaca and California, the building resembles a Greek temple — an appropriate reference to Bacchus. "I always liked the Greek Revival architecture that is so prevalent in this area," says Mark. In the earliest planning stages he and the architect had talked about renovating an old barn on the property. "Then one day Bruce threw this drawing up on the wall and said we could use the barn for the winery, and put a Greek Temple on top of it for tasting."

Today, gazing out through the tall windows of the tasting room, one can look 20 miles north over the lake toward Geneva. Excellent rotating art exhibits grace the walls, making this one of the most attractive spots in which to taste wine — and it's great wine, too!

There are 4,300 cases of wine produced annually by talented winemaker Rob Thomas. They include a superb blend called, simply, Estate White. "A nice Monday through Thursday wine," says Mark. He also makes Chardonnay, a dry Riesling, and an excellent Pinot Noir.

Picnic benches and tables provide an inviting spot for lunch.

Profile: Mark Wagner

Mark Wagner has spent his entire life working with grapes. "My father was growing labrusca when I was born. Then he switched to French-American varietals. Now I've added vinifera to the property." Mark's interest in grapes expanded to include wine at about the time he reached legal drinking age. "I had grown up with grapes and I had learned a lot about winemaking by association with the wineries we were growing for. At some point, I decided I'd like to have my own name on the bottle. It bothered me that other people were taking my grapes and doing who knows what with them."

Mark knew he wanted to concentrate on vinifera almost from the beginning. "I didn't want to do it halfway. I wanted to keep the quality up. Since I knew I didn't need to be the biggest winery in the world," he explains, "I set my eye on where I wanted to go — to make quality wine and to expand only as I'm able." He seeks a 25% annual growth. One way he ensures quality, says Mark, is by having control over the grapes. He supervises the vines' every aspect, from the day they're planted until the fruit is turned into wine.

The glacial till in the Finger Lakes, Mark explains, makes a superb environment for vineyards. "Deposits left in the Ice Age are of mixed-up soils," he says. "There is pure sand in one spot, gravel right next to it, then clay and loam. You can have all of these in a single vineyard." This is an unusual situation, says

$\rightarrow$

Mark, and he likes it very much. "Every soil gives the grapes a different character. "We're still experimenting here by mixing up the vines in different soil types and watching carefully. We're experimenting with different clones to discover which do best here."

The rigorous canopy management Mark has been practicing is proving to be particularly effective. Vines, he maintains, are like most plant life in the East. "Winter is so bleak. Then, suddenly, everything opens up and it's amazingly lush, and then it dies. The same thing happens in a vineyard, and if you don't control it properly you end up with problems."

In addition to Chardonnay, Mark has been having excellent results with Riesling, Cabernet Franc, and Pinot Noir. This last, he says, is the trickiest to grow and to make into wine. "It's so finicky. It plays with your mind. One day you go down to the cellar and taste it and think, 'Wow!' The next week you wonder what you can do with it. Just driving Pinot Noir home in your car can interfere with it."

Actually, there is only one major vinifera grape that strikes Mark as truly problematic. "Cabernet Sauvignon is the one I feel most uneasy about in this climate," he confesses. "One year in every five or ten might be a great year. The other years we'll use the grapes in our Red Table Wine. It really hasn't been planted here long enough for us to learn much about it, though," he adds.

Does the challenge of making premium wine in the East bother him? Not much, it seems. "The strategy is just to develop an idea of where you want to be, and then make it happen," he says with equanimity. And what's the first step for getting where you want to be? "Recognize that you can't make good wine from bad grapes," says Mark firmly.

As far as the future is concerned, Mark Wagner is optimistic. "Fifteen years ago," he says, "there wasn't much to write about. Now we're an up-and-coming region with the ability to do great things. We're making wines that can compete anywhere."

NEW LAND VINEYARD
Rating: 👤👤👤
315-585-4432 or
  315-585-9844;
  fax 315-585-9844.
577 Lerch Road, Geneva,
  NY.
Directions: From NY Rte.
  17 take exit 32 to Rte. 14
  north. In Watkins Glen
  take Rte. 414 north to Rte.
  96A in Ovid. Travel
  north on 96A to Lerch
  Road. Turn left. The
  winery is just past the
  junction with Rte. 336.

The fact that New Land's production is about one-third red wine is unusual for this region that specializes in whites. Owners and winemakers Andrew and Nancy Burdick were the last of Dr. Konstantin Frank's students, and the master's touch is clearly tasted in New Land's exceptional wines.

The 10-acre vineyard is particularly well situated on a protected bluff east of Seneca Lake. The site, Nancy insists, is one of the reasons their wine is so good. At any time of year the tiny tasting room affords a dramatic view over the open countryside and sparkling lake, but I can tell you from personal experience that to be there in the midst of a sum-

Nancy Burdick, co-owner, New Land Winery, Geneva, New York.

Marguerite Thomas

Owners: Andrew and
Nancy Burdick.
Open: May through Nov.,
Mon.–Thurs., noon–5 PM,
Fri.–Sun., 11 AM–6 PM;
Apr. & Dec., Sat. & Sun.,
noon–5 PM; Jan. through
Mar., by appointment
only.
Price Range of Wines: $12
for Chardonnay to $20
for Cabernet Sauvignon.
Special Features:
Spectacular view.

mer storm is particularly thrilling — like riding out a tempest in a trim little boat. Thunder crashed, lightening flashed, and a curtain of rain-drenched clouds descended over the lake as we sat it all out snugly, tasting the Chardonnay (Nancy calls it American Meursault), the Sauvignon Blanc (perhaps the only one in the Finger Lakes), the Pinot Noir ('93 was an exceptional vintage, with hints of cherry and spice), the Merlot ("It goes very quickly," warns Nancy about this understandably popular wine), and the rich and complex Cabernet Sauvignon. This up-and-coming winery presently turns out only 2,000–3,000 cases of wine a year. Picnickers will enjoy the open skies and lake views at New Land.

PREJEAN WINERY
Rating: 🍷🍷🍷
315-536-7524.
2634 Route 14, Penn Yan,
NY.
Directions: From I-90 take
exit 42 to Rte. 14 south.
The winery is south of
Dresden.
Owner: Elizabeth Prejean.
Open: May through Oct.,
daily, 10 AM–5 PM; Nov.
through Apr., daily,
10 AM–4 PM.
Price Range of Wines: $5.99
to $14.99.

Elizabeth Prejean and her late husband, Jim, started producing estate-grown Merlot, Chardonnay, Riesling, Gewürztraminer, Maréchal Foch, Cayuga, and Vignoles wines when they came to the Finger Lakes in 1986. Today Prejean turns out 5,000 cases of wine from its 39-acre vineyard.

The wines are among the region's best, but raising vines for making good wine is by no means a "given" here, as Libby Prejean is quick to point out. Take Gewürztraminer, for example, a fussy vine that many other Finger Lakes vintners have given up trying to grow. Prejean has devised a method of protecting the vines from winter damage by

Special Features: Picnic
  area.
Special Events: Annual
  Cajun Fest with food,
  wine, and music.

putting an extra wire on the trellis for the Gewürz.
When the vines have hardened off at the approach
of winter, the wire is dropped to the ground and
buried; in spring, workers stationed at both ends of
the wire give it a sharp tug, causing wire and vine
to pop up. "We've never lost a vine, even during
the very cold winters of 1992, 1993, and 1994," asserts Libby. But why go to
this labor-intensive trouble in the first place? "Prejean is a Cajun name, and
Gewürztraminer is the best wine to drink with Cajun food," explains Libby,
smiling.

The fact is, most vinifera grapes in the Finger Lakes region require a certain
amount of coddling. "Merlot is another one of our problem-children," sighs
Libby, "but we feel the rewards are worth it." She says that even the hybrid
Seyval has to be cluster-thinned every year. If it's allowed to over-produce, the
wine suffers and the vines weaken. "On the other hand, almost everyone can
produce good Riesling here," Libby adds brightly.

Buy a bottle of Prejean Riesling, or another of the Prejean wines and enjoy it
on the deck overlooking the lake. Or, bring a picnic of Cajun-style chicken
breasts to the winery, and drink a bottle of Gewürztraminer.

*Marti Macinski of Standing Stone Vineyards, Valois,
New York.*

Marguerite Thomas

**STANDING STONE
  VINEYARDS**
Rating: 🍷🍷🍷🍷
607-582-6051.
9934 Route 414, Valois, NY.
Directions: From NY Rte.
  17 take exit 32 to Rte. 14
  north. In Watkins Glen
  take Rte. 414 north. The
  winery is north of Valois.
Owners: Martha and Tom
  Macinski.

One of the newest of the Finger Lakes wineries,
Standing Stone has shot out of the starting
gate with the clear indications of a winner. This is
partly because talented winemaker, David Whiting, has been the consultant here from the beginning. Another reason, according to owners Martha
(Marti) and Tom Macinski, is that the soil is particularly well suited to grapes. Marti claims the wine
is already half-made when the grapes are harvested.

Open: Sat. 10 AM–6 PM, Sun. noon–5 PM, from harvest until the wines sell out (sometimes before Thanksgiving).

Price Range of Wines: $5.50 for dry Vidal to $9.50 for Gewürztraminer.

Special Features: Picnic area.

Special Events: Monthly Winemakers' Dinners.

Even so, the winery has expanded at a faster rate than the Macinskis had anticipated. "We certainly never dreamed we would sell all our wines 12 weeks after we opened," exclaims Marti. Despite this initial success, both Macinskis continue to pursue other full-time jobs. She is a lawyer and he works for IBM. "We could keep the winery going without having other jobs, but expansion would be much slower," says Marti.

Standing Stone has been garnering awards as far away as California for its exceptional Gewürztraminer and Riesling. The recently-released Cabernet Franc and Merlot are also expected to race into the limelight. The winery also makes a dry Vidal.

The tasting room is in a handsomely restored chicken coop, embellished with a large wooden terrace with picnic tables overlooking the vineyards and lake.

WAGNER VINEYARDS

Rating: 🍷🍷🍷

607-582-6450.

Route 414, Lodi, NY 14860.

Directions: From NY Rte. 17 take exit 32 to Rte. 14 north. In Watkins Glen take Rte. 414 north. The winery is between Valois and Lodi.

Owner: Bill Wagner.

Open: Daily 10 AM–5 PM.

Price Range of Wines: $3.99 for Reserve Red and Reserve White, $5.99 for Melody, $12.99 for Reserve Chardonnay.

Special Features: Gift shop, cafe.

Special Events: Oktoberfest, Pig Roasts, Champagne Weekends, Mulled Wine Weekends, Deck the Halls parties, and more.

Wagner Winery is just plain big. It produces 40,000 cases of wine a year, it maintains 240 acres of vines, and it is enormously popular, with its tasting room perennially crowded with visitors tasting the vast selection of Wagner wines. Not surprisingly, the Wagner gift shop is larger than most.

Bill Wagner first got into agriculture in the Finger Lakes region in 1947, when he started a vegetable and dairy farm. He also raised grapes that he sold to various wineries, and he continues to sell about half his grapes. In the 1960s, he eliminated his other crops to concentrate on grapes, and in 1978 he released his first vintage.

Wagner wines are made from native American, French-American hybrid, and European vinifera grapes. The variety includes three different Chardonnays, four or more Rieslings, a bunch of blushes, and Pinot Noir in various guises. Several wines are produced from grapes unique to the Finger Lakes region. Wagner's Melody, for example, is made from the Melody grape, a cross between Seyval and Geneva White, which, itself, is a cross between Pinot Blanc and Ontario. The Melody grape was developed in the late 1960s by the New York State Experiment Station in Geneva. Wagner winemaker Ann Rafetto describes the white, intensely fruity Melody as "fruit salad in a glass, a perfect summertime wine."

HERMANN J. WIEMER VINEYARD, INC.

Rating: 🍷🍷🍷
607-243-7971 or
607-243-7983.
Route 14, Dundee, NY.
Directions: From I-90 take exit 42 to Rte. 14 south. The winery is between Dresden and Starkey.
Owner: Hermann Wiemer.
Open: Apr. through Nov., Mon.–Sat., 10 AM–5 PM, Sun. 11 AM–5 PM; Dec. through Mar., Mon.–Fri., 10 AM–5 PM.
Price Range of Wines: $6.75 for Chardonnay, $10 for Pinot Noir, $13.99 for sparkling wines.

One reason Hermann Wiemer started his own winery was because of a dispute with Walter S. Taylor, his boss at Bully Hill Vineyards. Taylor, like most Finger Lakes winemakers in the mid-1970s, was adamantly committed to hybrid grapes, which he believed were the only grapes that could survive the region's cold winters. Hermann, who came from the cool Moselle region of northern Germany, was convinced that vinifera could grow in the Finger Lakes, where the hills slope gently to the water as they do in the Moselle, and the slatey glacial soils are also comparable. He was profoundly influenced by Konstantin Frank's success with European vinifera grapes.

In 1979, he bought an abandoned 145-acre soybean farm on the shores of Seneca Lake, and he began planting Riesling, Pinot Noir, and other vinifera grapes. As the vineyard grew, it first became successful because of the young vines it supplied to other vineyards. In this endeavor he was following in the footsteps of his father, who had run Germany's largest nursery and supervised the replanting of that country's vineyards after World War II. Today, Hermann Wiemer Vineyard supplies some 200,000 vines a year to vineyards in Latin America and the U.S., including such notable California wineries as Buena Vista, Caymus, and Kendall Jackson.

Wiemer wines are now becoming as well known as the vines. The winery produces 12,000 cases annually, including several good Rieslings, ranging from dry to semi-dry, as well as a very special Individual Bunch Select Late Harvest Riesling made in the German Trockenbeerenauslese (TBA) tradition from hand-selected grapes that have been affected by the noble botrytis mold. Other selections to try here are sparkling wines, Chardonnay, and Pinot Noir. The handsome winery, designed by Simon Ungers of UZK Architects of Ithaca, is actually built inside an old dairy barn. The grounds provide a nice backdrop for a picnic.

KEUKA LAKE

BULLY HILL VINEYARDS

Rating: 🍷
607-868-3610 or
607-868-3210.

The saga of Walter S. Taylor and his quirky winery, with its colorful, fun-filled labels, is the stuff of American legend. As a nation, we hail the maverick; we root for the underdog; and we hold a grudging admiration for the guy who thumbs his

Patio restaurant at Bully Hill Vineyards, Hammondsport, New York.

Marguerite Thomas

8843 Greyton H. Taylor Memorial Drive, Hammondsport, NY
Directions: From I-17 take exit 38 to Rte. 54. In Hammondsport, take Rte. 54A along west side of lake to County Rte. 76. Follow Rte. 76 for 1.5 miles to Greyton H. Taylor Memorial Drive and winery.
Owner: Walter S. Taylor.
Open: Mon.–Sat., 9 AM–5 PM, Sun. noon–5 PM.
Price Range of Wines: $6.50 for Harbor Lights to $8 for Red Wine.
Special Features: Picnic area, cafe, gift shop, museum.

nose at authority, particularly when he ends up making lots of money despite the odds against him.

This particular folk hero's chronicle began in the late 19th century when his grandfather, also named Walter Taylor, arrived in Hammondsport. He purchased a vineyard and established a winery. Taylor's wine was shipped 22 miles up Keuka Lake by steamboat to Penn Yan, then transported across to Seneca Lake and over to the Erie Canal. From there, it made its way to the large markets in New York.

The Taylor winery expanded rapidly in the 1920s and it began purchasing grapes from local growers. The original site atop Bully Hill was sold and the operation was moved to larger quarters. The firm rode out Prohibition by switching to grape juice, which was also shipped down the river in barrels. Taylor audaciously wrote on them: "Please do not add sugar or keep in a warm place or contents will ferment."

By the 1950s, Taylor Wine had become a leader in the New York wine industry, but success was somewhat tarnished for Walter S. Taylor by disputes with the rest of the Taylor clan over the quality of the wine. Walter argued that they should switch from native American labrusca grapes to the more universally appealing hybrid grapes. Furthermore, he believed they should stop adulterating the wine with additives such as sugar and water. "It's easy to tell when the Taylor Company is making wine," he used to joke, "because the level of Keuka Lake drops several feet." His relatives were not amused.

The Taylor Wine Company, by now made up of numerous relatives who had had enough of his zeal for reform, invited him to leave the firm in 1970. So, Walter and his father, Greyton, bought back the original Taylor site on Bully Hill and began their own winery. Little did Walter know his troubles were just beginning.

When the Coca-Cola Corporation purchased the Taylor Wine Company, they immediately filed, and eventually won, a lawsuit forbidding Walter to use the Taylor name on his wine. So Walter threw a party. He provided his guests with marking pens and plenty of wine to drink, and they spent the night inking out the word "Taylor" on thousands of bottles of wine. Unable to use the family name, Walter proceeded to design labels using portraits of his ancestors instead of their name. When Coca-Cola got a court order forbidding him to do that, he put masks on their faces, but — you guessed it — he was hauled back to court for another losing battle.

The denouement of the drama came when Walter was ordered to turn over everything he owned that related to the Taylor family. He led a motorcade hauling paintings, documents, and a host of other objects down the road to the Taylor Wine Company, where he dumped everything in a large pile on the front steps of the winery. Then he persuaded his goat, named Guilt Free, to pose on top of the heap. "They got my name and heritage, but they didn't get my goat," was Walter's now legendary quip.

Of course all of these legal wrangles cost Walter a bundle, but did any of it hurt Bully Hill sales? Absolutely not. Walter may have lost the battles, but he won the war. The Taylor Wine Company, which changed hands several more times, has now disappeared. Bully Hill, however, produces an enormous assortment of very popular wines.

Bully Hill wines are all made from French-American hybrid grapes. Harbor Lights is a semi-sweet white blend of Vidal, Cayuga, and Verdelet, and Red Wine is made from Baco Noir, Chancellor, and Chelois. Writer John Baxavanis said of this particular wine, "For those with a taste for French-American, this wine may be as important as a religious experience."

Walter S. Taylor, while confined to a wheelchair as the result of an automobile accident a few years ago, is still involved in running the winery. Bully Hill, which is part theme park and part winery, is enormously popular, receiving thousands of visitors each year. It offers unusually entertaining tours and it has an abundantly stocked gift shop and a museum. There's a cafe that serves pizza and other informal meals, as well as a picnic area with a view of the lake.

DR. FRANK'S VINIFERA WINE CELLARS/ CHATEAU FRANK
Rating: 👤👤👤👤
607-868-4884.
9749 Middle Road,
   Hammondsport, NY.

Vinifera Wine Cellars is where the eastern American wine industry was really born, and Dr. Frank himself exemplifies the story of the American dream come true. An immigrant from the Soviet Union, Dr. Frank arrived in New York with his family in 1951. Although he was a profes-

Willy Frank, owner of Dr. Frank's Vinifera Wine Cellars/Chateau Frank and son of legendary vintner Konstantin Frank.

Marguerite Thomas

Directions: From Rte. 17 take exit 38 to Rte. 54 north. Travel north for six miles to Hammondsport. Take Rte. 54A north for 6 more miles, take the first left past the Hammondsport Motel onto County Rte. 76 (Middle Road).
Owner: Willy Frank.
Open: Mon.–Sat., 9 AM–5 PM, Sun. noon–5 PM.
Price Range of Wines: $5.95 for Premiere Blush to $22 for Cabernet Sauvignon.

sor of plant sciences in the U.S.S.R., the only job Konstantin Frank could find in America at first was hoeing blueberries at the New York State Agricultural Experiment Station in Geneva. This is where Charles Fournier, of Gold Seal Vineyards, discovered him.

Recognizing Frank's talents, Fournier hired him to plant and manage vinifera grapes at Gold Seal. By 1962, Konstantin Frank had purchased his own land, where he proved to a skeptical world that European vinifera grapes could be successfully cultivated in the Finger Lakes region.

Next he went on to produce critically acclaimed wine from his grapes, including a Chardonnay and a Riesling, as well as almost 60 other varieties. Soon other prospective eastern vintners sought Dr. Frank's advice and encouragement. Untold numbers of wineries today owe their success, directly or indirectly, to Konstantin Frank's visionary work.

Vinifera Wine Cellars is now run by Willy Frank, who assumed control ten years ago when his father died at the age of 86. Approximately 20,000 cases of wine are produced here, from grapes grown on the property's 79 acres. The wines include a Riesling ("my father's favorite wine," says Willy. "He fought the general opinion that Chardonnay is the best wine,") and Gewürztraminer. "Gewürztraminer is the favorite grape of wild turkeys, but our sweet revenge is to serve Gewürz. with Thanksgiving turkey," he chuckles. Pinot Noir, made from the oldest Pinot Noir vineyard in the Finger Lakes region, is excellent. "The mature vine roots go down 15-20 feet to find minerals and other elements," said Willy. "A young vine can't possibly give you the color, body, or complexity of older vines."

Other winners include Salmon Run Riesling, Chardonnay, and Cabernet Sauvignon. "Growing Cabernet here is almost self flagellation," sighs Willy. And don't miss the Rkatsiteli, made from the unique Russian grape which is almost unknown in this country, or the late harvest Sereksia and Muscat Ottonel, made only in exceptional years. Chateau Frank, another winery under the same management but not open to the public, makes sparkling wines that are also superior.

The bell at Heron Hill Winery, overlooking Keuka Lake near Hammondsport, New York.

Marguerite Thomas

HERON HILL WINERY
Rating: 🔔
607-868-4241.
8203 Pleasant Valley Road, Hammondsport, NY.
Directions: From Rte. 17 take exit 38 to Rte. 54 north. Travel north for six miles to Hammondsport. Take Rte. 54A north for 6 more miles, take the first left past the Hammondsport Motel onto County Rte. 76 (Middle Road). Follow winery signs.
Owners: Peter Johnstone and John Ingle.
Open: May through Oct., Mon.–Sat., 10 AM–5 PM, Sun. noon–5 PM; closed Nov. through Apr.

Peter Johnstone was a New York advertising writer when the Finger Lakes captured his heart. In the late 1960s he bought property on a hillside with a spectacular view of Keuka Lake and went into partnership with John Ingle, a grape grower with vines on Canandaigua Lake. Peter ripped out the hybrid vines on his property and replanted with vinifera grapes. The winery has 25 acres of vines on Lake Keuka and another 20 on Canandaigua.

Heron Hill has long been known for white wines, but it recently began introducing a few reds as well. Recent vintages have been decent, if uninspired. The winery produces 17,000 cases annually, including the best-selling light, dry White Table Wine; Eye of the Heron, a dry, salmon-colored blush; Chardonnay Ingle Vineyard, a vanilla scented wine; and a fruity Pinot Noir. Simple box

Price Range of Wines: $3.36
for White Table Wine,
$4.29 for Eye of the
Heron, $9.99 for
Chardonnay Ingle
Vineyard, and for Pinot
Noir.

Special Features: Picnic
area, box lunches, gift
shop.

lunches may be purchased at Heron Hill to be
enjoyed at tables overlooking the panoramic view
of vineyards and lake. Attractive local stoneware
embellished with a heron theme is available at the
winery gift shop.

*Entrance to Hunt Country
Vineyard, Branchport, New
York.*

Marguerite Thomas

HUNT COUNTRY VINEYARD

Rating: 🍷🍷
315-595-2812;
   fax 315-595-2835.
4021 Italy Hill Road,
   Branchport, NY.
Directions: From I-17 take
   exit 38 to Rte. 54. In
   Hammondsport, take
   Rte. 54A along the west
   side of Lake Keuka to
   Branchport. Turn onto
   Italy Hill Road and
   continue straight up the
   hill to the winery.
Owner: Art Hunt.
Open: Jul. through Oct.,
   Mon.–Sat., 10 AM–6 PM,
   Sun. noon–6 PM; Apr.
   through June, Nov. &
   Dec., Mon.–Sat., 10 AM–

Art Hunt is the sixth generation of his family to
live on this farm above Keuka Lake. Art's
father was raised here, but during the Depression
he left the farm to work at the Corning Glass Company. Art grew up in Corning, but spent summers
on the farm, which he ultimately inherited from his
uncle.

While not a farmer himself, Art had a keen
attachment to the farm and the land. In the 1960s,
when local wineries were looking for premium
grapes, he decided that his sloping acreage of deep,
well-drained soil was ideally suited for grapes.
With borrowed money, he started planting vines
and learning about viticulture. Then, in the 1970s,
everything changed. Popular taste shifted from red
to white wine. The Taylor Wine Company, which
had purchased crops from local growers, was
acquired by Coca-Cola.

5 PM, Sun. noon–5 PM; closed Jan through Mar.
Price Range of Wines: $4.99 for Foxy Lady, $7.99 for the Riesling, $11.99 for the Barrel Reserve Chardonnay, and $18 for the Vidal Ice Wine.
Special Features: Picnic area, gift shop.
Special Events: Panorama Horse Sanctuary Benefit, a fundraiser to benefit a sanctuary for abused and unwanted horses.

The Finger Lakes area, like most of the rest of the country, was being swept from a regional economy into global economics. "Banks didn't even want to hear you knock on their door. In the early 1970s the cost of everything tripled," says Art. "Most growers had to start their own winery or get out of the grape business."

In 1981, the Hunts opened a winery. "The growers who survived had to learn to be more efficient, though in our case, it was more groping than brilliant management," Art says with a wry smile, "but we did learn how to do it. We learned how to hedge the vines, for example, and reduce the acreage of grapes that don't have a long-time future, such as Delaware."

Art Hunt, Hunt Country Vineyard.

Marguerite Thomas

While the Hunt vineyard still features native and hybrid species on its 55 acres, experimentation is being conducted here with other grapes, as well. Art Hunt, one of the few Finger Lakes vintners to tackle the thorny problem of how to sell wine in an already crowded market, travels every week to the Farmer's Market in New York City to sell his wines.

Despite the difficulty of adjusting to the changes, Art remains essentially upbeat. "When you stand back and look at things from a distance, you realize this whole premium wine thing couldn't have happened any other way. We could still be growing the same grapes for Taylor."

The future, he thinks, looks good. Hunt Country produces around 10,000 cases of commendable country wine annually, which, as Art points out, gets better all the time. "And look at that tasting room," he says, nodding towards the refurbished farm outbuilding that now houses a well-stocked gift shop and tasting bar. "I've never seen it as busy as this year." Among the wines to be sampled are Foxy Lady (blush), Riesling, Barrel Reserve Chardonnay, and Vidal Ice Wine.

There is a lovely spot for a picnic on the deck, or visitors might like to set out from the vineyards for a bike ride or a hike.

KEUKA SPRING VINEYARDS

Rating: 🍷
315-536-4711.
273 East Lake Road (Route 54), Penn Yan, NY.
Directions: From Rte. 17 take exit 38 to Rte. 54 north. Travel north for six miles to Hammondsport. Continue on Rte. 54 to the winery, which is three miles south of Penn Yan.
Owners: Judy and Len Wiltberger.
Open: June through Aug., Mon.–Sat., 11:30 AM–5 PM, Sun. noon–5 PM; Sept. & Oct. & May, Sat. 10:30 AM–5 PM, Sun. noon–5 PM; Nov. through Apr. closed.
Price Range of Wines: $6 to $14.
Special Features: Picnic area.

Keuka Spring's winery and tasting room are located in an old barn overlooking the lake. Owners Judy and Len Wiltberger commute between their home in Rochester and the winery. He is another of the Finger Lakes vintners who works at Eastman Kodak.

"We concentrate on what we feel is a good cross section of wine for the variety of folks who come in the door," says Judy. The wide range of styles includes a selection of whites such as classic Chardonnay and Riesling, and some reds, including Crooked Lake Red, a fruity red blend that, in Judy's words, "is the wine people want to take home to serve with their pasta." Like many eastern vintners, the Wiltbergers say that visitors to the winery often say they don't like sweet wine, "but then they walk out with Vignoles," laughs Judy, referring to a semi-sweet wine with a fruity flavor reminiscent of apricots.

Keuka Springs owns a six-acre vineyard, and it purchases about 30% of its grapes from local growers. The winery produces 1,500 cases annually. Picnic tables in front of the winery look out over the lake.

McGREGOR VINEYARDS & WINERY

Rating: 🍷🍷🍷
800-272-0192;
fax 607-292-6929.
5503 Dutch Street, Dundee, NY.
Directions: From Rte. 17 take exit 38 to Rte. 54 north. Travel north for six miles to Hammondsport. Continue on Rte. 54 to Hyatt Hill Rd. Turn up

McGregor Winery has the unusual distinction of raising hardy Russian vinifera varietals, as well as European vinifera grapes. "They seem to tolerate the winters here," observes Robert McGregor, "and they produce unusually deep red wine."

Robert, who retired early from Kodak in 1986, had planted vines on this slope of land in 1971. Today, from its 28-acre vineyard, McGregor produces about 7,000 cases of very good wine. Don't miss the Muscat Ottonel, a luscious sweet wine made in limited amounts. Late Harvest Vignoles is another fine dessert wine made here.

McGregor Vineyards &
Winery, Dundee, New York.

Hyatt Hill Rd. to Dutch
St. Turn left. The winery
is 1 mile further.
Owner: Robert McGregor.
Open: Apr. through Dec.,
  Mon.–Sat., 10 AM–6 PM,
  (Jul. & Aug., Thurs.
  11 AM–8 PM), Sun. 11
  AM–6 PM; Jan. through
  Mar., daily, 11 AM–5 PM.
Price Range of Wines: $6.99
  for Riesling to $14.99 for
  the Vintner's Reserve
  Chardonnay.
Special Features: Picnic
  area.
Special Events: Harvest
  Brunch Series, December
  Gourmet Dinner, regular
  food & wine pairings.

Visitors may picnic outside on the terrace or, if
the weather is cool, sit at tables inside the cozy tasting room overlooking the lake.

CAYUGA LAKE

**CAYUGA RIDGE
  ESTATE WINERY**
Rating: 🍷
607-869-5158.
6800 Route 89, Elm Beach
  Road, Ovid, NY.
Directions: From Ithaca
  take Rte. 89 north for 22.5
  miles to the winery.

Tom Challen had almost 20 years of wine background and vineyard management experience
in Canada, when he and his wife Susie purchased
Cayuga Ridge in 1991. Winery and vineyards were
established in 1980 by Bob and Mary Plane.

Tom's judgement is that the Finger Lakes region
is one of the best for producing fine wines. Rather

Owners: Tom and Susie
  Challen.
Open: May through Oct.,
  daily, noon–5 PM; Nov.
  through Apr., Sat. &
  Sun., noon -4 PM, or by
  appointment.
Price Range of Wines: $5.95
  for Duet to $9.95 for
  Chardonnay.
Special Features: Picnic
  areas.
Special Events: Monthly
  food & wine events, fall
  harvest events.

than make sweeping changes, the Challens have
elected to carry on the traditions started by the
Planes. Their labels still sport a quatrefoil, an
ancient symbol for quality. They carry on the winery's *vigneron* tradition, a program allowing partic-
ipants to lease vines and harvest their own grapes,
which the winery will then vinify if the owners
wish.

The Challens are also continuing to produce the
same respectable, if not dazzling, wines as the
Planes, including a buttery Chardonnay, Riesling,
Vignoles, and several red wines, such as Pinot Noir
and Cabernet Franc. Duet is a semi-sweet, Cayuga-
Vignoles blend that the Challens recommend serv-
ing with barbecue. They have a 36-acre vineyard
and bottle 4,500 cases of wine a year.

Cayuga Ridge's tasting room is in an enormous old barn, which has a deck
with picnic tables, and overlooks the lake. There are also picnic tables under a
tree in front of the winery.

*Door of tasting room, with
the signature grape-leaf of
Hosmer Winery, Ovid, New
York.*

OPEN

Marguerite Thomas

HOSMER
Rating: 🍷
607-869-5585.
6999 Route 89, Ovid, NY.
Directions: From Ithaca
  take Rte. 89 north for 22
  miles to the winery.
Owners: Cameron and
  Maren Hosmer.

This lakeside farm was purchased by the
Chicago-based Hosmer family in the 1930s as a
vacation retreat. Cameron Hosmer, who studied
fruit sciences (Pomology) at Cornell, began his current career as a home winemaker. He made wine
for friends and family from grapes his father
planted in 1972. In 1985, Cameron and his wife,
Maren, opened their winery. They now produce

Open: Apr. through Dec.,
Mon.–Sat., 10 AM–5 PM,
Sun. noon–5 PM; Jan.
through Mar. by
appointment.
Price Range of Wines: $6 to
$15.
Special Features: Picnic
area, gift shop, snack
shop.
Special Events: Asparagus
Day in June.

12,000 cases a year from their 40-acre vineyard, and they also supply grapes to other local wineries.

Hosmer wines include a Riesling with a pretty, floral aroma and a Cayuga that would be a good match for spicy Asian or Mexican dishes. Hosmer's young Cabernet Franc has bold tannins, that will probably mellow with time.

The tasting room, which is entered through a carved door that displays the Hosmer's signature grape-leaf pattern, includes a large gift shop where prospective picnickers can stock up on cheese, chips, and snack food, to enjoy with a bottle of wine at the picnic tables outside.

**KNAPP VINEYARDS
WINERY**
Rating: 🌲🌲🌲
607-869-9271.
2270 County Road 128,
Romulus, NY.
Directions: From I-90 take
exit 41 to Rte. 414, follow
Rte. 414 south to Rte.
20/5, go east on 20/5 to
Rte. 89, go south on Rte.
89 to Rte. 128, turn west
onto Rte. 128 (Ernsberger
Rd.) to the winery.
Owners: Doug and Suzie
Knapp.
Open: Apr. through Dec.,
Mon.–Sat., 10 AM–5 PM,
Sun. noon–5 PM; closed
Jan. through Mar.
Price Range of Wines: $5 to
$14.
Special Features:
Restaurant.

Doug and Suzie Knapp met in Panama while he was working for an electronics firm. They got married and eventually, in 1971, decided to buy a chicken farm in the Finger Lakes region, which they converted to vineyards.

"Like most growers around here, we were supplying grapes to the Taylor Wine Company," recalled Suzie. "And, like most growers in the region, we were growing native American grapes. These grapes had been the backbone of the American wine industry for 150 years," she continued. "Besides, most people felt that since we didn't have a Mediterranean climate, we couldn't grow anything else."

By the mid 1970s, everything had changed. "The Taylor family was no longer involved in the business. Under the ownership of Coca-Cola, and then Seagrams, the company was no longer responsive to local growers." As Suzie explains it, the large

Special Events: Harvest festival, winemaker's dinners, Champagne brunch.

corporation started allocating grapes and dropping prices. "Grapes aren't like corn," she points out. "You can't just change your crop from year to year according to the whims of the market. By 1976, a lot of people could see the writing on the wall."

Once the New York Farm Winery Act was passed a lot of growers started their own wineries. Those growers who changed — the ones who ripped out their vineyards of American grapes, replanted with more currently popular varieties, and opened their own winery — have mostly survived. "Of the others, few stayed in business," Suzie says.

Suzie is quick to point out, however, that while the wine industry has reinvented itself in the Finger Lakes region, the wineries are not owned by wealthy investors. Unlike other areas of the country, "we don't have Wall Street types and advertising executives buying up the vineyards. Here, land remains cheap and we're still mostly just farmers," she explains. Although this may be true, these "farmers" have become increasingly savvy. They now produce wines that are fine enough to please the most discriminating palate.

Knapp Vineyards' winemaker Dana Keeler is a significant force behind the high quality of this establishment's wine. Like a surprising number of Finger Lakes winemakers, Dana is from the area. He grew up in nearby Corning. His winemaking skills were acquired principally under the tutelage of Hermann Wiemer, first at Bully Hill, then at Wiemer's own winery.

Along with other vintners in the region, Dana believes the Riesling grape represents the strength of the Finger Lakes. As far as red wine goes, he would bet on Pinot Noir, but Cabernet Franc is also high on his list. Dana is convinced that the special conditions of the Finger Lakes yield grapes that mature completely without becoming overripe, a quality that lends structure and finesse to the wines.

Knapp's excellent wines include Chardonnay, Riesling, Pasta Red, Pinot Noir, Cabernet Franc, and Dutchman's Breeches, a combination of Vidal and Vignoles. This also is one of the first eastern wineries to produce a classic Italian Grappa. Don't even think of picnicking here — the restaurant at Knapp, one of the best in the entire region, is much too good to pass up.

LUCAS VINEYARDS
Rating: 🍷
607-532-4825 or
  800-682-WINE (in NYS).
3862 County Road 150,
  Interlaken, NY.
Directions: From Ithaca,
  take Rte. 89 north to
  County Rd. 150, travel
  west to the winery.
Owners: Bill and Ruth
  Lucas.

Lucas Vineyards is the oldest winery on Cayuga Lake, founded by the Lucas family in 1974. They moved to the 68-acre site from New York City and planted grapes which they sold to the Taylor Wine Company. In 1980 the Lucas's opened their own winery.

Owner Bill Lucas is a tug boat captain, who still pilots boats in New York Harbor, working a schedule of two weeks on and two weeks off. His wife, Ruth, makes the wines, assisted by their daughter

Stephanie Lucas, Lucas Vineyards, Interlaken, New York.

Marguerite Thomas

Grapes grown: Cayuga, Riesling, and Chardonnay.

Open: May through Dec., Mon.–Sat., 10:30 AM– 5:30 PM, Sun. noon– 5:30 PM; Apr., Sat. 10:30 AM–5:30 PM, Sun. noon–5:30 PM; closed Jan. through Mar.

Price Range of Wines: $5.50 Seyval and Captain's Belle, $6 for Tug Boat Red, $8.99 for Brut, $10.50 for Chardonnay.

Special Features: Picnic area with view.

Special Events: Summer Captain's Table Celebration.

Ruthie Crawford. The youngest Lucas daughter, Stephanie, runs the tasting room.

Lucas Vineyards currently has 22 acres planted in vines, from which it produces 10,000 cases of wine annually. The wines at Lucas are first rate, including a very dry Chardonnay; a good Brut sparkling wine; a clean, lemony Seyval; a blush called Captain's Belle; and Tug Boat Red, a slightly sweet hearty wine made from Dechaunac grapes. What's the most popular wine at Lucas? "Evening Tide is a real crowd pleaser," acknowledges Stephanie, referring to a semi-sweet blend of Cayuga and oak-fermented Vidal, and named after one of the boats her father pilots. Stephanie also claims that Lucas is the only major winery on Cayuga Lake with a view of the lake from the tasting room. The picnic tables overlooking the vineyards also afford a glimpse of the lake.

SWEDISH HILL VINEYARD & WINERY

Rating: 🍷🍷🍷

315-549-8326; fax 315-549-8477.

4565 Route 414, Romulus, NY.

Directions: From I-90 take exit 41 to Rte. 414, follow Rte. 414 south. The

Swedish Hill is one of the Finger Lakes' best wineries. Owners Dick and Cindy Peterson planted their first vines on this site in 1969, while she was still working for a bank and he had a job with the Seneca Falls school system. They produced their first vintage in 1985, and it was so successful that the Petersons quit their other jobs to devote themselves full time to the winery.

winery is eight miles south of Seneca Falls.

Owners: Dick and Cindy Peterson.

Open: Daily 9 AM–6 PM.

Price Range of Wines: $5.99 for Cayuga, $8.99 for Merlot, and $14.99 for Brut.

Special Features: Picnic area, gift shop, home winemaking equipment for sale.

Special Events: Horse-drawn wagon tours May–Oct.

Today the Petersons produce 25,000 cases of wine annually in their high-tech winery, and their goal is 50,000 cases. They have 35 acres of vines that provide them with about 40% of the fruit they need. They purchase the rest locally. The praise they've received since their very first release will become even more enthusiastic now that David Whiting has become the winemaker at Swedish Hill.

Swedish Hill has a large, new tasting room with three separate tasting bars, a well-stocked gift shop, and a selection of home-winemaking equipment for sale. The wines range from Cayuga, to Merlot, and they also make Brut, a classic sparkling wine. A superior late-harvest Vignoles is $11.99 for a 376-ml. bottle. Visitors are urged to bring a picnic lunch to enjoy with a bottle of chilled wine on the deck or in one of the other picnic areas.

CANANDAIGUA LAKE

CANANDAIGUA WINE COMPANY

Rating: 🍇

716-394-7680.

Sonnenberg Gardens, 151 Charlotte Street, Canandaigua, NY.

Directions: From I-90 take exit 44 and travel south on Rte. 332 toward Canandaigua. Turn onto Gibson Street and follow this to Charlotte St. Follow signs to winery.

Owners: A corporation.

Open: June through Aug., daily, noon–4 PM; May, Sept., and Oct., Sat. & Sun., noon–4 PM; closed Nov. through Apr.

Price Range of Wines: $3.29 to $12.99.

Special Features: Tasting room in manor house, gardens.

In contrast to the family-run establishments that characterize the Finger Lakes, Canandaigua is a mega-winery — the third largest winery in the United States. It was established in 1946. Today the corporation owns a host of other companies including such familiar labels as Cooks Champagne, Cribari, Italian Swiss Colony, Manischewitz Wines, Almaden, Le Domaine Champagne, Wild Irish Rose, and Canandaigua's other major winery, Widmer's Wine Cellars. It also imports Mateus and Marcus James, among other brands. The Canandaigua Wine Company produces millions of gallons of wine each year. Many of these may be tasted at Sonnenberg Gardens, a large estate in Canandaigua that also includes several landscaped gardens on its 50 acres of land. The tasting room, set in an old manor house, and decorated with stained glass windows and a fountain, is a popular tourist destination.

WIDMER'S WINE CELLARS

Rating: ♭
716-374-6311.
1 Lake Niagara Lane, Naples, NY.
Directions: From I-390 take exit 2 to Rte. 371 north. In North Cohocton, take Rte. 21 north. Watch for winery signs before the town of Naples.
Owners: Canandaigua Wine Company.
Open: June through Oct., Mon.–Sat., 10 AM–4 PM, Sun. 11:30 AM–4:30 PM; Nov. through May, daily, 1 PM–4 PM.
Price Range of Wines: $4.99 to $29.95 for sherry.
Special Features: Museum, gift and wine shop.
Special Events: Grape Festival, wagon rides, wine and food festivals featuring local chefs.

Perhaps Swiss immigrants are attracted to the Finger Lakes because the landscape, punctuated by green hills sweeping down to idyllic lakes, reminds them of their own country. While we don't know for certain why John Jacob Widmer moved here in 1882, he certainly made a success of it once he settled on this site.

Widmer planned to plant table grapes on his property, but since refrigeration was not sophisticated enough in those days to assure safe passage of such a fragile product to the markets in Manhattan and Philadelphia, he decided to raise wine grapes instead, and to open his own winery. As it turned out, Widmer's shale-based soil proved a boon for vines, enabling their roots to penetrate deep into the earth.

Widmer was innovative. Rather than making only table wine, he established a solera system for making sherry that is still in use today. Based on traditional Spanish techniques, the sherry is placed in seven-year-old Tennessee and Kentucky bourbon barrels. These are stored on the winery's roof, where the wine ages in the sun from four to six years. Visitors to the winery will see about 1,000 barrels, each holding 50 gallons, basking in the sun on the roof of the main building. The winery makes a full range of sherries, from pale dry versions to rich, sweet cream sherries. While this wine will certainly not put the fine sherries of Spain out of business, Canandaigua's sherries, particularly the sweeter ones, can be very pleasant sippers.

Widmer also produces an enormous range of sparkling and still wines, many of them based on Niagara, Elvira, and other native grapes that were the backbone of the original wine industry here. Winemaker Bonnie Abrams is also expanding a line of classic premium wines. In addition to her winemaking expertise, Bonnie is a popular songwriter and local TV and radio performer, who sings her own creations, such as "Winemaker's Blues."

Widmer produces 250,000 cases a year and it owns 250 acres of vines that are planted with 24 different grape varieties. It also procures fruit from about 1,200–1,500 additional acres of leased land.

The winery, now owned by the huge Canandaigua Company, is well equipped to receive the great numbers of visitors that flock to its doors. It offers very knowledgeable tour and tasting guides, and has a museum of early winemaking tools. The well-stocked gift and wine shop includes a large selection of kosher wines.

OTHER FINGER LAKE WINERIES

AMERICANA VINEYARDS (607-387-6801 or 607-387-4367, East Covert Rd., Interlaken, NY) is another small, family-operated winery that produces pleasant wines from native American and hybrid grapes.

FRONTENAC POINT VINEYARD (607-387-9619, Route 89, Trumansburg, NY). Owners Jim and Carol Doolittle produce Chardonnay, Riesling, Chambourcin, and a Late Harvest Vignoles, plus a handful of other good, dry table wines. The Doolittles have also played an active role in promoting the region's wines. Jim was a major force in getting the Farm Winery Bill of 1976 passed, and the couple continue to educate the public about the benefits of moderate wine consumption.

Six Mile Creek Vineyard.

Marguerite Thomas

SIX MILE CREEK VINEYARD (607-273-6219 or 607-273-1551, Slaterville Rd, Route 79, Ithaca, NY) is the first winery one passes when driving to the Finger Lakes from Binghampton. An attractive introduction to the region, this small, family-run winery is housed in a restored Dutch-reform barn. There's a large deck overlooking the vineyard. A variety of wines, from Chardonnay to Chancellor, is produced here.

RESTAURANTS AND LODGING

The Finger Lakes has numerous attractive bed and breakfast establishments and some are associated with wineries.

RESTAURANTS AND LODGING

TURBACKS
607-272-6484.
Elmira Road, Ithaca, NY.
Price: Moderate.

What sets Turbacks apart from many good restaurants in Ithaca is its exceptional wine list. There are over 100 selections, and all are from New York. The beer list is also devoted exclusively to New York. This is a regional restaurant and every dish features New York meat, produce, and seasonings. Turback's is located in a classic house of seven gables and staffed by enthusiastic young folks who love wine and who regularly taste the regional offerings.

The restaurant at Knapp Vineyards, Romulus, New York, serves lunch and dinner and offers both Knapp wines and other selections.

Marguerite Thomas

THE RESTAURANT AT KNAPP VINEYARDS
607-869-9481.
2770 County Road 128, Romulus, NY.
Price: Moderate.
Open: Lunch and dinner.

From the time it opened in 1992, this restaurant was recognized as one of the finest in the region. It's run by Chef Jeffrey Adema, the son of winery owner Suzie Knapp, and his wife, Louise Alimahomed. The dining room, a pleasant, light-filled space decorated with paintings by local artists, overlooks vineyards and flower gardens. In addition to Knapp wines, the list includes a handful of other alluring selections, such as Les Folatières 1990 Puligny Montrachet. Chef Adema shows off his Culinary Institute of America training with selections such as shrimp and brandy bisque, smoked salmon pesto pizza with aged Provolone cheese, roasted duck with raspberry–Cabernet Sauvignon sauce, and grilled beef tenderloin with saffron-Gorgonzola sauce. Simpler fare is also available. One summer day, for example, I lunched on cold roasted pepper and cucumber soup garnished with chopped fresh sage and crème fraîche, followed by a cheeseburger on a homemade roll, accompanied by a glass of

Brut Champagne. I ended with a delicious berry confection and a glass of Knapp Grappa. The restaurant is located a few steps from the winery.

**CASTEL GRISCH
ESTATE WINERY &
RESTAURANT**
607-535-9674.
3380 County Rte 28,
 Watkins Glen, NY.
Price: Inexpensive–
 Moderate.
Open: Lunch and dinner.

The building that houses Castel Grisch's tasting room and restaurant looks like a chalet that was transported directly from the Alps. Perched high above Seneca Lake, the whole mise-en-scène resembles a little corner of Switzerland. The menu may also transport one back to central and northern Europe, as the selections include creamed herring, cheese fondue, Hungarian goulash soup, Wiener schnitzel, spätzle, and Zurich Geschnatzelts, a classic Swiss veal dish. For less adventuresome diners, there is also a range of more familiar items, from shrimp cocktail to filet mignon. Kids can choose from the childrens' menu, which has such favorites as peanut butter and jelly sandwiches. Naturally, Castel Grisch offers a comprehensive wine list.

The lakeside Ginny Lee Cafe at Wagner Vineyards, Lodi, New York, is open for lunch.

Marguerite Thomas

**GINNY LEE CAFE (at
WAGNER
VINEYARDS)**
607-582-6574.
9322 Route 414, Lodi, NY.
Price: Inexpensive–
 Moderate.
Open: Lunch.

Named for Bill Wagner's daughter, the cafe has a splendid view of the lake. The fare ranges from light to robust, and includes such imaginative items as Garlic Decadence, an appetizer with garlic, cream cheese, and nuts, and salmon that's been smoked over barrel shavings from the winery. Except for special occasions, such as the annual Harvest Dinner, the cafe closes at 4 PM.

**GLENORA WINE
CELLARS WINE
GARDEN CAFE**
607-243-5511.
Route 14, Dundee, NY.
Price: Moderate.

The view from the dining room and the terrace, across the vineyards to Seneca Lake, surely rivals that of any restaurant in the world. Lunch at Glenora provides a perfect mid-day refresher between winery visits. There are cheese boards, salads, appetizing sandwiches, (grilled portobello mushrooms, smoked salmon, crab cakes, and sliced Black Angus Beef are only a few), and hearty main courses, such as shrimp and mussel scampi over pasta or chicken saté over rice. Dinner might include an appetizer of wild mushrooms baked in a puff pastry and an entree of sea scallops with leeks and saffron. The perfect accompaniment would be a bottle of Glenora Brut.

**BELHURST CASTLE
RESTAURANT AND
INN**
315-781-0201.
Route 14 South,
Geneva, NY.
Price: Moderate–Expensive.
Open: Lunch, dinner, and
Sunday brunch.

This 1885 gothic red stone structure, decorated with an abundance of towers and turrets, is the subject of many picturesque tales and legends. One of the most colorful features the doomed romance between a Spanish Don and a beautiful Italian opera singer, who was killed when a secret tunnel running from the house to the lake shore collapsed on her. In its varied history, Belhurst has been a stop on the Underground Railway during the Civil War, a speakeasy during Prohibition, and a gambling casino in the 1950s.

Today it is a romantic inn and restaurant, where diners can enjoy starters such as venison pâté, lobster and artichoke salad, or three-onion soup. Entrees range from rack of boar to ravioli primavera, with such traditional standbys as chicken Kiev and tournedos with béarnaise also sharing the menu. The extensive wine list covers most of the world, including several Finger Lakes wines by the glass or the bottle. Sunday brunch at Belhurst Castle is a popular local tradition.

Belhurst's rooms and suites set a romantic mood. They are decorated with antiques, Oriental rugs, and gas fireplaces. Air conditioning and modern plumbing provide the necessary modern comforts.

**GENEVA ON THE
LAKE–INN AND
RESTAURANT**
315-789-7190 or
800-3-GENEVA;
fax 315-789-0322.
1001 Lochland Rd, Route
145, Geneva, NY.
Price: Expensive.

With marble fireplaces, coffered ceilings, paneled rooms, and formal Italianate gardens sweeping down to Seneca Lake, this grand estate is a replica of an ancient villa in Frascati, outside of Rome. Built between 1910 and 1914 as a private residence for Byron Nester, the estate served as a Capuchin Monastery between 1949 and 1974. It was restored as a private residence between

Open: Year-round,
breakfast, Sun. brunch;
Jul. & Aug., Mon.–Sat.,
lunch on the terrace;
year-round, Fri., Sat., and
Sun., dinner with live
music.

1979–80 and later converted to luxury apartments. Today it's a country inn.

Some of the luxury suites have kitchens, fireplaces, and balconies. You may even stay in the suite where Paul Newman and Joanne Woodward once sojourned.

PART THREE
The Mountains

I. The Virginia Highlands

II. Central Pennsylvania

PART THREE
The Mountains

Statue at Chateau Morrisette on the Blue Ridge Parkway in Virginia.

Marguerite Thomas

Except for a few isolated areas, the weather in the mountainous regions of the East is too extreme for grapes to grow. In certain places, however, specific microclimates offer a more hospitable environment. Small viticultural regions in the mountains of Pennsylvania and Virginia, for example, have relatively high altitudes that keep the summer temperatures warm during the day and cool at night, conditions in which grapes thrive.

Here, the mountain air tends to be drier than in the muggier Uplands and Benchlands, which discourages fungus and molds from proliferating in the vineyards. Because the growing season in the mountains is long and relatively cool, grapes ripen slowly and develop intense color and flavors that are imparted to the wine.

From the traveler's perspective, these mountains still convey the sense of isolation and wild beauty for which this nation is noted. There are hundreds of lakes, thousands of forested acres, and miles and miles of hiking trails that charm sportsmen and nature lovers from all over the world.

THE VIRGINIA HIGHLANDS

The bell at Rockbridge Vineyards, Raphine, Virginia.

Marguerite Thomas

Virginia's western border is framed by the spectacular Blue Ridge, Shenandoah, Allegheny, and Cumberland Mountains. The spectacular beauty of the 105-mile Blue Ridge Parkway and Skyline Drive is one of the finest sights in America. This two-way road is devoid of buildings, billboards, villages, restaurants, or motels, allowing travelers to savor mile after mile of uninterrupted natural splendor.

Late spring is a fine time to travel here, when the white dogwoods, the orange- and lemon-colored rhododendron, and the delicate pink wild azalea bloom. The cloud shadows are scattered like pancakes across the foothills and the Shenandoah Valley below. Each season presents its own charms along this ribbon of road. To enhance any visit, it's also possible to segue over to some of the best wineries in Virginia.

As in the rest of Virginia, history plays a strong role in this region. There is a common thread that links the entire Monticello appellation, which includes wineries in both the Uplands and the Mountains. As Afton Vineyard's Tom Corpora put it, "At some point, Jefferson traversed it all on horseback."

Bob Harper, owner of Naked Mountain winery, is a walking encyclopedia of geological, culinary, and historical facts and trivia about the area, that he'll share in an inspired moment. Here are some of the things I learned from Bob in a single afternoon: Route 688, where his winery is located, is the same road Robert E. Lee took on his way to Gettysburg. Lee caught influenza along the way and had to spend a few days recuperating in Markham. Sweet Georgia Brown is buried in the local cemetery. Revolutionary War hero Daniel Morgan was painted only in profile because one of his ears was bitten off in a barroom brawl. The town of Pumpkinville, where George Washington lived, changed its name to Paris after Lafayette came to visit in the 1790s. The Shenandoah Valley is one of the largest lamb-producing regions in the U.S. Flint Hill, Virginia, still has the original white post set by George Washington when he surveyed the area.

Tom and Shinko Corpora, owners, Afton Mountain Vineyards, Afton, Virginia.

Marguerite Thomas

AFTON MOUNTAIN VINEYARDS
Rating: ♦♦♦
540-456-8667 (tel. and fax).
Route 631, Afton, VA.
Directions: From I-64, take exit 107 and go west on Rte. 250 for six miles to Rte. 151, then go south for three miles on Rte. 151 to Rte. 6, go west on Rte. 6 for 1.8 miles to Rte. 631, go south 1.2 miles to winery entrance.
Owners Tom and Shinko Corpora.
Open: Mar. through Dec., Wed.–Mon., 10 AM–6 PM; Jan. through Feb., Fri.–Mon., 11 AM–5 PM, or by appointment.
Price Range of Wines: $7 for Festiva Red and White, $13 for Gewürztraminer, $15 for Pinot Noir.
Special Features: Snack area.

Tom Corpora had a distinguished career as a journalist. He was with UPI for ten years and with NBC News for 18. During this time he covered six presidential campaigns and four wars on five different continents. Throughout it all, he entertained a vague fantasy about living on a farm.

When the "golden handshake" came from NBC, Tom seized the moment and began searching for his idyllic spot. As parents, Tom and his wife, Shinko, were particularly attracted to Virginia because of its publicly supported upper education system. They knew they didn't want to raise animals or start a new farm from scratch, but otherwise they hadn't any particular notion of what they *did* want to do.

Then, one day in 1988, a real estate broker drove Tom down a gravel road that cut through a gap in the eastern slope of the Blue Ridge Mountains, where the scenery is, as Tom described it, "almost sublime in its beauty." There was a six-acre vineyard, verdant in its early summer growth, and a 20-acre lake, large enough to have a moderating effect on the vineyard's microclimate. Tom's fate was sealed. "But we don't know anything about growing grapes or making wine," protested Shinko when Tom broke the news to her. "We can learn," he said.

Almost a decade later, Tom looks back at that moment and points out that the world consists of two kinds of people: those who grew up on a farm and those who didn't. "A corollary of that might be that those who grew up on farms are too smart to want to have anything more to do with them," he sighed. "I was in the second category, and though I knew people in the first, and had been warned by them about the hard work of farming, I still wasn't prepared for the reality."

In addition to the usual labor involved in farming, the Corporas were faced with a vineyard that had been sadly neglected and needed a massive amount of trimming and replanting. Gabriele Rausse, Virginia's pre-eminent vintner, became their vineyard advisor and, ultimately, their close friend. Gabriele taught Shinko how to make wine. The state enologist and viticulturist also provided invaluable advice.

The Corporas planted more vineyards, raising their total vineyard acreage to 17 acres, and they opened a winery. They now produce 2,000 cases of wine annually, which they hope to steadily increase. Clearly it has been a struggle, emotionally as well as economically ("It's not as lucrative as NBC News," says Tom drily).

This isn't to say that Tom and Shinko have stopped dreaming. "People say you can't make Gewürztraminer in Virginia. I'm hoping to prove them wrong," says Shinko and, after tasting her recent Gewürz, one can believe she'll do just that. "I tell people who like our dry, Chablis-style Chardonnay to just say no to oak and get the grape back into Chardonnay," Shinko smiles. Among the other very good wines at Afton are a delicate Pinot Noir and a Vouvray-style Chenin Blanc.

Visitors can enjoy a snack at cafe tables in the tasting room overlooking the sublime scenery.

CHATEAU MORRISETTE
Rating: 🍷🍷🍷
540-593-2865;
   fax 540-593-2868.
Milepost 171.5, Blue Ridge
   Parkway (Meadows of
   Dan), VA.
Directions: From the Blue
   Ridge Parkway, turn
   west at mile post 171.5,
   onto Rte. 726, take an
   immediate left on
   Winery Rd. to the winery
   on the right.
Owners: The Morrisette
   family.

Many changes have taken place recently at this fine winery. It moved to a dramatic new building and opened a restaurant on a stunning site on the Blue Ridge Parkway, just above the Rock Castle Gorge Wilderness Area. In 1990 it hired winemaker Bob Burgin. After earning a degree in enology and viticulture at Mississippi State, Bob opened his own winery in Mississippi. He soon realized, however, that 60% of Mississippi's residents held religious beliefs that required them to be teetotalers. It occurred to him that he might be in the wrong place.

Then he met David Morrisette, whose father owned the Virginia winery bearing his name. As

Bob Burgin, waiter at Le Chien Noir, Chateau Morrisette's restaurant.

Marguerite Thomas

Open: Mon.–Sat., 10 AM–5 PM; Sun. 11 AM–5 PM.
Price Range of Wines: $7.50 for Sweet Mountain Laurel to $11 for Chardonnay.
Special Features: Restaurant.

they were looking for a talented winemaker, they hired Bob, who brings more than winemaking skills to his job. He has a certain Southern sensibility that adds color to Chateau Morrisette's wines. For example, he defies a tradition among winemakers by admitting that he likes sweet wines, which he considers good quaffing wine as well as a nice beverage to accompany dessert. He specifically likes the much-maligned Niagara grape that grows spectacularly well in the mountainous climate of the Blue Ridge Mountains. "A lot of Fresno State grads might turn up their nose at making Niagara wine, but we know it pays the bills," he states pragmatically.

Bob is a believer in the advantages of blending grapes from different climates, as well as different vineyards. Chateau Morrisette's successful 1993 Chardonnay, for example, was made by mixing several wines that had been fermented and aged separately. Grapes from different vineyards were used: austere, high-acid mountain grapes blended with fatter, flabbier fruit from central Virginia, even a small amount of fruit from a North Carolina vineyard about 45 miles away. The result is a beguiling wine that combines a lemony tartness with the rich, round flavors of caramelized bananas.

The staff in the tasting room at Chateau Morrisette make a genuine effort to educate visitors. "Let the wine roll across your tongue, hitting both sides, then swallow it in small sips," advised the tasting room director, John Wilkins, to a group of enthralled visitors one afternoon. He poured samples of Mountain Laurel, a sweet Niagara wine, saying, "This is great porch wine. Keep it well chilled, and sip it a little at a time." "Sweet wine makes my tongue thick," mutters one skeptic, but after tasting it, she decides to buy a bottle. "Serve this with pecan pie or cheese cake," John tells her, "or try whizzing a cup or two of

Mountain Laurel in the blender with a couple of scoops of vanilla ice cream, a few ice cubes and one and a half pints of fresh strawberries. It's a great daiquiri-type dessert."

Among the many winning Chateau Morrisette wines are Black Dog, a combination of Cabernet, Chambourcin, and Merlot, and Black Dog Blanc, a Chardonnay, Vidal, and Seyval blend, that is excellent with spicy foods, such as blackened catfish.

While the Blue Ridge Park is dotted with attractive picnic sites, it would be a shame to miss a top-notch meal at the Chateau Morrisette Restaurant.

Main house at Linden Vineyards, Linden, Virginia.

Marguerite Thomas

LINDEN VINEYARDS

Rating: 🍷🍷🍷🍷
540-364-1997.
3708 Harrels Corner Road, Linden, VA.
Directions: From Washington, D.C., take I-66 to exit 13 in Linden, go one mile east on Rte. 55, then turn right onto Rte. 638 and go two miles to the winery.
Owners: Jim and Peggy Law.
Open: Apr. through Dec., Wed.–Sun., 11 AM–5 PM; Jan. through Mar., Sat. & Sun., 11 AM–5 PM.
Price Range of Wines: $10.50 for Seyval to $14 for Cabernet Sauvignon.
Special Events: July Blueberry picking.

Jim and Peggy Law have science and agricultural backgrounds, which helped them know what to look for when they decided to plant a vineyard in Virginia. "We knew we wanted a mountain site," Jim said, explaining that the cooler air in the mountains helps delay the ripening of the grapes, and that promotes more intense flavors. "When grapes grow in hot and humid climates, they ripen in August, and don't have a lot of finesse. In our area, the sunny days and cool nights allow the grapes to ripen over a longer period of time. We feel it adds elegance and harmony to the wine."

The Laws chose a spot at the 1,300 elevation in the Blue Ridge Mountains for their vineyard in 1985. "It's ideal for grapes," said Jim. "They ripen late in October, when the fruit has great intensity." The winery produces 5,000 cases of wine annually from its 25-acre vineyard, and the wines are widely accepted as some of the best in the state.

Linden Vineyards white wines include a barrel fermented Chardonnay, Seyval, Sauvignon Blanc, and a Riesling-Vidal blend. The lush, spicy reds are blends of Cabernet Sauvignon, Cabernet Franc, and Petit Verdot. The wines are terrific, but can the Laws hope to succeed in today's competitive market? "Let's put it this way," grins Jim. "Do you hear that hammering in the background? That's the sound of our $100,000 addition being built. We certainly wouldn't be doing that if we weren't optimistic about the future."

Bob Harper and his distinctive truck, Naked Mountain Vineyard, Markham, Virginia.

Marguerite Thomas

NAKED MOUNTAIN VINEYARD AND WINERY
Rating: ♦♦♦
540-364-1609.
2747 Leeds Manor Road., Markham, VA.
Directions: From Washington, D.C. take I-66 to exit 18 in Markham, go 1¹/₂ miles north on Rte. 688 to the winery.
Owner: Bob Harper.
Open: Mar. through Dec., Wed.–Sun., 11 AM–5 PM; Jan. & Feb., Sat. & Sun., 11 AM–5 PM.
Price Range of Wines: $10–$14.
Special Features: Picnic area, light snacks.

The name provokes a lot of speculation. "More than a few people get carried away by the name Naked Mountain," admits winery owner Bob Harper, flashing a wicked grin. In fact, the name, which is found in the original 1765 deed to the property, aptly describes the mountain, whose soil composition is mostly schist and decomposed rock.

Because of a thermal inversion, the eastern slope of the Blue Ridge Mountains is relatively sheltered from winds and it enjoys milder winter temperatures and cooler summers than many other areas in the state. "It is the best place in Virginia for grapes," says Bob simply. Of course, there are certain problems, such as the Clipper, a wind-born cold front that sometimes whips through here. Bob seems unfazed when such topics are mentioned. "This is agriculture," he shrugs. "There are no freebies."

Naked Mountain Winery produces 5,000 cases of vinifera wine annually from grapes grown in its 40-acre vineyard. The winery specializes in white wines, with Chardonnay accounting for 75% of its production. It also produces some Sauvignon Blanc and Riesling. Bob believes Riesling does better at this elevation than in the lower parts of the state. Among its red wines, it makes a Cabernet Sauvignon, and may soon plant Shiraz. Naked Mountain's mobile bottling unit travels to smaller wineries all over the East that don't have their own bottling equipment.

Bob is a former lubricants engineer with Texaco. "I'm just working with another kind of lubricant now," he jokes. The winery is less than an hour from Washington, D.C and Bob is proud to point out that Naked Mountain wine has been served in the Clinton White House.

There is an attractive picnic area. Cheese and other light fare are sold in the tasting room.

Oakencroft Vineyard & Winery, Charlottesville, Virginia.

Courtesy Oakencroft Vineyard

OAKENCROFT VINEYARD & WINERY

Rating: 🍷
804-296-4188 (weekdays)
804-295-8175 (weekends);
fax 804-293-6631.
Route 5, Charlottesville, VA.
Directions: From Rte. 29, go 3¹/₃ miles west on Barracks Rd. (Rte. 654), to Garth Rd. The winery entrance is on the left.
Owner: Felicia Warburg Rogan.
Open: Apr. through Dec., daily, 11 AM–7 PM; Jan. & Feb., 11 AM– 5 PM by

Felicia Warburg Rogan and her late husband, John, were owners of Charlottesville's famous Boar's Head Inn when they first became interested in making their own wine. They planted an experimental vineyard and made Seyval Blanc, Chardonnay, and Merlot with amateur equipment in a converted tool shed.

Then, in 1982, Felicia Warburg Rogan got serious. She hired a vineyard manager, planted a 17-acre vineyard, and began producing a variety of wines from hybrid and vinifera grapes. One of her smartest moves was to hire Shepherd Rouse, an outstanding Virginia winemaker. Although Shep now devotes most of his time to Rockbridge, his own winery, he continues to serve as consultant at appointment; mid-Mar. to Apr., Sat. and Sun. 11 AM–5 PM.

Price Range of Wines: $7.50 for Countryside White, $11 for Chardonnay, $12 for Merlot.

Special Events: Rites of Spring Open House, Spring Fiesta, Holiday Open House, Christmas Open House and Candlelight Tour.

Oakencroft. The wines, reflecting his skillful touch, are improving all the time.

In their brief history, Oakencroft wines have managed to travel far. They went to Moscow in 1988 with President Reagan, who presented Mikhail Gorbachev with a gift of Oakencroft Seyval Blanc. Oakencroft wine has also been poured at diplomatic events in Taipei, Hawaii, and at the American Embassy in Paris.

In the United States, the wines can be tasted at the winery. Pack a picnic and go to the winery, where you can buy some of the same kind of Seyval Blanc that went to Moscow. It's now called Countryside White. Other popular Oakencroft wines are the Chardonnay and Merlot.

Jane Rause at Rockbridge Vineyard, Raphine, Virginia.

Marguerite Thomas

ROCKBRIDGE VINEYARD
Rating: 🍇🍇🍇
540-377-6204.

Route 606, Raphine, VA.

Directions: From I-81/I-64 take exit 205 and go west on Rte. 606 for one mile to the winery.

Owners: Shepherd and Jane Rause.

Open: May through Oct., Fri. & Sat., 11 AM–5 PM; Sun. noon–5 PM; Apr., Nov. & 1st 2 weeks in Dec., Sat. 11 AM–5 PM;

At 2,000 feet above sea level, Rockbridge grapes tend to ripen later than the fruit in other regions. Chardonnay, for example, is about two weeks behind the Chardonnay in other areas. This gives it ample time to develop full, rich flavors. This is one of the reasons that Shepherd and Jane Rause share a quiet optimism about the future of their new winery.

Shep, who previously worked at wineries in Germany, Virginia, and in California's Napa Valley, where he specialized in sparkling wines, is well qualified to make excellent wines. His name is

closed Jan. through Mar.
Price Range of Wines: $6
for apple wine to $14 for
Pinot Noir.
Special Features: Picnic
area.
Special Events: Almost May
Celebration (1st tasting of
the barrel fermented
apple wine), Summer
Breeze Fete, End of
Summer Solace, Fall
Harvest Fest, Holiday
Open House.

inevitably at the top of the list whenever Virginia winemakers are discussed.

Visitors to the Rause's big, restored dairy barn and seven-acre vineyard can discover these classy, award-winning wines for themselves. There's an intensely aromatic Moselle-style Riesling, for example, and a flavorful and harmonious Chardonnay. Tuscarora White, a Riesling/Vidal blend with a touch of sweetness, is named after the Tuscarora White sandstone deposits that are prevalent in the region. Tuscarora was also the name of the Iroquois tribe who migrated south from New York to hunt in the Blue Ridge Mountains. Tuscarora Red is a full-bodied wine that would be a nice partner for steak. Rockbridge currently produces about 2,300 cases of wine annually, but with quality this high, growth is inevitable.

For an exceptional picnic in a pastoral setting, bring some smoked salmon or smoked turkey, a loaf of crusty bread, and some rich, ripe cheese to enjoy with a bottle of Rockbridge St. Mary's Blanc, a dry, spicy wine made from Vidal that was fermented in French oak. It's named after the nearby St. Mary's Wilderness Area, which is a beautiful place to go hiking after the picnic.

SHENANDOAH VINEYARDS

Rating: 🍷
540-984-8699;
fax 540-984-9463.
3659 South Ox Road,
Edinburg, VA.
Directions: From I-81 take
exit 279, go west at the
bottom of the ramp onto
Stony Creek Rd. Take the
first right onto South Ox
Rd., go 1^1/2 miles to the
winery on the left.
Owner: Nathan Randall.
Open: Daily, 10 AM–6 PM.
Price Range of Wines: $7
for Shenandoah Blanc to
$17.95 for Pinot Noir.
Special Features: Picnic
area in grape arbor.
Special Events: Harvest
Festival the first weekend
after Labor Day, Pig
Roast in July.

Nestled in the Blue Ridge Mountains of the Shenandoah Valley, this winery has been producing premium wines since it opened 20 years ago. It was the first commercial winery in the Shenandoah Valley, and one of the first in Virginia. Today, Shenandoah Vineyards makes about 8,000 cases of vinifera and hybrid wines, mostly from grapes raised in the winery's own 30-acre vineyard.

Virginia wines are dramatically improving, and Nathan Randall, the youngest generation to enter the family business, is convinced that the future looks good. "A few years ago the wine here wasn't much, but now we're definitely able to compete with the rest of the country. Of course, there's still room for improvement, but that's a never-ending mission," he says with a smile. "Quality and excellence are the future of the Virginia wine industry."

Quality and excellence describe Shenandoah's wines. Shenandoah Blanc, a medium-dry white blend and Pinot Noir are both excellent. Surrounded by vineyards, and with great views out over the Blue Ridge Mountains, visitors will enjoy relaxing at the picnic tables under the grape arbor.

Mike Riddick of Wintergreen Vineyards & Winery, Nellysford, Virginia.

Marguerite Thomas

WINTERGREEN VINEYARDS & WINERY

Rating: 🍷🍷🍷
804-361-2519.
Route 664, Nellysford, VA.
Directions: From Charlottesville, go south on Rte. 151 for 14 miles to Rte. 664, turn west and go ¹/₂ mile to the winery. From the Blue Ridge Parkway, exit onto Rte. 664 east at mile post 13. The winery is 5 miles on the left.
Owners: Mike and Kathy Riddick.
Open: Apr. through Dec., daily, 10 AM–6 PM; Jan. through Mar., Wed.–Mon., noon–5 PM.
Price Range of Wines: $6.49 for Mill Hill Apple Wine to $15.99 for Black Rock Reserve Chardonnay and Cabernet Sauvignon.

Mike and Kathy Riddick bought a 400-acre farm in the Blue Ridge Mountains in 1988. "Before long," said Mike, "We were tired of watching cows eat grass." In 1989 they planted vines, knowing that by 1992, when it was time for the first harvest, they would have to decide whether to hire a winemaker or to learn winemaking themselves.

They spent the intervening years reading everything they could about wine and traveling to wineries in California, the Finger Lakes, and Long Island. "Even then, of course, we didn't know what we were doing," acknowledges Mike cheerfully.

Mike is an upbeat kind of guy, who clearly enjoys life. "It's fun making wine," he says. "It's especially fun now that we're getting some recognition, and it's fun hearing the cash register ring." Every year the cash register rings twice as often as it did the year before.

Mike only makes the kind of wine he likes to drink. "I like a big buttery California-style Chardonnay," he says, "so that's what I strive for here." He likes a semi-dry (i.e. slightly sweet) Riesling. "I can't think of a wine I'd rather have with Maryland crabcake."

Mike gives full credit for the success of his wines to his vineyard. Planted in an old apple orchard with rocky, clay loam, it is, he says, a great place to grow vines. "The old-timers recognized that it was a frost-free microclimate, without really understanding the implications. No matter how we make the wine, we constantly win awards."

The winery is next to Wintergreen Resort where summer hiking and golf, and winter skiing attract tourists year-round.

RESTAURANTS AND LODGING

For additional places to stay and eat, please refer to the Central Virginia section of the Uplands chapter.

RESTAURANTS AND LODGING

**L'AUBERGE
PROVENÇALE**
540-837-1375 or
800-638-1702.
Rte. 340, White Post, VA.
Price: Moderate–Expensive.

Alain and Celeste Borel have created a little bit of Provence in this picturesque section of Virginia which, in so many ways, is similar to the landscape of Provence where Alain was raised and learned his craft. He is an acclaimed chef, and a trip out from Washington, D.C. for one of his Provençal meals is well worth the effort. The dining rooms, as well as the ten guestrooms, are decorated with bright provincial fabrics and antiques. Naturally, a fine selection of Virginia wines is on the list.

SAMPSON EAGON INN
540-886-8200 or
800-597-9722.
238 E. Beverley St.,
Staunton, VA.

Frank and Laura Mattingly have lovingly restored a historic 1840 Greek Revival house on Staunton's Gospel Hill, right across the street from the Woodrow Wilson Museum. The four guestrooms are decorated with personal remembrances of former owners of the house, in an elegant and sophisticated style with canopy beds lavishly draped in chintz. Although there is no restaurant, Frank and Laura are very knowledgeable about Virginia wines and will be happy to direct guests to local restaurants that feature them.

**LE CHIEN NOIR
RESTAURANT
(CHATEAU
MORRISETTE)**
540-593-2865.
Milepost 171.5, Blue Ridge

The name of this attractive restaurant refers to the black lab, who is the winery's mascot. It might also call to mind the dog days of summer, when one wants the kind of simple but flavorful fare offered here: a sandwich of grilled eggplant,

Parkway, (Meadows of Dan,) VA.
Open: Lunch: Wed.–Sun., 11 AM–2 PM; dinner: Sat. & Sun. only (reservations requested).
Price: Moderate.

onion, roasted red pepper, anchovy aioli, and goat cheese on a baguette, for example, accompanied by a glass of well chilled Chardonnay. Or, a bowl of red lentil soup with dried cherries and apricots, followed by grilled shrimp Szechuan style with warm sesame noodles, might be just the thing. Actually, a buffalo burger from a local buffalo farm, or blackened catfish, from a fish farm owned by Chateau Morrisette, are equally appealing. At any time of year the Black Dog's menu is full of temptations, and the view of the mountains from the deck rates five stars by itself.

The Mabry Mill.

Marguerite Thomas

MABRY MILL COFFEE SHOP
540-952-2947.
Milepost 176.1, Blue Ridge Parkway, VA.
Price: Inexpensive.

The gristmill built by E. B. Mabry in 1935 is the most photographed thing on the Blue Ridge Parkway. In addition to the place's photogenic virtues, the mill, as well as the blacksmith shop and sawmill, are interesting to visit, particularly on days when they are in operation. They are run by the Eastern National Parks and Monuments Federation. The funky old coffee shop dishes up real indigenous breakfasts of ham, eggs, grits, and biscuits, plus corn cakes made from grain ground on the property. Try a country ham or barbecued pork sandwich for lunch.

Profile: Cheese

MONASTERY COUNTRY CHEESE (3365 Monastery Drive, Crozet, VA 22932).

Picture a fat round of Gouda cheese encased in a protective coat of gleaming red wax. Picture the cheese's soft, smooth texture, its nutty aroma, and its mild, creamy taste that harmonizes so aptly with wine. Now picture the people who make this cheese. No, not Dutch farmers in a flat, tulip-filled landscape. These cheesemakers are nuns, who work on a farm in the foothills of the Blue Ridge Mountains.

The sisters belong to an order that requires them to earn their own living rather than rely on charity. They learned to make cheese from the farm's original owner, a Dutch woman who had learned her craft in Holland. The sisters produce almost 20,000 pounds of cheese a year, and most of it sells out by Christmas.

The sisters practice the ageless technique of heating milk (which they obtain from dairy farmers in the nearby Shenandoah Valley) and adding cultures to produce curds that are then cut by hand, packed in forms called hoops, and pressed. The finished wheels of cheese are immersed in salt brine and cured in a refrigerated room, where they are turned and inspected daily. When they are finished, each wheel is dipped in its protective red wax coating.

Intrepid travelers can make their way to this remote spot, but it's simpler to buy the cheese by mail order. There is no telephone. The address is: Our Lady of the Angels Monastery, Rte. 2, Box 288 A, Crozet, VA 22932.

RHODES FARM INN
804-361-1200.
Wintergreen, VA.
Price: Inexpensive.

After a long morning of lifting countless glasses of wine, I can't begin to describe how good that big ole' plate of impeccably fried chicken with fluffed up potatoes, green beans, and scarlet rounds of tomatoes bathed in vinegar tasted. There's no menu at Rhodes Farm; guests just make their way into the brick farmhouse, settle down at one of the communal tables, pour themselves a glass of iced tea from one of the perpetually-filled pitchers on the table or order some local wine, and wait for the platefuls of mouthwatering country fare to arrive. Trust me, this is the real thing, not some gussied up version of rural vittles, and not a sleazy cut-rate imitation. The ingredients are fresh, wholesome, and prepared in traditional fashion. For heaven's sake, please don't start carrying on about how the green beans ought to be *al dente*. It's just not that kind of place. One gets the feeling that "city folk" have never ventured out to this unspoiled spot, but in fact lots of Rhodes fans have made the pilgrimage out here over the past 20 years to chow down and shoot the

Marguerite Wade on the porch of the inviting Rhodes Farm Inn in Wintergreen, Virginia.

Marguerite Thomas

breeze with Marguerite Wade, the charming proprietress — Muhammad Ali, John Lennon, Mick Jagger, and Virginia's own U.S. Senator John Warner among them. Did I mention the hot buttered rolls, the homemade applesauce, and the warm gingerbread topped with real cream? The inn also has guest cottages for anyone who had the good sense to reserve one in advance.

CENTRAL PENNSYLVANIA

Pennsylvania's Huntingdon County is known as "the land of a thousand hills" because of the mountainous spine that rolls through central Pennsylvania on its way down to Virginia. The region is a paradise for hikers, fishermen, hunters, enthusiasts of water sports, and everyone else who loves nature and the outdoors. There are three state parks in Raystown and Huntingdon counties, with hundreds of miles of hiking trails and dozens of lakes, including the 22-acre lake in Whipple Dam State Park.

Intellectuals, as well as nature lovers, have found inspiration here. Edgar Allen Poe, for example, got the idea for his famous poem "The Raven" while he strolled along Raven Rock Trail in Trough Creek State Park. Geology buffs won't want to miss the Indian or Lincoln Caverns.

Railroad devotees will enjoy seeing the famed Horseshoe Curve, a railroad engineering marvel. Tracks were carved into the Allegheny Mountains at Altoona, connecting Philadelphia and Pittsburgh for the first time. The Hunt Railroad Signal Tower Museum is also interesting (call 814 643 6308 for directions and hours).

Fans of antique cars will be fascinated by the Swigart Museum, where the largest private collection of antique steam, gas, and electric automobiles in the

U.S. are displayed. How many other places can you see a 1930 Dusenberg? It's located on Route 22 east of Huntingdon.

If all this invigorating activity has made you hungry, head for the Benzel Pretzel Factory for some samples and a self-guided tour through the bakery (Route 764 in Altoona). There are also numerous candy factories in the area.

People on the wine trail, of course, will devote much of their time to the region's wineries. To the uninitiated, the steep slopes and extreme weather in this region may make it appear like an unlikely place to raise grapes, but local vintners would disagree. "This region has the greatest soil in the world. California would kill for it," insists Don Chapman, who owns Brookmere Farm Vineyards, in Belleville. In a candid moment Don will then add, "Of course, we'd kill for their weather."

Marguerite Thomas

Brookmere Farm Winery is in the Big Valley of central Pennsylvania.

BROOKMERE FARM VINEYARDS

Rating: ♦
717-935-5380.
Route 655, Belleville, PA.
Directions: From Rte. 322 take Rte. 655 southwest for five miles to the winery.
Owners: Don and Susan Chapman.
Open: Mon.–Sat., 10 AM–5 PM; Sun. 1 PM–4 PM.
Price Range of Wines: $4.25 for Autumn White, $8 for Chardonnay.

Brookmere is located in the Kishaquillas Valley, more commonly known as "Big Valley." The valley is only three miles wide by 35 miles long, but it's framed by seven mountains. It is quietly lovely, fertile and verdant, with farmhouses standing guard over fields and an occasional Amish family clip-clopping along the road in a horse and buggy.

Don Chapman is clearly at home here in Big Valley. He and his wife, Susan, are relative newcomers, having purchased this farm 20 years ago. The farm itself is part of a 700-acre original land grant dating back to William Penn. Before they moved here, the Chapmans lived in Connecticut, where Don, who has a background in engineering,

Special Features: Gift shop, picnic area.

owned a company that manufactured various metal objects, ranging from hatchets to fans.

A home-winemaker whose hobby got out of control, Don took courses in enology at Cornell, U.C. Davis, and Pennsylvania State College while easing into the business professionally with, as he puts it, "more guts than brains." Reducing the art of making wine to a simple description, Don said, "You're just solving chemistry problems, shooting for a balance between the acidity and the sugar content." Pointing out that Pennsylvania is full of limestone caves, Don explained that the local land is ideal for grapes since it is rich in potassium and calcium.

Brookmere produces 3,500 cases of wine from grapes grown on its own five-acre vineyard, plus additional grapes purchased from other Pennsylvania growers. About 20,000 people visit the winery each season. The Chapmans' goal has been to produce a wide range of wines, from dry to semi-sweet to sweet (about 16 selections in all), so that people can try different styles in order to find out what they like.

What they mostly like now is sweet, so that's what Brookmere's wines tend to be. Happily, they are well-crafted enough to appeal to experienced wine drinkers, as well as those less experienced. Valley Mist is a pleasant blend of Seyval, Vidal, and Chardonel. Brookmere Riesling usually exhibits a good balance between sweetness and acidity. Tears of the Goose, a blush wine that is more interesting than many blushes offered by well-known producers, is made in honor of Goose Day, a favorite local holiday related to the British Michaelmas feast. As this September holiday is supposed to honor debtors, people who are invited out to dinner traditionally bring money and a goose to the host.

Bring your own picnic fare (a goose might be messy), buy a bottle of wine after tasting the selections, and enjoy an afternoon of picnicking in Brookmere's vineyard. Autumn White is a fairly sweet white, but Chardonnay is drier. Save some time for visiting the gift shop, which has unusually appealing selections made by local artists and craftspeople.

OAK SPRINGS WINERY
Rating: 🍷
814-946-3799.
Old Route 220,
   Altoona, PA.
Directions: From Altoona take Rte. 220 north for three miles to the Pine Croft exit. Turn right at the light and continue to the winery, which will be $^1/_2$ mile on the right.
Owners: John and Sylvia Schraff.

This family-operated winery, owned by John and Sylvia Schraff, makes about 5,000 cases of wine annually from grapes grown in its own three-acre vineyard, plus those purchased from other Pennsylvania growers. The vineyard, at a 1,200-foot elevation, is planted on a hillside that maximizes sunlight and takes advantage of the morning breeze.

"This is a good growing area," said winemaker Scott Schraff, John's son. "Yes, the weather is sometimes extreme — we got over 100 inches of snow during two recent consecutive winters. But even

Open: Daily 11 AM–6 PM.
Price Range of Wines: $6
to $9.

then we only lost a couple of vines, and that was from the wind."

The advantages of the area include the fact that with thousands of reservoirs in the region there has never been a drought. There is also less humidity here than in many other eastern regions, thanks to the altitude and the breezes. In fact, the prevailing winds are so prevalent in the region, that the annual world hang-gliding championships are held here. Folks theorize that it would be possible to take a glider from here to Kentucky and back on the same current.

"Actually, conditions may be good enough here that we could grow vinifera," said Scott, "but Chambourcin is probably the best red-wine grape for the region. You can get your Bordeaux-style wines from California, but Chambourcin is the recognizable Pennsylvania wine."

What prompted a successful, young photojournalist to leave New York to become a vintner in the Pennsylvania mountains? Scott did this partly out of a desire to move his young family from the city to a congenial rural area, and partly because his stepmother, Sylvia Schraff, had started the winery. It captured his interest. "We learned to make wine by doing it," he said. "My stepmother and I work together on it."

Scott was also drawn to this area because his grandfather had come to Altoona to help build the railroad. "In those days immigrants put down roots," said Scott, describing how the German, Italian, and Polish men, who built the railroad, settled here when the job was finished.

Visitors to Oak Springs can ponder these issues as they taste the wines. What the winery lacks in quaintness it makes up for in convenience, as it is located on a major road. There are no picnic grounds, but the surrounding region is full of sylvan spots for an al fresco meal.

OREGON HILL WINERY

Rating: 🍷
717-353-2711.
Morris, PA.
Directions: From
  Wellsboro, follow
  Rte. 287 for 17 miles
  south. When you reach
  the log cabin restaurant
  "Inn 287," turn right
  onto the paved road.
  Go one mile to the
  winery.
Owner: Eric Swendrowski.
Open: Daily, 10 AM–5:30 PM.

Eric Swendrowski was a child prodigy in the world of wine. At the age of 12, he made his first wine. (His Belgian-born father had always made wine at the family farm in Pennsylvania while Eric was growing up.) At the age of 18, he formed a corporation, and at 19, he opened his winery.

Now 29 years old, Eric purchases his grapes from local farmers, as Oregon Hill's own vinifera vineyard was phased out after six years of struggling to maintain it in this inhospitable spot. "We get June frosts up here," said Eric. "We're basically at the top of a crater, with poor soil and poor drainage. But, as one of our neighbors, who's a farmer, said, 'Just because I don't have my own chickens doesn't

Price Range of Wines: $4.95 for Mountain White and Mountain Red to $14.95 for Cabernet Sauvignon.

mean I can't make an excellent omelette.'"

Eric produces about 2,000 cases of wine a year in 17 different varieties, and all are for sale at the winery. They range from a dry, oak-aged Cabernet to Niagara. Mountain White and Mountain Red, both Niagara-based wines, are popular.

Located near the Pennsylvania Grand Canyon, in one of the state's most remote areas, Oregon Hill attracts hikers, hunters, and nature lovers. There are no picnic facilities at the winery, but it is surrounded by hundreds of acres of idyllic picnic sites.

OTHER CENTRAL PENNSYLVANIA WINERIES

Travelers to the Pittsburgh region can swing by **LAPIC WINERY** (412-846-2031, 682 Tulip Dr., New Brighton, PA), where a variety of dry to semi-sweet wines has been produced for the past two decades. When the steel mills in this area shut down years ago, young people left in droves to seek work elsewhere. Today, when they return to visit families in the region, they are apt to stock up on Lapic Wine to carry back to their new homes in Texas, Arizona, or even Australia.

Appendixes

I. How Wine is Made

II. When is Wine Ready to Drink?

III. Tasting Wine in a Winery

IV. Where to Buy Eastern Wines

V. Touring the Eastern States Wine Regions

VI. Wineries Listed Alphabetically by State

VII. Best Wines of the East - Selected Favorites

VIII. Bibliography

HOW WINE IS MADE

The best way for consumers to learn about winemaking is to visit a few wineries. A first-hand glimpse at the various winemaking steps — from vineyard practices through the bottling operation — leads to a better understanding of the process. While the precise methods of making wine may vary from winery to winery, the fundamental techniques are the same everywhere.

Although the equipment used in winemaking in now high-tech, and winemakers have become better at controlling the forces of nature, the basics of winemaking have not changed significantly since the dawn of civilization. When it was first discovered that fermented fruit juice tasted good and could have a pleasant effect on anyone who drank enough of it, wine became a magic potion; it still is today. The various steps, then and now, for converting grapes into the alcoholic beverage we call wine, can be easily understood.

Harvesting the grapes: Grapes are picked, either by hand or by machine. Ideally, the fruit has reached a maximum degree of ripeness by the time it is harvested. Vintners can tell how ripe the grapes are and what the sugar content is through a refractometer, which measures fruit on the vine in "degrees Brix." Underripe fruit yields thin-flavored, overly acidic juice; overripe fruit lacks the touch of acidity that gives a wine backbone, and it may even have acquired off-flavors because of mold or rotting.

Crushing: The harvested fruit is transferred to the winery, where weight is applied via some device such as human feet or the mechanical crushers used by virtually all modern wineries. Crushing splits the grape skins, thereby releasing the juice.

Pressing: In the case of white wines a press is used to gently squeeze the juice away from the skins and seeds before beginning fermentation. Red wines are generally fermented for a time along with their skins, which lends both flavor and color to the wine. Most grapes, even those with red skins, are white inside.

Fermenting: After pressing, the juice, which is called "must" at this point, is transferred for fermentation to large, open, wood vats, concrete vats or, more commonly today, large cylindrical stainless steel tanks. Certain premium wines, both red and white, may be fermented in small oak barrels. This is riskier, and requires more attention than fermenting in stainless steel, but complex and pleasing flavors picked up from the wood can be transmitted to the wine.

Yeasts (either man-made or natural yeasts clinging to the fruit) feed on the sugars in the grape juice. As the sugar is consumed, it is converted to alcohol and carbon dioxide. One of the most significant advances in modern winemaking is the vintner's ability to control the temperature of fermenting must. For white wines, particularly, going through a longer, cooler fermentation has resulted in fruitier, fresher wines.

The skins are left in the tank with fermenting red wine until the desired color has been extracted from them, then the must is "racked," or transferred, away from the skins into another tank.

Good rosé wine, incidentally, is made by leaving the skins in the fermentation tank just long enough to create a rosy color. Cheap rosé wine is often a mixture of red and white wine.

Wine sometimes undergoes a second fermentation, called "malolactic fermentation." This procedure converts harsh and astringent malic acid (the kind found in apples) into supple, softer lactic acid (the kind found in milk).

After fermentation: Fermentation stops when all of the sugar molecules have been converted to alcohol. The resulting alcoholic content of the wine varies from an average of 7–9% (especially where grapes are grown in very cool regions such as Germany) to 10–14% (most of the table wines we drink fall in this latter range). When all the sugar in the wine has been used up, we say it is a "dry" wine as opposed to "sweet."

In actuality, it is almost impossible for all of the different types of sugar in grape juice to be converted to alcohol. The few remaining sugar cells are called "residual sugar," or RS. The amount of RS in wine can vary from 1 gram per liter to 2.5 grams or more, but most wine that contains less than 2 grams of residual sugar will be perceived as dry; obviously, the higher the amount of residual sugar, the sweeter the wine will taste.

Aging: Wine that has just finished fermenting may look cloudy and smell gassy or yeasty. Red wine usually leaves a rough, abrasive feel in the mouth from the tannins that have been extracted from the skins and seeds. All wine needs a period of "aging" to allow these unpleasant side-effects of fermentation to dissipate or at least to have their rough edges smoothed over.

White wine is frequently aged for a few months in stainless steel tanks before it is bottled. The resulting wine will, ideally, taste as crisp and bright as a fresh apple or pear. Some premium white wines, especially those made from Chardonnay and, increasingly, Seyval grapes, are matured in small oak barrels. The oak can add complex and appealing nuances, often described as vanillalike, to the flavor of the wine. When aged in oak, wine is usually left "*sur lie.*" This means it is left on the lees, the sediments left behind by the yeasts. This also adds richness and depth of taste to the wine.

Red wine may be aged from a few weeks to three years or more before bottling. Longer maturing usually takes place in oak barrels, also called "*barriques.*" The *barriques* favored by the majority of winemakers today hold about 225 liters, or 60 gallons. This follows the example set in Burgundy and Bordeaux.

Aging in oak helps to soften and round out the harsh tannins in red wine. The oak also imparts certain desirable flavors to wine that remind people of vanilla, various spices, or toasted bread. Some winemakers like to use new oak barrels, which impart a stronger "oaky" flavor. After three or four years, they may sell their barrels to other vintners, who prefer the subtler impact of older, seasoned oak.

Classic *barriques* are usually made from French oak, but many American winemakers are turning to less expensive American oak. There are various arguments on each side of the issue, ranging from, "American oak is better for American wine," to "American oak is too tannic" or "too sappy." American oak, incidentally, is widely used in the viticultural regions of South America, Australia, and Spain, where its more aggressive flavor is counteracted by the potent wines from these warm countries.

An alternative to expensive oak barrels is the use of oak chips — little nuggets of wood that are usually added to wine during fermentation to impart some of the desirable characteristics provided by oak barrels.

Clarifying the wine: Wine is left with a certain amount of sediment after maturing, and various methods have been employed over the ages to remove them. This is known as "clarifying" the wine. One of the oldest techniques, and one still commonly used, is the application of beaten eggs whites which attract particles suspended in the wine. Other methods for "fining" wine include the addition of gelatin or various kinds of clay, such as bentonite.

Filtering: Before bottling, most wines are passed through a filter to remove any remaining particles. It should be pointed out that many winemakers, and consumers as well, object to rigorous clarification and filtration of wine, claiming that these procedures rob wine of some of its character and complexity. The American public, particularly, has been accused of demanding a squeaky-clean product — a beautifully transparent wine, but one perhaps lacking some of its personality. The trend today, at least in certain wineries, is away from obsessive fining and filtration.

Adding sulphites: Preservatives have been used in winemaking since antiquity. Sulphite, which includes various compounds of sulfur, notably sulfur dioxide (SO_2), is the chemical used for this purpose. It is a sterilizing agent, usually added during bottling, to protect wine against harmful bacteria and spoilage. Although regulations permit adding up to 220 parts per million of sulphite to wine, most wineries today bottle with only 40 to 60 parts per million. It is virtually impossible to make drinkable wine on a commercial scale without adding sulphites. For that matter, since SO_2 is one of the natural by-products of fermenting grapes, wine, like bread dough, contains certain sulfites inherently.

Aging in the Bottle: Unless it has been pasteurized, wine continues to evolve even after it has been bottled, as tannins, pigments, alcohols, and certain microscopic elements act, react, combine, and interact with the wine.

WHEN IS A WINE READY TO DRINK?

Numerous factors determine when a wine is ready to drink: the type of wine, the year the grapes were grown, the vintner's skills, and even the storage conditions. Most white wines and rosés are ready to drink when they are purchased. A year or two after they have been released they may become oxidized, acquiring a brownish tint and a tired flavor resembling unpleasant sherry. A few of the best oak-aged white wines may gain richness and intensity of flavor over a period of a few years. Some of the greatest whites are still good after ten years or more, but these are exceptions.

Red wines vary even more in their ability to improve with age. Most eastern American reds are best consumed right away or within a few years of their release, for they are unlikely to improve significantly, if at all, over the years. A few wines, like certain people, get better as they get older, improving in complexity and depth of character after ten or even twenty years.

In the eastern states more than in temperate California, the climate of any given year will affect the outcome of the wine to a greater or lesser degree. Frost-kill during bud development can significantly decrease grape production, while cool, rainy days around harvest time can limit the fruit's sugar production. Long stretches of warm summer days and cool evenings promote grapes with a good sugar/acid ratio, while too much rain at the wrong time can lead to flabby flavors.

In the northeastern viticultural regions particularly, summers are sometimes too cool and short for many grape varieties to ripen properly. Pinot Noir, for example, may perform beautifully in good years, but fail to ripen when conditions are unfavorable. This is where winemaking skills are important, as vintners must decide whether to produce the wine, perhaps under a second, less expensive label; to sell the crop to another winery; or simply to write it off as a loss. "Vintage conditions put the house to the test," observes Chaddsford Winery's Eric Miller. "In trying times, a house should never relinquish responsibility to excellence."

TASTING WINE IN A WINERY

Most wineries have a tasting room, where visitors are invited to sample the wines. There is usually no fee for tasting, although a few wineries have begun to charge a modest amount, usually a couple of dollars, for this age-old custom. Tasting enables consumers to try the wines of a given region without making a heavy capital investment.

While every vintner entertains the fond hope that tasters will become buyers, there is little pressure to buy in the tasting room. After all, it is in a winery owner's best interests to acquaint as many people as possible with the product he is selling. In actuality, most visitors do end up buying at least a bottle or two if they like what they've sampled.

It makes good business sense for a winery to introduce people, especially those who are unfamiliar with wine, to the pleasures of drinking it. Sampling a variety of selections at different wineries is one way to learn more about wine and to discover the kind of wine the consumer likes best.

Tasting at a winery used to involve standing around a chilly wine cellar that was undecorated except for the barrels of wine and a dim light bulb, and the winemaker himself, who would dribble wine into glasses that might or might not have been washed. Many wineries in France and Italy are still like this, but in America, owners sometimes invest in their tasting rooms as soon as they plant their vines.

American tasting rooms range from a simple counter in a corner of the winery, to vast, barnlike rooms where the customer can indulge in gift-shopping as well as tasting. In addition to wine, there may be corkscrews and other wine-related products, posters, food items, or books for sale.

There will probably be a bar in the tasting room, and behind the bar, a person who knows something about the wines being poured. The best thing that can happen is that the winemaker himself or herself will be on duty pouring. In some of the bigger wineries there may be a young "intern" who can rattle off a series of memorized facts, but who won't necessarily be able to help much with detailed questions. But never mind — you're here to taste the wine. Here's how to do it.

Selecting the wines to taste: Tasting wine and drinking wine are two different activities — the former a somewhat unnatural imitation of the latter. One thing that differentiates the two is that in most wine drinking situations, such as a dinner party, one generally consumes only a few different wines. In an average tasting room, the selection may range from six to 12, or even more.

For those interested in sampling an entire range of wines, the general rule of thumb is to start dry and finish sweet. In other words, begin with the simplest, driest white wine, moving on to more complex whites that have, perhaps, been aged in oak. Then it's on to light and medium-bodied reds, finishing with the fullest, most complex red wines. If the winery makes dessert wines, try these at the very end of the tasting.

Another difference between tasting and drinking is that wine is meant to go with food. In a tasting room, there is rarely any food except perhaps a dish of bread chunks or crackers. These are not really meant as hors d'oeuvres — they're for cleansing the palate between wines.

Looking at the wine: Several character traits can be revealed by studying the wine in the glass for a moment. For example, one of the first things people may notice is a film of clear liquid on the glass just above the wine, forming droplets that trickle down the sides of the glass back into the wine. This occurrence, known as "tears," or "legs," is not related to viscosity or to glycerol, as is commonly assumed; it is a complicated phenomenon having to do with interfacial tensions between liquid and glass, and with the evaporation of alcohol from water. One thing it tells us is that the wine has a fairly high level of alcohol — at least 12%.

To see the wine's color precisely, it helps to look at it against a light-colored surface. Tipping the glass at a slight angle reveals a concentration of color around the edge. Certain grape varieties produce lighter- or darker-colored wines.

Color also indicates something about a wine's age. Young white wines, for example, are usually pale yellow, often deepening in color as they age. Full-bodied whites, especially those that have been aged in oak, tend to take on a rich, golden color. A brownish tinge is a warning sign. Just as oxidation turns a cut apple brown, it will also cause white wine to discolor, indicating it is too old.

Unlike white wines, reds *lose* color intensity as they age. A young red wine is usually drenched in deep purplish colors, evolving into translucent ruby or garnet hues over time. With further aging, the density of color fades; older wines are often a clear brick-red. They may have brownish tones around the edges, which isn't necessarily a sign of trouble, but may indicate instead that the wine has matured into a fine, mellow vintage ready to be savored.

Smelling the wine: The way experienced wine tasters swirl their glass and sniff, swirl again and sniff, sniff and swirl, may seem like obsessive concentration on this aspect of the wine, but in fact aroma can reveal far more than taste alone. Swirling air through the wine by rotating the glass in gentle circles fans the perfumes up toward the top of the glass (to prevent wine from sloshing over the side, glasses should never be more than half-filled). After swirling the wine, some tasters plunge their entire nose over the rim of the glass to inhale the released scents; others dip one nostril at a time over the glass or pass the glass back and forth under their nose.

Most of what we call "taste" is really smell, which is why food tastes so bland when we have a cold. Taste buds can actually perceive only four different sensations: sweet, bitter, salty, and sour, while the nose is capable of detecting at least 10,000 different aromas. One of the body's most important recipients of pleasurable sensations, the nose can tell us whether the wine is young or old: young wines tend to have a simple fruity smell, while older wines can develop complex aromas.

Experienced wine drinkers recognize and describe these nuances in terms of similar odors. White wines, for example, may exude aromas that resemble pineapple, mango, melon, and other tropical fruits, or even butterscotch and caramel. The typical odor of Sauvignon Blanc is said to be "herbaceous" or "grassy." Some white wines, particularly Riesling, may smell like flowers, and a fine Riesling sometimes has a distinctive, oily odor described as "petrol." When a wine gives off only a very faint aroma, or none at all, it is said to be "closed," or going through a "dumb" phase. If it is a good wine, it may develop an aroma after a few moments, or it may require further bottle aging before that particular wine develops a bouquet.

The aroma of red wine may resemble any number of red fruits, including cherries and various berries. It may smell like roses, or violets, or like certain trees, such as cedar or eucalyptus. An earthy odor resembling mushrooms or wet leaves might also be detected. A whiff of black pepper can often be picked up, or of licorice, mint, smoke, or tobacco. Certain vegetable smells are often associated with red wine — green peppers or beets, for example. Many fine red wines give off hints of cheese rinds, or "wet dog," or the oft- encountered "barnyard smell." While many of these descriptions may not sound appealing — and overbearing doses of any one of them would be considered a flaw — they are part of the subtle, evocative appeal of wine.

A myriad of aromas are found in the best wines, to be released by a swirl of the glass, the way a gust of wind sends forth the full fragrance of an apple tree in blossom. The better the wine, the more layers of half-hidden perfume are there awaiting discovery. Beginning tasters usually wonder what the fuss is all about, but those who persist soon discover that it takes both experience and concentration before one begins to recognize and identify a variety of aromas in wine. This is part of the fun and the challenge of wine tasting.

Of course, sometimes one encounters an unpleasant or "off" smell in the wine glass. Two of the most easily recognizable of these are "corkiness," an odor like wet cardboard that indicates a cork has gone bad, and the presence of sulfur, which smells like hard-boiled eggs. Hints of sulfur often dissipate after a few moments, while a "corked" wine never fully recovers.

Tasting: Having gained an impression of the wine through its aroma, the time has finally come to taste it. The standard procedure is to take a sip, allowing the wine to sit for a few moments on the tongue while the taste buds do their job of sorting out sweetness, acidity, astringency, bitterness, and tannin. The mouth registers spritziness, an indication of carbon dioxide, and it evaluates whether the wine feels thin, or if it has viscosity or "body." The sum of these impressions is known as "mouth feel."

At this point some tasters swish the wine around in their mouth. They may "chew" the wine, or aerate it by carefully (sometimes noisily) inhaling air through their mouth. These activities send aromas to the brain via the olfactory receivers, and perceptions from both the mouth and nose are synthesized into the sensation we call "taste."

Most experienced wine tasters spit each wine out after "mouthing" it. While novices find this a bizarre and unappetizing practice, its advantage for the professional wine taster, or anyone else who plans to taste many different wines in one day, is obvious. And remember, especially if you're driving, all those little sips can add up.

What are some of the impressions one might expect to get from all the swirling and sipping? While each winery produces wines with its own distinctive characteristics, certain generalizations might be made in identifying wines from the eastern states.

First, it's important to remember that this is mostly a cool-weather growing region. The wines, therefore, will be typically crisp and lively rather than rich and opulent except, perhaps, when they come from some of the warmer regions, such as Virginia, or when they have been blended with wine from other warm areas, such as California.

Eastern wine tends to be delicate and subtle, rather than bold and overbearing. It may not be as intensely colored as wine made from warm-weather grapes. Because of the cool weather and shorter growing season, eastern wines may be relatively high in acidity, which, when balanced with other flavor components such as fruitiness or tannins, makes them a good match for food. Thanks to this hint of acidity, many of the slightly sweeter wines are clean-tasting rather than cloying, which also makes for an appealing accompaniment to food.

The best eastern late-harvest wines and eiswein-style wines, those made from grapes that have a high concentration of sugar — either because they have been picked after fully ripening or because they have been frozen — can be nice after-dinner sipping wines. These are excellent whether on their own or with dessert.

The attentive consumer will soon discover that wine from the eastern states, like all good wine, can be as mysterious, elusive and multi-faceted, in its own way, as a Shakespearean sonnet.

WHERE TO BUY EASTERN WINES

Most of the wine produced in the East is purchased right at the individual winery. As I travel around the various wine regions in the East, I am often reminded of France, where Parisian, Italian, German, and English customers make annual pilgrimages to Bordeaux or Burgundy to buy wine. Some of these customers visit a variety of wineries every year to taste and compare the new vintages, while others head straight for their favorite winery, whether it is a renowned chateau or an obscure country wine cellar. The goal, for all, is the same: to load up the back of the car with enough cases of wine to last until they return again the following year.

In the eastern United States, similar rituals occur. Some loyal consumers come to stock up at their local winery because they like driving out into the countryside, tasting a variety of wines right where they were made, and chatting with the winemaker about that particular vintage. In short, they like the personal contact.

Many folks travel to wineries simply because a wine has captured their fancy, and it is only available at the winery. Indeed, the majority of wines produced in the eastern states are available *only* from the winery itself. Those relatively few vintners who make enough wine to sell outside the winery may also distribute their products in local wine shops, while a few of the largest producers may reach markets outside their own region, particularly in large urban centers such as New York, Boston, Washington, D.C., or even, in a handful of rare cases, in California and Europe.

Nevertheless, the fact remains that the usual and most dependable way to buy wines made in the eastern states is to pick it up in person at the individual winery, or to have the winery ship it to you (a telephone call will generally reveal the shipping policy).

TOURING THE EASTERN STATES WINE REGIONS

Many dedicated wine buffs like to focus an entire weekend or even a week-long holiday, exclusively on wineries. Most vacationers, however, prefer to intersperse winery visits with other activities. Following are a variety of suggested wine country tours — from one-day visits to week-long outings — that can be tailored to meet almost everyone's idea of a great visit to the wine regions of the eastern states.

DAY TRIPS

I. From Washington, D.C.: One way to break up a visit to the capital's historic monuments and political shrines is to escape for an entire day to the idyllic countryside of northern Virginia. Heading directly west from the capital, one can comfortably take in Tarara, Loudoun, and Willowcroft wineries, with plenty of time to enjoy a picnic along the way. Alternatively, head south on the Beltway toward Swedenburg, Piedmont, and Meredyth wineries.

II. From the Connecticut shore or from New York City: A quick ferry ride across Long Island Sound or a short drive east from New York City brings one to the wine country of the North Fork. Because the North Fork's wineries are spaced closely together along two main roads, it is possible to visit virtually all of them at a fast clip in a single day. On the other hand, visitors who wish to adopt a more leisurely pace can concentrate on four or five wineries during a one-day outing, with plenty of time to savor each one.

III. From Buffalo/Niagara Falls: Honeymooners and other visitors to this region will enjoy a pleasant day trip driving along Lake Erie, with stops at Woodbury Winery and Johnson Estate Wines.

IV. From Cleveland: A day's outing to the Lake Erie wineries near Cleveland should lay to rest any doubts about whether good wine can be made in this area. Start at Firelands Winery in Sandusky, then hop a ferry to Put-In-Bay, for a visit to Heineman Winery.

V. From Atlantic City or Philadelphia: After spending too many hours playing the slot machines in Atlantic City, a breath of fresh air is called for. From either Atlantic City or Philadelphia, one can easily fit in visits to Tomasello,

Amalthea, and Sylvin Farms wineries. Alternatively, from Philadelphia, one can head northwest to Smithbridge, Chaddsford, and Twin Brooks wineries for an easy day's outing.

WEEKEND TRIPS

I. From New York: The Delaware River region has long been a popular weekend getaway for New Yorkers who are attracted by the superb scenery and good restaurants. A winery tour can add yet another dimension to the enjoyment of this area that stretches along the New Jersey–Pennsylvania border. Stop at Unionville winery in New Jersey, and then head across the river to Sand Castle and Buckingham Valley Vineyards in Pennsylvania. Or work your way down the Delaware River from Franklin Hill Vineyards to Peace Valley, both in Pennsylvania.

II. In New England: Fall, which is the peak season for sightseeing in New England, is also an ideal time to visit the region's wineries. Spend the first day visiting Westport Vineyards, in Massachusetts, and Sakonnet in Rhode Island. The next day, drive to Connecticut, stopping in at Stonington Vineyards and Chamard Vineyards. There will be plenty of fall foliage to take in along the way. If it's a three-day weekend, one might then head west, to the charming town of Litchfield, for more leaf-peeping plus visits to Haight, Sandy Hook Vineyards, and Hopkins Winery.

III. The Hudson River region: A wealth of scenic and cultural sights have attracted weekend visitors to the magnificent Hudson River for hundreds of years. Winery touring is yet another reason to travel to this area. Highlights include visits to Benmarle, set in one of the world's most spectacular landscapes, and to Millbrook's impressive winery.

TRIPS OF A WEEK OR LONGER

I. The Blue Ridge Mountains: While it is entirely possible to zip through all the Blue Ridge wineries in a couple of days, there are few trips quite as rewarding as a slow-paced, leisurely drive through this region. A trip could begin at Naked Mountain, heading south toward Wintergreen, both in Virginia. Stop along the way at some of the country's loveliest historical sights, most notably Monticello.

II. The Finger Lakes: So many fine wineries have emerged in the past few years in the Finger Lakes region that a week-long visit, interspersed with activities such as boating, fishing, and antiquing, is the best way to do justice to all of them. Alternatively, spend a few days concentrating on Lake Seneca's wineries, starting at Fox Run and driving completely around the lake to New Land.

III. Pennsylvania's Appalachian Trail: The mountainous country of Pennsylvania is a paradise for nature lovers who can travel up to the high altitude of Altoona, where Oak Spring Winery, one of the East's highest wineries, is located. It's possible to drive from there to Brookmere in a couple of hours, but why not stop along the way to explore the landscape, hike, swim, sail, or fish? This country is a paradise for nature lovers.

WINERIES LISTED ALPHABETICALLY BY STATE

CONNECTICUT

Chamard Vineyards - Benchlands
DiGrazia Vineyards & Winery - Uplands
Haight Vineyards, Inc. - Uplands
Hopkins Vineyard - Uplands
McLaughlin Vineyards, Inc. - Uplands
Stonington Vineyards, Inc. - Benchlands

MARYLAND

Boordy Vineyards - Uplands
Catoctin Vineyards - Uplands
Fiore Winery and La Felicetta Vineyards - Uplands
Woodhall Vineyards & Wine Cellars - Uplands

MASSACHUSETTS

Mellea Vineyard - Benchlands
Nantucket Vineyard - Benchlands
Westport Rivers Vineyard & Winery - Benchlands

NEW JERSEY

Amalthea Cellars - Benchlands
Amwell Valley Vineyard - Uplands
Balic Winery - Benchlands
Cream Ridge Winery - Uplands
Four Sisters Winery - Uplands
King's Road Winery - Uplands
LaFollette Vineyard & Winery, Inc. - Uplands
Poor Richard's Winery - Uplands
Renault Winery - Benchlands
Sylvin Farms - Benchlands
Tamuzza Vineyards - Uplands
Tomasello Winery, Inc. - Benchlands
Unionville Vineyards - Uplands

NEW YORK

Adair Vineyards - Uplands
Americana Vineyards - Uplands
Anthony Road Wine Company, Inc. - Uplands
Arcadian Estate Vineyards - Uplands
Baldwin Vineyards - Uplands
Bedell Cellars- Benchlands
Benmarl Wine Company - Uplands
Bidwell Vineyards - Benchlands
Bridgehampton Winery - Benchlands
Brimstone Hill Vineyard - Uplands
Brotherhood Winery, Ltd. - Uplands
Bully Hill Vineyards, Inc. - Uplands
Canandaigua Wine Company, Inc. = Uplands
Cascade Mountain Winery - Uplands
Castel Grisch Estate Winery - Uplands
Cayuga Ridge Estate Winery - Uplands
Chateau LaFayette Reneau - Uplands
Clinton Vineyards - Uplands
Dr. Frank's Vinifera Wine Cellars / Chateau Frank - Uplands
Duck Walk Vineyards - Benchlands
Fox Run Vineyards - Uplands
Frontenac Point Vineyard - Uplands
Glenora Wine Cellars, Inc. - Uplands
Gristina Vineyards - Benchlands
Hargrave Vineyard - Benchlands
Hazlitt Vineyards - Uplands
Heron Hill Winery - Uplands
Hosmer - Uplands
Hunt Country Vineyard - Uplands
Jamesport Winery - Benchlands
Johnson Estate Wines - Benchlands
Keuka Spring Vineyards - Uplands
Knapp Vineyards Winery - Uplands
Lakewood Vineyards - Uplands
Lamoreaux Landing Wine Cellars - Uplands
Lenz Winery - Benchlands
Lucas Vineyards - Uplands
Mattituck Hills Winery - Benchlands
McGregor Vineyards & Winery - Uplands
Millbrook Vineyards & Winery - Uplands
New Land Vineyard - Uplands
Palmer Vineyards - Benchlands
Paumanok Vineyards - Benchlands

Peconic Bay Vineyards - Benchlands
Pellegrini Vineyards - Benchlands
Pindar Vineyards - Benchlands
Prejean Winery - Uplands
Pugliese Vineyards - Benchlands
Riverview - Uplands
Royal Kedem Winery - Uplands
Sagpond Vineyards - Benchlands
Six Mile Creek Vineyard - Uplands
Standing Stone Vineyards - Uplands
Swedish Hill Vineyard & Winery - Uplands
Wagner Vineyards - Uplands
Widmer's Wine Cellars, Inc - Uplands
Hermann J. Wiemer Vineyard - Uplands
Woodbury Winery & Vineyards - Benchlands

OHIO

Chalet Debonne Vineyards, Inc. - Benchlands
Firelands Winery - Benchlands
Grand River Wine Company - Benchlands
Harpersfield Vineyard - Benchlands
Heineman Winery - Benchlands
Klingshirn Winery, Inc. - Benchlands
Lonz Winery - Benchlands
Markko Vineyard - Benchlands
Steuk Wine Company - Benchlands

PENNSYLVANIA

Adams County Winery - Uplands
Allegro Vineyards - Uplands
Blue Mountain Vineyards - Uplands
Brookmere Farm Vineyards - Mountains
Buckingham Valley Vineyards - Uplands
Calvaresi Winery - Uplands
Chaddsford Winery - Uplands
Clover Hill Vineyards & Winery - Uplands
Conneaut Cellars Winery - Benchlands
Fox Meadow Farm - Uplands
Franklin Hill Vineyards - Uplands
French Creek Ridge Vineyards - Uplands
Hunters Valley Winery - Uplands
Mazza Vineyards - Benchlands
Naylor Vineyards & Wine Cellar - Uplands
Nissley Vineyards & Winery Estate - Uplands

Oak Springs Winery - Mountains
Oregon Hill Winery - Mountains
Peace Valley Winery - Uplands
Penn Shore Winery & Vineyards - Benchlands
Presque Isle Wine Cellars - Benchlands
Rushland Ridge Vineyard & Winery - Uplands
Seven Valleys Vineyard & Winery - Uplands
Sand Castle Winery - Uplands
Slate Quarry Winery - Uplands
Smithbridge Cellars - Uplands
Twin Brook Winery - Uplands
Vynecrest Winery - Uplands

RHODE ISLAND

Diamond Hill Vineyards - Benchlands
Sakonnet Vineyards - Benchlands

VIRGINIA

Afton Mountain Vineyards - Mountains
Barboursville Vineyards - Uplands
Chateau Morrisette - Mountains
Dominion Wine Cellars - Uplands
Gray Ghost Vineyards - Uplands
Horton Vineyards, Inc. - Uplands
Ingleside Plantation Vineyards - Benchlands
Jefferson Vineyards - Uplands
Linden Vineyards - Mountains
Loudoun Valley Vineyards - Uplands
Meredyth Vineyards - Uplands
Montdomaine Cellars - Uplands
Naked Mountain Vineyard & Winery - Mountains
Oakencroft Vineyard & Winery - Mountians
Oasis Vineyards - Uplands
Piedmont Vineyards & Winery - Uplands
Prince Michel and Rapidan River Vineyards - Uplands
Rockbridge Vineyard - Mountains
Shenandoah Vineyards - Mountains
Swedenburg Estate Vineyard - Uplands
Tarara Vineyard & Winery - Uplands
Totier Creek Vineyard & Winery - Uplands
Williamsburg Winery, Ltd. - Benchlands
Willowcroft Farm Vineyards - Uplands
Wintergreen Vineyards & Winery - Mountains

BEST WINES OF THE EAST:
THE AUTHOR'S 17 PERSONAL FAVORITES

Bordeaux-style red blend ....Linden Vineyards
Cabernet Franc...Barboursville Vineyards
Cabernet Sauvignon...............................Allegro Vineyards
Chambourcin..Naylor Wine Cellars
Chardonnay..Chaddsford "Philip Roth Vineyard"
Gewürztraminer ....Harpersfield Vineyard
Late Harvest (blend)...............................Pellegrini Vineyards "Finale"
Merlot...Bedell Cellars
Muscat Otonell Eiswein.........................McGregor Vineyards Winery
Pinot Gris ....Markko Vineyard
Pinot Noir ....New Land Vineyard (1993 Vintage)
Riesling..Dr. Frank's Vinifera Wine Cellars
Sangiovese ....Millbrook Vineyards and Winery
Sparkling Wine ....Oasis Brut Cuvée d'Or and Pindar
                                                                    Cuvée Rare
Vidal Blanc..Sakonnet Vineyards
Viognier ....Horton Vineyards, Inc.
White Table Wine ....Lamoureaux Landing "Estate White"

BIBLIOGRAPHY

ADAMS, Leon D., *The Wines of America*, Mc Graw Hill, NY, 1985.

BELTRAMI, Edward J., and PALMEDO, Philip F., *The Wines of Long Island- Birth of a Region*, Waterline Books, Great Falls, VA, 1993.

BORELLO, Joe, *Wineries of the Great Lakes*, Raptor Press, Lapeer, MI, 1995.

BRENNER, Leslie, *Fear of Wine: An Introductory Guide to the Grape*, Bantam Books, New York, Toronto, London, 1995.

LEE, Hilde Gabriel, and LEE, Allan E., *Virginia Wine Country Revisited*, Hildesigns Press, Charlottesville, VA, 1994.

MARTELL, Alan R., and LONG, Alton, *The Wines and Wineries of the Hudson River Valley*, Countryman Press, Woodstock, VT, 1995

McCARTHY, Edward, and MULLIGAN, Mary Ewing, *Wine for Dummies*, IDG Books, Worldwide, Inc., Boston, MA, 1995.

WIENER, Susan, *Finger Lakes Wineries*, Mc Books Press, Ithaca, NY, 1992.

Index

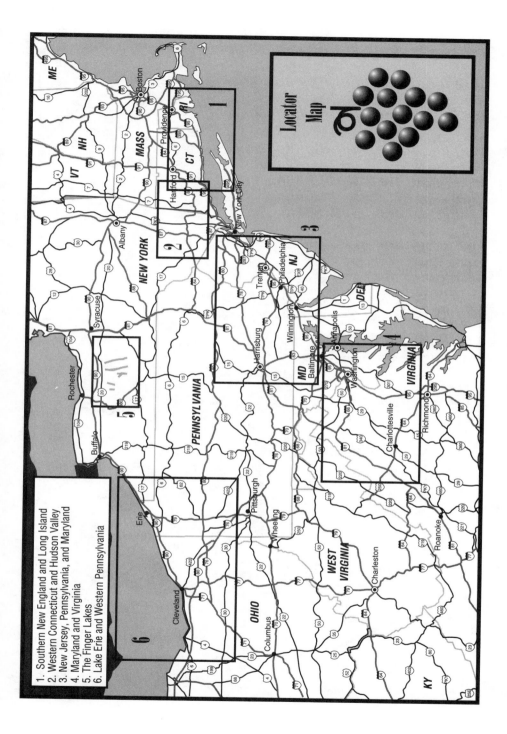

Locator Map

1. Southern New England and Long Island
2. Western Connecticut and Hudson Valley
3. New Jersey, Pennsylvania, and Maryland
4. Maryland and Virginia
5. The Finger Lakes
6. Lake Erie and Western Pennsylvania

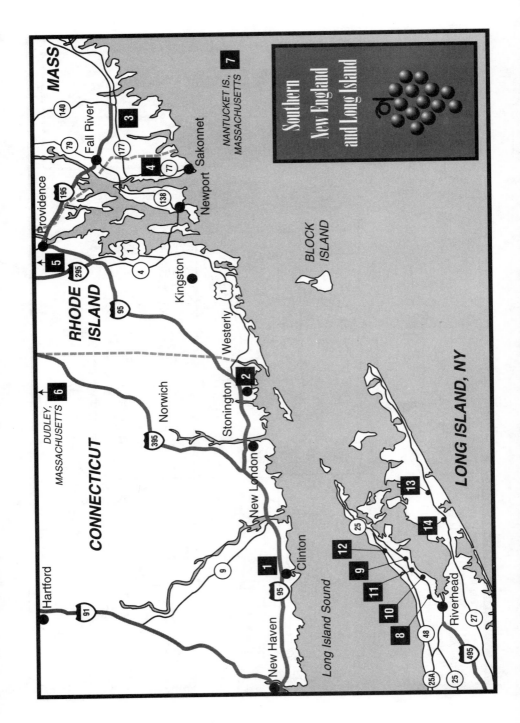

Southern
New England
and Long Island

MASS

Fall River

Providence

RHODE
ISLAND

Kingston

Westerly

Newport

Sakonnet

NANTUCKET IS.,
MASSACHUSETTS 7

BLOCK
ISLAND

DUDLEY,
MASSACHUSETTS 6

CONNECTICUT

Hartford

Norwich

New London

Stonington

Clinton

New Haven

Long Island Sound

LONG ISLAND, NY

Riverhead

1
2
3
4
5
6
8
9
10
11
12
13
14

140
79
177
77
195
138
1
4
295
95
1
395
9
95
91
25
25A
25
48
495
27

Map Legend — SOUTHERN NEW ENGLAND AND LONG ISLAND

Southern New England (Benchlands)

1. Chamard Vineyards, 115 Cow Hill Rd., Clinton, CT
2. Stonington Vineyards, Taugwonk Rd., Stonington, CT
3. Westport Rivers Vineyard and Winery, 417 Hixbridge Rd., Westport, MA
4. Sakonnet Vineyards, 162 West Main Rd. (Rte. 77), Little Compton, RI
5. Diamond Hill Vineyards, 3145 Diamond Hill Rd., Cumberland, RI
6. Mellea Vineyard, 108 Old Southbridge Rd., Dudley, MA
7. Nantucket Vineyards, Bartlett Farm Rd., Nantucket, MA

Long Island (Benchlands)

North Fork (by town)

8. Aquebogue:
   Palmer Vineyards, Sound Avenue, Aquebogue, NY
   Gaumanok Vineyards, Main Road (Rte. 5), Aquebogue, NY

9. Cutchogue:
   Bedell Cellars, Main Road (Rte. 25), Cutchogue, NY
   Gristina Vineyards, Main Road (Rte. 25), Cutchogue, NY
   Hargrave Vineyard, Rte. 48, Cutchogue, NY
   Pellegrini Vineyards, Main Road (Rte. 25), Cutchogue, NY

   Bidwell Vineyards, Rte. 48, Cutchogue, NY
   Peconic Bay Vineyards, Main Road (Rte. 25),Cutchogue, NY
   Pugliese Vineyards, Main Road (Rte. 25), Cutchogue, NY

10. Jamesport:
    Jamesport Winery, Main Road (Rte. 25), Jamesport, NY

11. Mattituck:
    Mattituck Hills Winery, Bergen Ave., Mattituck, NY

12. Peconic:
    Lenz Winery, Main Road (Rte. 25), Peconic, NY
    Pindar Vineyards, Main Road (Rte. 25), Peconic, NY

South Fork (by town)

13. Bridgehampton and Sagaponack:
    Sagpond Vineyards, Sagg Road, Sagaponack, NY
    Bridgehampton Winery, Bridgehampton, NY

14. Water Mill:
    Duck Walk Vineyards, Mauntauk Hwy, Water Mill, NY

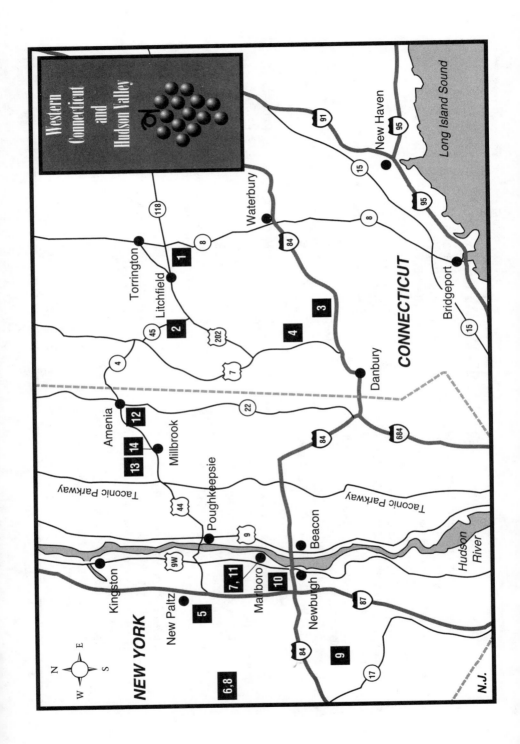

Western Connecticut and Hudson Valley

NEW YORK

CONNECTICUT

Long Island Sound

Hudson River

N.J.

New Haven

Waterbury

Bridgeport

Danbury

Torrington

Litchfield

Amenia

Millbrook

Poughkeepsie

Beacon

Newburgh

Marlboro

New Paltz

Kingston

Taconic Parkway

Taconic Parkway

95

15

91

8

84

118

45

202

7

4

22

684

84

87

84

9

9W

44

17

15

15

95

1

2

3

4

5

6,8

7,11

9

10

12

13

14

N
W E
S

Map Legend — WESTERN CONNECTICUT AND HUDSON RIVER VALLEY

Western Connecticut (Atlantic Uplands)

1. Haight Vineyard, 29 Chestnut Hill Rd., Litchfield, CT
2. Hopkins Vineyard, Hopkins Rd., New Preston, CT
3. McLaughlin Vineyards, Inc., Albert Hill Rd., Sandy Hook, CT
4. DiGrazia Vineyards and Winery, 131 Tower Rd., Brookfield, CT

The Hudson River Valley (Atlantic Uplands)

West Side of the Hudson River

5. Adair Vineyards, 75 Allhusen Rd., New Paltz, NY
6. Baldwin Vineyards, 176 Hardenburgh Rd., Pine Bush, NY
7. Benmarl Wine Company, 156 Highland Ave., Marlboro, NY
8. Brimstone Hill Vineyard, 49 Brimstone Hill Rd., Pine Bush, NY
9. Brotherhood Winery, 35 North St., Washingtonville, NY
10. Riverview, 656 Rte. 9W N., Newburgh, NY
11. Royal Kedem Winery, 1519 Rte. 9W, Marlboro, NY

East Side of the Hudson River

12. Cascade Mountain Winery, Flint Hill Rd., Amenia, NY
13. Clinton Vineyards, Schultzville Rd., Clinton Corners, NY
14. Millbrook Vineyards & Winery, Wing Rd., Millbrook, NY

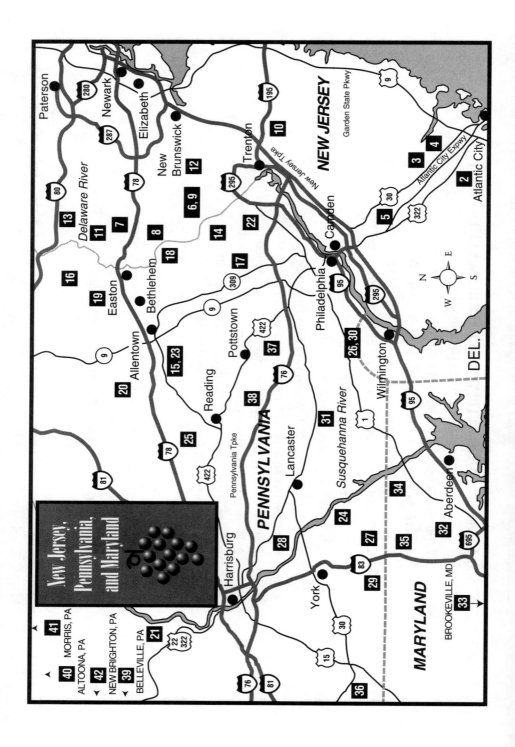

Map Legend — NEW JERSEY, PENNSYLVANIA, AND MARYLAND

Southeastern New Jersey (Benchlands)

1. Amalthea Cellars, 267 Hayes Mill Rd., Atco, NJ
2. Balic Winery, Rte. 40, Mays Landing, NJ
3. Renault Winery, 72 N. Bremen Ave., Egg Harbor City, Galloway Township, NJ
4. Sylvin Farms, 24 Vienna Ave., Germania, NJ
5. Tomasello Winery, 225 White Horse Pike, Hammonton, NJ

Northern New Jersey and the Delaware River Region (Atlantic Uplands)

New Jersey Side of the Delaware River

6. Amwell Valley Vineyard, 80 Old York Rd., Ringoes, NJ
7. King's Road Winery, Rte. 579, Asbury, NJ
8. Poor Richard's Winery, 220 Ridge Rd., Frenchtown, NJ
9. Unionville Vineyards, 9 Rocktown Rd., Ringoes, NJ
10. Cream Ridge Winery 145, Rte. 539, Cream Ridge, NJ
11. Four Sisters Winery, Rte. 519, Belvidere, NJ
12. LaFolette Vineyard and Winery, 64 Harlingen Rd., Belle Mead, NJ
13. Tamuzza Vineyards, Cemetary Rd., Hope, NJ

Pennsylvania S.Je of the Delaware River

14. Buckingham Valley Vineyards, 1521 Rte. 413, Buckingham, PA
15. Clover Hill Vineyards & Winery, 9850 Newtown Rd., Breinigsville, PA
16. Franklin Hill Vineyards, Franklin Hill Rd., Bangor, PA
17. Peace Valley Winery, 300 Old Limekin Rd., Chalfont, PA
18. Sand Castle Winery, 755 Rover Rd., Erwinna, PA
19. Slate Quarry Winery, 460 Gower Rd., Nazareth, PA
20. Blue Mountain Vineyards, Grape Vine Drive, New Tripoli, PA
21. Hunters Valley Winery, Rtes. 11 & 15, Liverpool, PA
22. Rushland Ridge Vineyard & Winery, 2665 Rushland Rd., Rushland, PA
23. Vyncrest Winery, 172 Arrowhead Lane, Breinigsville, PA

Southern Pennsylvania and Maryland (Atlantic Uplands)

Pennsylvania

24. Allegro Vineyards, Brogue, PA
25. Calvaresi Winery, 107 Shartlesville Rd., Bernville, PA
26. Chaddsford Winery, Rte. 1, Chadds Ford, PA
27. Naylor Vineyards & Wine Cellar, Ebaugh Rd., Stewartstown, PA
28. Nissley Vineyards and Winery Estate, 140 Vintage Dr., Bainbridge, PA
29. Seven Valleys Vineyard and Winery, Gantz Rd., Glen Rock, PA
30. Smithbridge Cellars, 159 Beaver Valley Rd., Chadds Ford, PA
31. Twin Brooks Winery, 5697 Strasburg Rd., Gap, PA

Maryland

32. Boordy Vineyards, 12820 Long Green Pike, Hydes, MD
33. Catoctin Vineyards, 805 Greenbridge Rd., Brookeville, MD (See map of Maryland and Virginia)
34. Fiore Winery and La Felicetta Vineyard, 3026 Whiteford Rd., Pylesville, MD
35. Woodhall Vineyards & Wine Cellars, 17912 York Rd., Parkton, MD

Other Wineries in Southern Pennsylvania

36. Adams County Winery, 251 Peach Tre Rd., Orrtanna, PA
37. Fox Meadow Farm, 1439 Clover Mill Rd., Chester Springs, PA
38. French Creek Ridge Vineyards, Grove Road, Elverson, PA

Central Pennsylvania (Mountains)

39. Brookmere Farm Vineyards, Rte. 655, Belleville, PA
40. Oak Springs Winery, Old Rte. 220, Altoona, PA
41. Oregon Hill Winery, Morris PA
42. Lapic Winery, 682 Tulip Dr., New Brighton, PA (See map of Lake Erie and Western Pennsylvania)

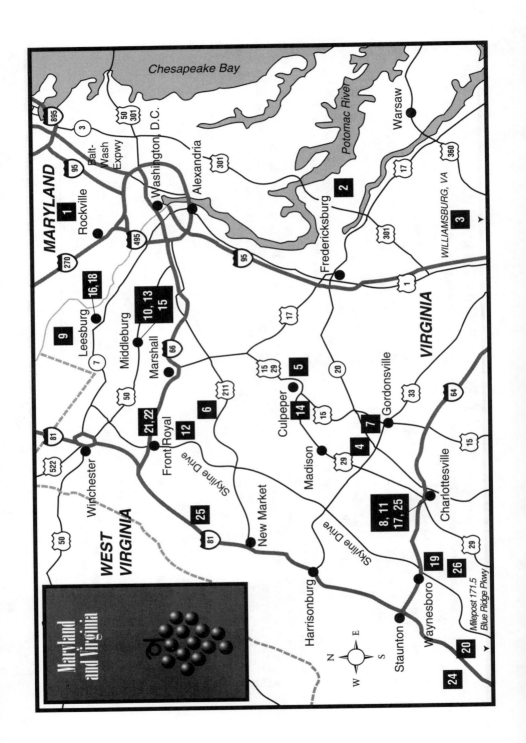

Map Legend — MARYLAND AND VIRGINIA

Maryland (Atlantic Uplands)

1. Catoctin Vineyards, 805 Greenbridge Rd., Brookeville, MD

Virginia (Benchlands)

2. Ingleside Plantation Vineyards, Rte 638, Oak Grove, VA
3. Williamsburg Winery, 2638 Powell Rd., Williasburg, VA

Northern and Central Virginia (Atlantic Uplands)

4. Barboursville Vineyards, 17655 Winery Rd. (Rte. 777), Barboursville, VA
5. Dominion Wine Cellars, 1 Winery Ave., Culpeper, VA
6. Gray Ghost Vineyards, 14706 Lee Highway, Amissville, VA
7. Horton Vineyards, Rte. 33, Gordonsville, VA
8. Jefferson Vineyards, Highway 53, Charlottesville, VA
9. Loudoun Valley Vineyards, Rte. 9, Waterford, VA
10. Meredyth Vineyards, Rte. 628, Middleburg, VA
11. Montdomaine Cellars, Rte. 720, Charlottesville, VA
12. Oasis Vineyards, Highway 635, Hume, VA
13. Piedmont Vineyards & Winery, Rte. 626, Middleburg, VA

14. Prince Michel & Rapidan River Vineyards, Rte. 29, Leon, VA
15. Swedenburg Estate Vineyard, Rte. 50, Middleburg, VA
16. Tarara Vineyard and Winery, 13648 Tarara Lane, Leesburg, VA
17. Totier Creek Vineyard & Winery, Rte. 720, Charlottesville, VA
18. Willowcroft Farm Vineyards, Rte. 797, Leesburg, VA

Virginia Highlands (Mountains)

19. Afton Mountain Vineyards, Rte. 631, Afton, VA
20. Chateau Morrisette, Milepost 171.5 (Meadows of Dan), Blue Ridge Parkway, VA
21. Linden Vineyards, 3708 Harrels Corner Rd., Linden, VA
22. Naked Mountain Vineyard and Winery, 2747 Leeds Manor Rd., Markham, VA
23. Oakencroft Vineyard and Winery, Rte. 5, Charlottesville, VA
24. Rockbridge Vineyard, Rte. 606, Raphine, VA
25. Shenandoah Vineyards, 3659 South Ox Rd., Edinburg, VA
26. Wintergreen Vineyards & Winery, Rte. 664, Nellysford, VA

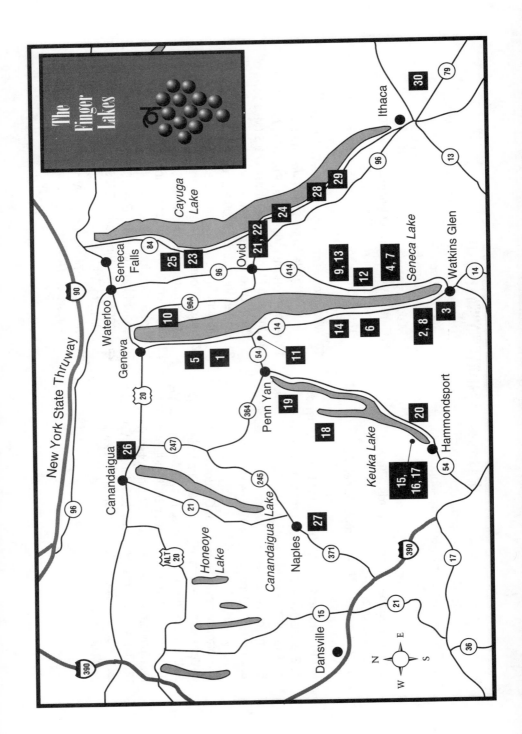

Map Legend — THE FINGER LAKES

Seneca Lake

1. Anthony Road Wine Company, 1225 Anthony Rd., Penn Yan, NY
2. Arcadian Estate Vineyards, 4184 Rte. 14, Rock Stream, NY
3. Castel Grisch Estate Winery, 3380 County Road 28, Watkins Glen, NY
4. Chateau LaFayette Reneau, Rte. 414, Hector, NY
5. Fox Run Vineyards, 670 Rte. 14, Penn Yan, NY
6. Glenora Wine Cellars, 5435 Rte. 14, Dundee, NY
7. Hazlitt Vineyards, Rte. 414, Hector, NY
8. Lakewood Vineyards, 4024 Rte. 14, Watkins Glen, NY
9. Lamoreaux Landing Wine Cellars, 9224 Rte. 414, Lodi, NY
10. New Land Vineyard, 577 Lerch Rd. Geneva, NY
11. Prejean Winery, 2634 Rte. 14, Penn Yan, NY
12. Standing Stone Vineyards, 9934 Rte. 414, Valois, NY
13. Wagner Winery, Rte. 414, Lodi, NY
14. Herman J. Wiemer Vineyard, Inc., Rte. 14, Dundee, NY

Keuka Lake

15. Bully Hill Vineyards, 8843 Greyton H. Taylor Memorial Drive, Hammondsport, NY
16. Dr. Frank's Vinifera Wine Cellars/Chateau Frank, 9749 Middle Rd., Hammondsport, NY
17. Heron Hill Winery, 8203 Pleasant Valley Rd., Hammondsport, NY
18. Hunt Country Vineyard, 4021 Italy Hill Rd., Branchport, NY
19. Keuka Spring Vineyards, 273 East Lake Rd. (Rte. 54), Penn Yan, NY
20. McGregor Vineyard Winery, 5503 Dutch St, Dundee, NY

Cayuga Lake

21. Cayuga Ridge Estate Winery, 6800 Rte. 89, Elm Beach Rd., Ovid, NY
22. Hosmer, 6999 Rte. 89, Ovid, NY
23. Knapp Vineyards Winery, 2270 County Road 128, Romulus, NY
24. Lucas Vineyards, 3862 County Rd. 150, Interlaken, NY
25. Swedish Hill Vineyard, 4565 Rte. 414, Romulus, NY

Canandaigua Lake

26. Canandaigua Wine Company, 151 Charlotte St., Canandaigua, NY
27. Widmer's Wine Cellars, 1 Lake Niagara Lane, Naples, NY

Other Finger Lakes Wineries

28. Americana Vineyards, East Covert Rd., Interlaken, NY
29. Frontenac Point Vineyard, Rte. 89, Trumansburg, NY
30. Six Mile Creek Vineyard, Slaterville Rd., Rte. 79, Ithaca, NY

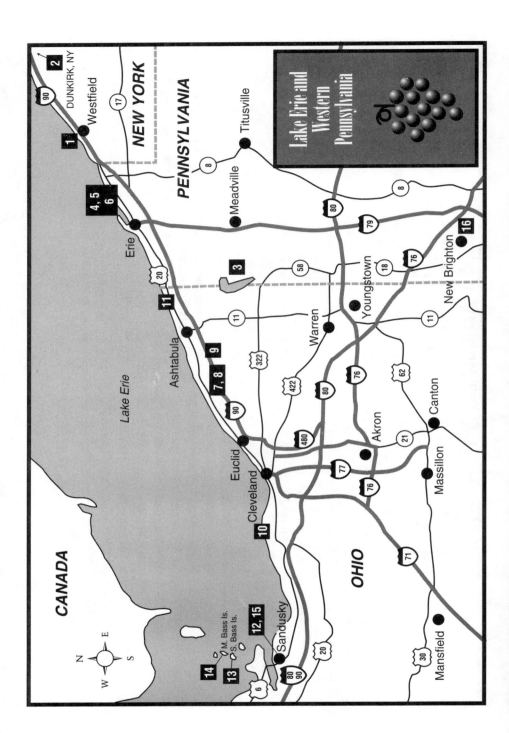

Lake Erie and Western Pennsylvania

DUNKIRK, NY
Westfield
NEW YORK
PENNSYLVANIA
Titusville
Meadville
Erie
Ashtabula
Euclid
Cleveland
Sandusky
Lake Erie
CANADA
OHIO
Warren
Youngstown
New Brighton
Akron
Canton
Massillon
Mansfield
M. Bass Is.
S. Bass Is.

Map Legend — LAKE ERIE AND WESTERN PENNSYLVANIA

Lake Erie Region (Benchlands)

New York

1. Johnson Estate Wines, Rte. 20, Westfield, NY
2. Woodbury Winery & Vineyards, 3230 South Roberts Rd., Dunkirk, NY

Pennsylvania

3. Conneaut Cellars Winery, Rte. 322, Conneaut Lake, PA
4. Mazza Vineyards, 11815 East Lake Rd. (Rte. 5), North East, PA
5. Penn Shore Winery & Vineyards. 10225 East Lake Rd. (Rte. 5), North East, PA
6. Presque Isle Wine Cellars, 9440 Buffalo Rd., North East, PA

Ohio

7. Chalet Debonne Vineyards, 7734 Doty Rd., Madison, OH
8. Grand River Wine Company, 5750 South Madison Rd., Madison, OH
9. Harpersfield Vineyards, 6387 State Rte. 307, Geneva, OH
10. Klingshirn Winery, 33050 Webber Rd., Avon Lake, OH
11. Markko Vineyards, 2 South Ridge Rd., Conneaut, OH
12. Firelands Winery, 917 Bardshar Rd., Sandusky, OH
13. Heineman Winery, Put-in-Bay (South Bass Island), OH
14. Lonz Winery, Middle Bass Island, OH
15. Steuk Wine Company, 1001 Fremont Ave., Sandusky, OH

Western Pennsylvania (Mountains)

(For other Pennsylvania wineries, see map of New Jersey, Pennsylvania, and Maryland)

16. Lapic Winery, 682 Tulip Dr., New Brighton, PA

About the Author

Marguerite Thomas writes about food, wine, travel, and people for a variety of publications. She is the travel editor of *The Wine News* and a regular contributing writer for *The Wine Enthusiast*. She is the author of a cookbook, *The Elegant Peasant*. She was raised in California and in France, and she presently lives in Connecticut and New York.